The
# Challenge
of
# Children's
# Rights
for
# Canada

## Studies in Childhood and Family in Canada

A broad-ranging series that publishes scholarship from various disciplines, approaches, and perspectives relevant to the concepts and relations of childhood and family in Canada. Our interests also include, but are not limited to, interdisciplinary approaches and theoretical investigations of gender, race, sexuality, geography, language, and culture within these categories of experience, historical and contemporary.

*Series Editor:*
Cynthia Comacchio
History Department
Wilfrid Laurier University

The
# Challenge
of
# Children's
# Rights
for
# Canada

## 2ND EDITION

Katherine Covell

R. Brian Howe

J.C. Blokhuis

WILFRID LAURIER
UNIVERSITY PRESS

*Inspiring Lives.*

Wilfrid Laurier University Press acknowledges the support of the Canada Council for the Arts for our publishing program. We acknowledge the financial support of the Government of Canada through the Canada Book Fund for our publishing activities. This work was supported by the Research Support Fund.

| | | |
|---|---|---|
| Canada | Canada Council for the Arts / Conseil des arts du Canada | ONTARIO ARTS COUNCIL CONSEIL DES ARTS DE L'ONTARIO an Ontario government agency un organisme du gouvernement de l'Ontario |

**Library and Archives Canada Cataloguing in Publication**

Covell, Katherine, author
The challenge of children's rights for Canada / Katherine Covell,
R. Brian Howe, J.C. Blokuis. — Second edition.

(Studies in childhood and family in Canada)
Includes bibliographical references and index.
Issued in print and electronic formats.
ISBN 978-1-77112-355-6 (softcover).—ISBN 978-1-77112-357-0 (EPUB).—
ISBN 978-1-77112-356-3 (PDF)

1. Children's rights—Canada. 2. Children—Government policy—Canada.
3. Child welfare—Canada. 4. Convention on the Rights of the Child (1989
November 20). I. Howe, Robert Brian, author II. Blokhuis, J. C., author
III. Title. IV. Series: Studies in childhood and family in Canada

HQ789.C68 2018          323.3'520971          C2018-902141-1
                                               C2018-902142-X

Front-cover photo from Shutterstock, Inc. (ID 710840458).
Cover design by Cyanotype Book Architects. Interior design by Janette Thompson (Jansom).

This book is printed on FSC® certified paper and is certified Ecologo. It contains post-consumer fibre, is processed chlorine free, and is manufactured using biogas energy.

Printed in Canada

RECYCLED
Paper made from recycled material
FSC® C103567

**FOR TIM**

☙

and all other parents
who put the best interests
of their children first

# Contents

# Preface to the Second Edition

More than a quarter of a century has passed since Canada ratified the United Nations Convention on the Rights of the Child, and more than a decade and a half has passed since *The Challenge of Children's Rights for Canada* was published in its first edition.

*The Challenge* has served as an important resource for children's rights courses across the country and as a valuable reference for researchers and students. But the time is clearly ripe for updating. In this completely revised and expanded edition of *The Challenge*, we incorporate new material and add legal and philosophical perspectives to our interdisciplinary analyses of children's rights in Canada. We review decisions by the Supreme Court of Canada in which the Convention has been invoked to show how children's rights under the Convention have been judicially recognized. And we add new issues and cases that show the continuing gap between the promise and the reality of children's rights. For example, we examine Katelynn's Principle, which resulted from the inquest into the preventable maltreatment death of Katelynn Sampson, and we analyze the problems of Internet luring, as highlighted in the tragic sexual exploitation of Amanda Todd.

As in the first edition, we examine the gap between Canada's commitment to implementing the rights of children, as expressed in Canada's official approval of the Convention on the Rights of the Child in 1991, and the actual state of children's rights in Canada. In doing so, we incorporate the most up-to-date empirical and theoretical research in our respective fields. And as in the first edition, a key reference point for our analyses is developmental psychology. We use Bronfenbrenner's ecological systems theory to draw attention to the important influences of families, policies, and laws on children's capacity to enjoy their rights. Politically and philosophically, we remain firmly rooted in the liberal tradition, with its rejection of proprietary notions of children and its respect for all individuals as ends in themselves, as bearers of rights with inherent dignity and worth, and as the appropriate focus of our moral concern. Children's rights are, of course, human rights. International human rights instruments, including the Convention itself, would be unintelligible in the absence of widespread commitment to these basic liberal principles. We have also adopted a conceptualization of rights (including children's rights) as correlates of duties (including duties voluntarily assumed by the state), while acknowledging both the interest theory and the will theory of rights.

We note that cross-cultural and intersectional approaches to the rights and experiences of children who are members of particular groups are largely beyond the scope of this book. For these, we encourage interested readers to consult more specialized and multidisciplinary volumes, including volumes in which we have partnered with sociologists, criminologists, cross-cultural psychologists, social workers, and Indigenous scholars.

We trust that this new edition of *The Challenge of Children's Rights for Canada* will be of interest to academics, policy-makers, parents, teachers, social workers, and human service professionals—to everyone who cares about and for children.

‿

## CHAPTER 1

# The Challenge of Children's Rights

In April 2015, a freighter in Vancouver harbour spilled 2700 litres of bunker fuel oil.[1] The oil washed up on beaches along the harbour. Seemingly unaware of this, a local teacher took her class to a beach where the children began to play in the contaminated sand and water. Contact with bunker fuel oil is dangerous for children, who are far more sensitive to toxic chemicals than adults.[2] Vapours coming off the fuel are harmful if inhaled and can cause skin and eye irritation; prolonged exposure is considered carcinogenic. Fortunately, local resident Jeremy Board saw what was happening. He quickly alerted the teacher, who then ensured the children were removed from the toxic area. Board was widely praised for his action. The teacher, the children, their parents, and the general public were unanimous in their praise for his swift intervention.

This response is not surprising. Increasing diagnoses of childhood asthma, autism spectrum disorder (ASD), and attention-deficit/hyperactivity disorder (ADHD) have heightened concerns about the potential role of environmental toxins in children's development.[3] Interventions to protect children from environmental toxins, which may pose immediate or long-term threats to healthy development, are welcomed whether they come from governments, advocacy groups, or individuals.

Yet the comparably profound impact of harmful social conditions on children's development has not received the same attention. It is not that social causes of developmental difficulties are ignored. Media attention is given to children living in poverty, child abuse and maltreatment, and inadequate early childhood education and care programs. But efforts to protect children from harmful social environments, or to provide children with positive social environments, do not seem to receive the same widespread acceptance as efforts to ensure children have safe physical environments. Government policies aimed at improving children's social environments are sometimes criticized as too costly or too intrusive into family life. Groups that advocate for such policies may be dismissed as radicals or "morality police," and individuals may be told to mind their own business.[4]

As a consequence, many children in Canada today are being raised in social contexts that are as poisonous to their development as physical toxins. In this book, we argue that under the United Nations Convention on the Rights of the Child, children have a right to be raised free of any toxins, both social and physical. By ratifying the Convention in 1991, Canada recognized this right. However, the challenge is to put it into effect.

## The Socially Toxic Environment

This term was coined by the American child psychologist James Garbarino to describe rearing conditions such as poverty and violence.[5] Social toxins are any social-environmental conditions that are known to threaten the child's healthy development.[6] They are like physical toxins because their impact can be predicted, and because children are more susceptible to their effects than adults. Social toxins can reside within the family, for example, in the presence of alcoholic or abusive parents. Social toxins can be found in the community, for example, in unsafe play areas, inadequate housing, lack of quality daycare, and overcrowded schools.[7] And social toxins can be the product of laws and public policies, such as economic policies that leave parents underemployed or unemployed, and social policies that provide families with inadequate parental leave or child care.

In later chapters, we examine Canada's commitment to children's rights and the developmental impact of specific social toxins. Here, we provide a brief illustration of how social toxins affect the child's development. We use two relatively common social toxins, abuse and poverty. Children in street situations are exposed to both.

On any given night across Canada, there are about 6000 youths sixteen to eighteen years of age in street situations, and another 300 under sixteen.[8] Most of these young people are escaping from abusive families, foster care, or group homes. How they survive varies. Lacking in life experience, skills, and resources, some panhandle, some wash car windshields at stoplights, some sell drugs, and some work in the sex trade. Their survival strategies make them highly vulnerable to crime, exploitation, and further abuse. Children in street situations are one highly visible example of the impact of abuse in early childhood.[9] There are many more.

The impact of abuse in early childhood is also reflected in young children's behaviour disorders, aggression at school, lowered academic performance and achievement, poor peer relations, and adolescent antisocial behaviour.[10] The effects of early maltreatment persist well beyond childhood and adolescence. Consistently, the research evidence suggests a causal relation between early maltreatment and a range of criminal behaviours, psychiatric disorders, drug use, suicide attempts, and high-risk behaviours in adolescence and adulthood.[11] Such findings underscore the fact that exposure to social toxins in early childhood has effects that are cumulative and persistent.

The impact of social toxins associated with poverty follows the same developmental pattern. Poverty, and its correlates of single parenthood, low educational levels, and unemployment, has long-lasting negative effects on child development. As detailed in Chapter 5, children living in poverty tend to show difficulties in mental and physical health, in behaviour, and in academic achievement. Many of these difficulties are a result of physical, social, and school environments that lack adequate opportunity and age-appropriate stimulation.[12] Impoverished rearing conditions also affect child development through their impact on parenting. Poverty increases parental stress and impairs parental social support systems. As a result, effective parenting, the key determinant of favourable child outcomes, is made more difficult.[13] As with abuse, the impact of ineffective parenting is not restricted to childhood. Early disadvantage shows a cumulative effect across childhood with increasingly poor academic achievement and elevated levels of behaviour problems.[14] In fact, poverty experienced early in life is more predictive of negative outcomes such as high school dropout than is poverty experienced in later childhood.[15] Yet the number of children living in poverty in Canada remains high. Back in the 1998 federal budget, Paul Martin, then minister of finance, remarked that investments in children and youth would be made "when we can afford it." We are still waiting. The most recent data show that 17.4 percent of children in Canada are still living in poverty—more than in most other advanced industrial countries.[16] Recent neuroscience research tells us we cannot afford to keep waiting. We cannot continue to ignore the social toxins to which so many children are exposed.

## Exposure to Social Toxins

Why does early exposure to social toxins such as abuse and poverty have long-lasting effects? From Freud's early writings to the present, psychologists have noted the particular importance of the first three years of life in determining later outcomes for the child. The complex neural mechanisms by which early experience affects subsequent health, well-being, and social behaviour are now being identified.[17] Perhaps the most important discovery is that we are not simply the product of our genes, but of a gene–environment interaction in which early experience plays a major role.[18]

At birth, the infant's brain has the neural circuits laid out; an initial blueprint is there, ready for refinement. The subsequent development of the brain is guided by experience. An infant's brain structure and functioning grows with stimulation. In the absence of positive interactions such as cuddling, talking, and smiling, brain growth suffers. And in the presence of environmental adversities, the risk of developing emotional, physical, and mental health problems is high.[19] We have known for some time that toxic substances such as alcohol, drugs, and lead impair brain growth. We know now that toxic experiences alter brain development in ways that affect the child's ability to think, feel, and relate to others. Children are particularly vulnerable to toxic experiences during the first two or three years of life because of the rapidity and complexity of brain growth at this time.[20] The effects are long-lasting.

Much of the research has focused on the effects of early maltreatment—physical, sexual, and emotional abuse, and neglect—on the developing brain. This is because of the prevalence of child maltreatment. Over 200,000 cases are reported to child protection services in Canada each year.[21] Empirical research has established that maltreatment affects brain structure and function in areas that are implicated in a number of clinical disorders, the regulation of stress, and the control of aggression.[22] And consistently, the evidence points to a causal relation between early maltreatment and adverse outcomes that persist across adolescence and into adulthood.[23] Abused and neglected children are at elevated risk of a range of psychiatric and conduct disorders, drug and alcohol misuse, risky sexual behaviour, and criminal behaviour.[24] The extent to which maltreatment results in disorders varies with its severity and frequency in a dose-dependent manner.[25]

The most extreme manifestation of a severe history of maltreatment is seen in children who kill. In their study of children who have been convicted of homicide, Canadian researchers Katharine Kelly and Mark Totten show how the experiences of children who kill—the patterns of abuse, brutality, and neglect—in essence train them for violence.[26] Recall, for example, the horrific case of James Bulger in England. He was only two years old when he was murdered by two ten-year-olds, Jon Venables and Robert Thompson.[27] Although many in the media referred to them as evil, Jon and Robert shared a history of extreme family dysfunction and deprivation, with a failure of social or educational services to provide much-needed interventions.[28] In fact, the one commonality researchers find among children who kill is a history of severe and multiple maltreatment.[29] Evidence of the link between early childhood abuse and violent behaviour in adolescence was noted back in 1981.[30] Since then, advances in developmental neuroscience have shown that the link is through the effect of abuse on brain development.

Just as early negative experiences have a long-term impact on brain development and behaviour, so do early positive experiences. In his autobiography, neuroscientist James Fallon illustrates this in dramatic fashion.[31] Fallon was researching the neurological underpinnings of serial murderers and psychopaths when he made a startling discovery: He was genetically predisposed for psychopathy. He later learned that his ancestry included a long line of murderers. This knowledge led him to appreciate the importance of an early environment that is positive and nurturing. It was his loving, stable, and nurturing family, he concluded, that limited the expression of his psychopathy genes such that although he lacks empathy and tends to be irresponsible and impulsive, he is able to control his anger and avoid violence, and he has no criminal record. As Fallon came to realize, environments make a significant difference in gene expression. Not all children are as fortunate as he was, but poor outcomes are not inevitable. Early intervention programs, particularly home visitation and preschool enrichment programs, can make a significant difference to child outcomes.

The Dutch Nurse-Family Partnership, which has received considerable attention in Canada, shows significant promise as a means of preventing child maltreatment and improving developmental outcomes up to age fifteen.[32] The program involves the establishment of a mentoring and supportive relationship between a nurse with specialized training and a high-risk parent. The relationship starts with the pregnancy and continues until the child is two years old. During this time, there are frequent home visits as well as contact through social media, texting, and phone calls. Intensive enrichment programs in the United States, most notably the Abecedarian Project, the Perry Preschool Program, and the Chicago Child-Parent Centers, have also shown long-term benefits to children.[33] These programs involve a combination of social and cognitive skills development for children at risk and parenting skills training for their parents. These interventions have cumulative positive effects on children's development. For example, by age twenty-seven, the children who participated in the Perry Preschool Program, compared with their counterparts, had lower rates of welfare use and criminal activity, and higher rates of employment and earnings.[34]

Early intervention programs meet children's developmental needs not only directly by providing environmental stimulation appropriate to healthy brain development, but also indirectly through their impact on parents. Studies show that a corollary of early intervention programs is improved parenting.[35] Both effective parenting and healthy brain development in early childhood are protective factors in children's subsequent exposure to adverse experiences.[36] In essence, protective factors provide children immunization against social toxins that they may encounter later in their lives.

In addition to providing children with optimum conditions for early development, we must also ensure their needs are met in all the environments and institutions in which they develop. Even children whose development has been compromised by early disadvantage will more likely reach their potential if subsequent environments are designed to meet their needs. And although it is very important to provide for healthy development in the first three years, it is also important to address children's needs throughout childhood.

## Children's Developmental Needs

Throughout childhood, children need to be raised in conditions that allow them to grow dysfunction-free, to develop their skills and self-worth, and to become contributing members of their families and communities. Urie Bronfenbrenner's classic explication of the systems of development helps us identify optimal conditions for child development.[37]

Children are raised within systems that Bronfenbrenner described as a series of dynamically interacting social contexts or environments. At the core of all environments is the child with his or her at-birth health and temperament status. Surrounding the child is the family. In turn, the family is embedded within a community, which is embedded within a culture. Children have needs within each social context because their development is shaped by each, as well as by their birth status. Parenting and the development of the child, for example, may be affected by the child's health or temperament status at birth. But the child's development, the parenting the child receives, and the parent–child relationship are also affected by what happens in the workplace; by the safety, resources, and stability of the community; by the quality of schools; by the health and recreation facilities available; and by the supports provided to parents. In turn, laws and policies and the prevailing beliefs and values of the culture affect each of these.

Do Canadians place high value on parenting? To what extent do we provide assistance and supports to parents? What are our beliefs about children? What emphasis is given to rearing children and what to individual career development? What portion of social spending do Canadians want to go to promoting the healthy development of children? The answers to such questions help to determine our public policies. In turn, policies shape our neighbourhoods, schools, and supports provided for children and their parents, and as a result the developmental pathways of our children. We can support child-friendly and family-friendly environments, and healthy child development. Or we can remain a society in which some children are deprived of the nurturing environment needed for healthy development, and some suffer significant maltreatment. As noted in the 2015 movie *Spotlight* by Mitchell Garabedian, attorney for victims of sexual abuse, "It takes a village to raise a child, but it also takes a village to abuse a child." Children's needs are not met in socially toxic environments.

Across the contexts of development identified by Bronfenbrenner, children's needs can be categorized broadly into three overlapping domains of provision, protection, and participation. Provision needs are the necessities for the child's healthy physical and psychological growth. These needs start before birth. To promote the best possible birth status, a fetus needs a healthy environment free from toxic substances such as alcohol that will impair development regardless of the quality of postnatal environments. After birth, children's needs for adequate nutrition and healthy, safe homes and neighbourhoods are self-evident. Less apparent but as important are children's needs for healthy psychological growth. Here, a basic requirement is sensitivity to the individual child's needs, which tend to vary with temperament status. Other necessities for healthy development are parental love and acceptance, parental time, opportunity to develop talents and skills, support and guidance, age-appropriate demands and limits, and positive, supportive role models. Shortages of resources and shortages of time make meeting provision needs through childhood difficult. Poverty is associated with childhood health problems, with limited educational attainment, and with the development of antisocial behaviours.[38] It is difficult for children to develop their talents and skills when family, school, and neighbourhood resources are scarce, or when poverty disallows the child's participation in extracurricular activities. Sensitive parenting and the giving of time to children are difficult when parental-leave policies are inadequate, and when workplaces do not have flexible policies for parents or on-site child care.

Protection needs require that the child be protected from all physical and social toxins in the environment. Children require protection from family and societal contexts that are violent, abusive, neglectful, rejecting, or in any other way likely to compromise healthy development. At the family level these include chronic ineffectual parenting, harsh discipline practices, sexual or economic exploitation, parental alcoholism, and parental drug abuse.[39] In addition to strong preventive interventions, children need an effective child protection system, and they need protection from violence and instability in their schools and neighbourhoods. At the broader cultural level, children need protection from cultures that accept violence and from those that devalue children.

Children also have participation needs. These may be the least obvious of children's developmental needs. A positive sense of self and high self-regard develop not only with the protections and provisions noted above, but also through learning that it is possible to control the environment. Witness the joy of the five-month-old who realizes he can make his toy rattle, or the toddler who can make her dog sit on command. This sense of efficacy is a motivational factor in self-esteem that influences children's curiosity, confidence in approaching new tasks, acquisition of knowledge, and intellectual growth.[40] Children who, at home and at school, are encouraged to explore and to learn, who are given age-appropriate roles in family and school functioning, and who are given age-appropriate demands for independence have a strong sense of competence.[41]

Participation needs include teaching effective decision-making. This can be accomplished through allowing free play and peer interaction, and by giving the child age-appropriate choices. A toddler, for example, might be asked to choose between apple and orange juice, a ten-year-old between piano and guitar lessons, a fourteen-year-old between summer camp and an aunt's cottage. What is important is that the child learns how to make good decisions, and how to anticipate and accept the consequences of those decisions. This cannot happen without gradual age-appropriate training. Children who have not had opportunities to participate in their family life, or in the functioning of their classrooms and schools, are more likely to have low self-confidence. They are more vulnerable to negative influences and less capable of making rational decisions in later childhood and adulthood—times when the penalties for poor decisions typically are more severe. Participation in decision-making improves the child's sense of self-worth, and helps children meet their need to feel part of a family and a community.[42]

Meeting children's protection, provision, and participation needs across all the contexts of development requires policies and practices designed to provide environments that are free of toxins that threaten their development. Children's needs are met best when interventions and policies are proactive. The approach in Canada remains largely reactive. Maintaining a fundamental belief that parents are responsible for their children, our society remains reluctant to intervene. We react only when toxicity levels are chronic and high, often in a manner that is parent-centred rather than child-centred. It does not work. We know this from the number of high-profile cases brought to our attention by the media, including that of Phoenix Sinclair, returned to her parents despite their history of abuse; Serena and Sophia Campione, returned to their mother despite her psychiatric problems; Jackie Brewer, who died of dehydration and neglect in her crib despite repeated reports to child protection and medical authorities; Jordan Heikamp, whose homeless mother watered down his formula while assuring social workers he was fine; Sara Podniewicz, returned to her parents despite their history of abuse; Shanay Johnson, battered to death by a drug-addicted mother known to social workers; Jeffrey Baldwin, placed in the care of his maternal grandparents despite their long history of violence and abuse; Alex Radita, returned to his parents despite their refusal to provide him with insulin for his diabetes; and Melonie Biddersingh, whose murder was neither investigated nor prosecuted for almost two decades. The cruel deaths of these children underscore the importance of proactive approaches.

## The Challenge of Children's Rights

Children have not only needs, but they also have rights. They have both moral and legal rights to have their provision, protection, and participation needs met. This is recognized in the United Nations Convention on the Rights of the Child (hereafter the Convention). The Convention regards childhood as a protected part of the life cycle and prescribes the role of governments in ensuring optimum conditions for meeting children's developmental needs. In fact, as we discuss in Chapter 2, the Convention specifically takes children's developmental needs into account. The Convention tells us that children have a fundamental right to environments as free from social toxins as they are from physical toxins. In the Convention, children are acknowledged to be independent bearers of provision, protection, and participation rights. Although the Convention recognizes the importance of parenting and family life, it makes clear that children are not to be seen or treated as parental property or as objects of charity.[43] The challenge of children's rights, then, is twofold.

First, we must provoke a shift in culture. Rather than seeing children as the property of their parents or objects of pity, we need to understand and acknowledge them as independent bearers of human rights. This shift requires effective and comprehensive public education on the rights of the child, as called for in the Convention and by the UN Committee on the Rights of the Child and as discussed later in the book. The shift also requires recognition that it is neither appropriate nor desirable for individual parents or families to be solely responsible for the children in their care.[44] Although there may be some support in Canada for the principle of social responsibility for children, in practice there are too few supports for child-rearing, and too little attention to the needs and rights of children. As mentioned earlier, our society continues to leave children in socially toxic environments because of the pervasiveness of proprietarian views of children and of parental rights. This is why child protection agencies tend to see the parent rather than the child as their client. And this is why there is so little done for children whose development has been seriously compromised by prenatal exposure to toxic substances. Such beliefs prevent us from taking children's rights seriously. It is the children on whom we must focus, and it is their human rights and best interests that must guide our policies and practices in all contexts.

Second, we need a shift in laws, policies, and practices. We need to incorporate the rights of the child into our laws and policies to reduce social toxins and to promote resilience where we are unable to effect environmental change. Rather than policies and laws that are reactive and parent-focused, we need ones that are proactive and child-centred. Among the measures required are economic support, early childhood education and care, programs to protect children from maltreatment and sexual exploitation, and reforms to ensure that children can exercise their rights of participation. It is vitally important, and consistent with the Convention, that decisions about children be made in their best interests. Whether it is in the area of child protection, child custody, health care, or education, laws and policies need to be consistent with the best interests and rights of the child. In short, we need to take children's rights seriously. Nelson Mandela once remarked that the true character of a society is revealed in how it treats its children. The character of Canada is revealed by the measures it takes to implement the rights of the child.

In this book, we describe key areas where changes are necessary to meet the challenge of children's rights for Canada. In Chapter 2, after reviewing the historical background, we examine the contents of the Convention, its guiding principles, its provisions on the rights of children, and Canada's obligations to put the Convention into effect. In Chapter 3, we consider the moral and legal status of children, distinguishing moral rights from legal rights and addressing some enduring problems associated with the ascription of legal rights to minors in Canada. In Chapter 4, we review decisions by the Supreme Court of Canada in which the Convention has been invoked to show how children's rights under the Convention have been judicially recognized and reconciled with the *parens patriae* doctrine and the *Charter of Rights and Freedoms*.

In Chapters 5 through 7, we examine the key areas in which change is needed. In each chapter we first examine specific Convention rights and review Canada's progress in providing for these rights. We then examine the empirical literature to identify why it is critical that current laws and policies be changed to meet the challenge of children's rights. In Chapter 5, we examine provision rights. We consider three areas: child poverty rates, inadequacies of health care, and shortcomings in early childhood education and care. Changes are needed to ensure each child has a healthy start and optimal development. In Chapter 6, we focus on protection rights. Our attention is on child maltreatment, corporal punishment, and sexual exploitation. We find serious shortcomings in Canada's record for each domain. Evidence is presented to bolster our position that it is imperative proactive measures be taken to prevent all forms of violence against children, including sexual exploitation. Chapter 7 is focused on children's participation rights in families, schools, and legal proceedings. Finding little opportunity for children to exercise their participation rights, we call for changes to allow for children's meaningful participation in each domain. We urge that children be accorded respect, dignity, and the opportunity to develop a sense of efficacy and good decision-making skills by being given a voice in matters that affect them.

In our final chapter, we consider what accounts for Canada's failure to implement the rights of the child and the gap between the enthusiastic ratification of the Convention and its reality. We then consider what action needs to be taken to implement children's rights and the possibility that such action will occur.

Our focus in this book is on children's human rights in general. Guided by the principles of international human rights law and by the Convention, we look at the basic rights that children have in common—provision, protection, and participation rights—and the degree to which these rights have been realized in Canada. We also look at the social toxins that threaten these rights and the importance of countering these threats through putting children's rights into effect. We appreciate that members of particular groups may have additional interests and needs and corresponding rights. As stated in the Convention, children with special needs have the right to special care, and children who are members of minority groups have the right to enjoy their own culture and practise their own religion.[45] We also appreciate that different groups of children have different experiences. Indigenous children, for example, are affected by the legacy of colonization and residential schools. And many children who are refugees are affected by their experience of war and violence. As cross-cultural and intersectional approaches to the rights and experiences of children who are members of particular groups are largely beyond the scope of this book, we would encourage interested readers to consult more specialized and multidisciplinary volumes.[46] While we do give attention to children who are disproportionately affected by social toxins, our primary focus is on the rights of children in general and on the forces that threaten or violate these rights. We are mindful that under the Convention, the rights of *every* child matter and that *every* child is to be respected as an individual bearer of rights regardless of the child's family or culture or group membership. *All* children have the same provision, protection, and participation rights, and *any* child may experience harmful toxins such as poverty, maltreatment, exploitation, or the denial of expression.

More than a quarter of a century has passed since our federal, provincial, and territorial governments expressed their commitment to Canada's children by ratifying the Convention. It is time, long past time, to demonstrate that commitment with action. Imagine if social toxins received the same attention from governments as physical toxins. Imagine if laws, policies, and practices protected children from harmful social environments, provided for every child to develop to potential, and allowed for every child to experience the respect and dignity that come from meaningful participation. Imagine if every Canadian child were assured swift intervention if exposed to social toxins—intervention as timely, successful, and welcome as that of Jeremy Board when he spotted children playing on a contaminated Vancouver beach. Only then would the challenge of children's rights be met.

## CHAPTER 2

ॐ

# The Promise of Children's Rights

The early 1990s were important years for Canada's children. It was during this time that Canada officially embraced a public policy of providing for and advancing the human rights of children. This occurred with the approval of the Convention by all of the provinces except Alberta in 1991, and with Canada's subsequent ratification of the Convention on December 13, 1991. Alberta finally endorsed the Convention in 1999.[1]

In ratifying the Convention, Canada made a commitment to respect the rights of the child as outlined within its provisions. This constituted a very important promise that every effort would be made—through legislation, policies, and programs—to actualize the rights of children. To borrow a famous phrase from legal philosopher Ronald Dworkin, Canada committed itself to a policy of "taking children's rights seriously."[2]

We now analyze Canada's policy promise to children. Our analysis begins with a brief review of the historical evolution of Canadian policy and law in regard to the treatment of children. We then examine the guiding principles underlying the Convention and outline Canada's specific commitments under its various articles, the corresponding entitlements of children, and the processes established for advancing children's rights. We conclude with a look at the hopes of child advocates at the time of ratification, setting the stage for our assessment of Canada's progress since 1991 in later chapters.

## From Objects to Subjects

A review of the evolution of Canadian public policy on children and families shows that the incorporation of children's rights into policy is a relatively new development in Canada, as it is elsewhere. What is evident in this evolution is a shift away from a traditional policy in which children were seen as objects without rights to one in which they were viewed as subjects and persons with dignity and human rights. Traditionally, children were regarded as objects: first, of parental authority and control and then, with the rise of the social welfare state, as objects of concern, pity, and care by the paternalistic state. In early policy and law, children had no basic rights. But after the Second World War, in an era of expanding human rights consciousness, children came to be viewed as subjects and bearers of rights. The outcome was the emergence of a new policy of children's rights.

At the risk of oversimplification, we can divide Canadian policy developments into three overlapping stages: social laissez-faire, paternalistic protection, and children's rights.[3] It is important to note that in each of these stages, given Canada's constitutional structure, the provinces were the main policy and legislative actors. This was because of wide provincial jurisdiction in such child-related fields as social welfare, education, civil rights, family law, and the regulation of much of the private sphere, including family matters. But the federal government still was an important actor. Given federal jurisdiction in areas such as criminal law and divorce, the federal government played an important role in dealing with youth criminal justice and child custody. And given its spending power (its authority to spend in areas of provincial jurisdiction), the federal government also played a major role in providing funds for social programs involving children, either by itself or, more commonly, through cost-sharing arrangements with the provinces. It also is important to note that developments in Québec were unique given the civil law and Catholic tradition of that province. These developments are well documented elsewhere.[4]

In the first policy stage, roughly from colonial times to the nineteenth century, children in Canada were conceived largely as the objects of parental authority. As in the United States and Europe, they were regarded as parental property and as appendages or extensions of the father in patriarchal families.[5] Under social laissez-faire policies, while parents were required to provide their children with the necessities of life, they were given a relatively free hand in all matters of child-rearing. There were virtually no protective laws for children. For example, there was no legislation against abuse or neglect.[6] Parents were allowed to inflict harsh discipline, including beatings. Parents could do this under common law in reference to a parental right of "reasonable chastisement" that allowed them wide latitude in discipline.[7]

Children also had little protection outside the family. There were no laws against economic exploitation by employers. And there was no protective system of youth criminal justice. Youth in conflict with the law (over age thirteen) were treated much the same as adult offenders.[8] In short, a policy of social laissez-faire left children vulnerable to a socially toxic environment of abuse, neglect, and exploitation.

In the second stage, roughly from the time of Confederation to the mid-twentieth century, the property concept began to yield to a new conception of children as a separate and special class of immature persons who were vulnerable and in need of state paternalism and protection. Influenced by a rising tide of humanitarianism and sentimentality, Canadians increasingly believed that society, through state policies and laws, had a duty not only to prevent the abusive treatment of children, but also to provide them with a protective and nurturing social environment.[9] The assumption that parental authority should never be questioned was giving way to an assumption that the state must intervene when parents could not, or would not, fulfill their responsibilities.

A prime example was the enactment of provincial child welfare—or child protection—legislation at the turn of the nineteenth century, giving power to children's aid societies (or child protection agencies) to remove children from abusive homes.[10] Another was the creation of the federal *Juvenile Delinquents Act* in 1908, providing for a separate system of juvenile justice and giving authority to youth courts for the paternalistic treatment of youth in conflict with the law.[11] And in legal proceedings the *parens patriae* doctrine (the state as parent), developed by the Chancery Courts in England to safeguard the property interests of incompetent heirs, was reconstituted and extended by courts and legislatures in Canada to safeguard the publicly determined best interests of all children.[12]

Progressive though this new policy was, children still were regarded as objects in need of care either by their parents or by the paternalistic state. They were seen as "not-yets"—as future adults with future rights rather than as persons with present rights. The state would intervene not because children had rights but because their parents had failed. At best, while the policy of state paternalism offered children certain protection from abusive parents, it left them exposed to conditions that denied them voice and value as persons. At worst, because the state was so reluctant to intervene in family life, beyond the most severe cases, many children remained vulnerable to abuse and neglect. And when the state went too far, as it did with the establishment of residential schools for Indigenous children after 1880, the consequences were horrific.[13]

In the third stage that followed the Second World War, the concept of paternalism began to yield to a newly emerging conception of children as independent bearers of rights. Children gradually came to be considered less as objects and not-yets in occasional need of paternalistic state protection, and more as subjects or existing persons in the here and now with dignity and basic rights of their own. Children are now entitled to make claims not out of the sentiment or benevolence or duties of others, but because of their status as persons with rights to be provided with health care and an adequate standard of living; rights to be protected from maltreatment and exploitation; and rights to participate in decisions affecting them. Unlike the previous concepts, this was a conception consistent with respect for children as persons.[14]

This conception was gradually incorporated into new law and legal principles during the 1970s and 1980s, receiving full recognition in public policy with Canada's ratification of the UN Convention in 1991. In constitutional law, for example, the basic rights listed in the new 1982 *Canadian Charter of Rights and Freedoms* (hereafter the *Charter*) applied to children as well as to adults, subject to reasonable limits. In federal law dealing with youth justice, influenced by the *Charter*, children were given new legal rights in the 1984 *Young Offenders Act* and in the 2003 *Youth Criminal Justice Act*.[15] In marked contrast to the old *Juvenile Delinquents Act*, youth in conflict with the law had a right to legal counsel and a right to be heard in proceedings. And in family law and provincial child protection legislation, the *parens patriae* doctrine expanded the "best interests of the child" principle.[16] In child protection proceedings, the best interests principle became the basis for decisions regarding the placement of a child determined to be in need of protection. And in child custody disputes, the child's best interests became the paramount consideration rather than parental interests.

Finally, with Canada's ratification of the Convention in 1991, commitment to the principle of children's rights and the best interests of the child became official public policy. Earlier, in 1959, Canada signed the UN Declaration of the Rights of the Child. However, like other international declarations, this was a statement of broad moral principles, ideals, and aspirations rather than a legally binding treaty.[17] But conventions or covenants are different. A convention is an expression not only of a moral stand but also of a legal agreement and international obligation. As with other countries ratifying the Convention (all countries but the United States by 2015),[18] the treaty committed Canada to an official policy of recognizing and implementing the rights of the child, not merely aspiring to the practice of children's rights. This constituted a legally binding promise. But it also presented a formidable challenge and task. Where the previous policies of social laissez-faire and state paternalism failed to meet the developmental needs of children, the task of the new policy of children's rights was to meet the basic protection, provision, and participation needs of children.

It is important to note that Canada did have responsibility to provide for many of the rights described in the Convention before its ratification. In signing previous international documents dealing with human rights in general, Canada was obligated to protect and advance the rights of children as well as those of adults. A difficulty, however, was that in these older documents a distinction generally was not drawn between adults and children. Children were assumed to have many of the same rights as adults but this was not always clear. For example, many of the rights specified in the International Covenant on Civil and Political Rights and the International Covenant on Economic, Social, and Cultural Rights were assumed to apply to children. But this was not stated in a systematic and coherent manner. What is important about the UN Convention on the Rights of the Child, in addition to recognizing certain new rights for children, is that standards for children's rights are given clear, comprehensive, and systematic statement. It is unambiguous in the Convention that Canada and other signatory states must respect and implement the rights of the child as described in its provisions.

Gathering support for the Convention and the principle of children's rights was not easy. In Canada, as well as in other countries, the movement for children's rights encountered major resistance and internal division. Resistance was particularly strong by staunch defenders of the institution of the family.[19] According to their view—an updated version of social laissez-faire—state intervention in family life should be as limited as possible. Parents generally have the best interest of their children at heart. The role of the state should be limited to providing economic and other support for families, without intervening directly in family life in the name of children's rights. In cases of abuse and neglect, every effort should be made to preserve and support the family unit. If a child must be apprehended from the home, it should be done only as a very last resort, with the intention of reuniting the family as quickly as possible. Emphasis should be given not to children's rights but to the importance of families in providing stable and continuing care for children. In the view of defenders of the family, support for children's rights and the Convention would serve only to increase conflict in the family and to encourage unwarranted state intrusion into family life. This belief was influential in Canada. Apart from impeding progress toward the adoption of the Convention, it influenced the creation of policies such as ones of family preservation during the 1970s where child protection legislation was modified to make a greater effort to preserve the family unit in cases of child maltreatment.[20]

The children's rights movement also experienced major division within its own ranks.[21] In Canada, as elsewhere, there was a serious rift between child liberationists and child protectionists.[22] Both groups agreed with the essential point that children should have the status of persons with independent rights. And they agreed that these rights should include ones of protection and provision of welfare. But child liberationists argued that children should also have the right to self-determination.[23] The liberationists claimed that in order for children to overcome oppression and discrimination and to exercise autonomy, they should have the same rights as adults. Their argument was this: As gender and ethnicity are unjustifiable grounds for exclusion, children should not be excluded on the arbitrary basis of age. Should children wish, they should be able to work, to vote, and to have sexual relations. However, for child protectionists such self-determination should not be a right.[24] According to their view, a child is a person in the process of development, with limits on his or her abilities and maturity. Protection and nurturance are required until the child's capabilities for autonomy are developed. The best interests of the child need to be attended to in a protective way by parents and state authorities. While age is a somewhat arbitrary cut-off point, it is a necessary and practical means of separating childhood from adulthood. But it is important to determine age limits on a case-by-case basis and to constantly re-examine them to ensure that they are appropriate.

In order to gather support for the Convention, the framers of the document had to find sufficient common ground and to satisfy in some measure the many different sides within and outside of the children's rights movement. They had to provide a statement of children's rights that would find support among both protectionists and liberationists. They had to show to the defenders of the family that the Convention was not a threat to the institution of the family and parental authority. And they had to find appeal among countries with very different religious and cultural values.

## The UN Convention

The Convention on the Rights of the Child was unanimously approved by the UN General Assembly in 1989. It was then signed and ratified by almost all countries of the world during the 1990s, making it the most widely and most quickly ratified convention in world history.

Like other countries, when Canada approved the Convention, it committed itself to the principle that children have certain basic rights as individual persons and that parents, adults, and state authorities have responsibilities to provide for those rights. This is why the Convention is such a landmark document in the history of public policy vis-à-vis children. It officially puts to rest older assumptions about the fundamental rights of parents in child–parent relations and about the role of the paternalistic state in protecting the interests of children. The rights of children are now required to be the central objective of policy. It is children who have inherent and fundamental rights, and it is parents, adults, and state officials who have responsibilities to provide for those rights. To the extent that parents and adult authorities have rights, these are rights delegated to them under the Convention and connected to their duties and responsibilities to children.

In designing the Convention, the framers first had to address a key question: Who is a child? It was relatively easy for the framers to define the upper age of the child. In article 1, they stated that a child is every person under age eighteen unless the law of a nation grants majority at an earlier age. But what is the minimum age of a child? Is it at conception or at birth? With the abortion issue in the background, this was one of the most controversial issues in designing the Convention.[25] To reach a consensus and find common ground among nations with different religious and cultural values, the framers decided that in article 1, there would be no minimum age. Thus the minimum age could be at either birth or conception. But at the same time, the framers acknowledged the importance of the prenatal environment to the health and well-being of the child. Thus, in the Preamble to the Convention, it is stated that the child "needs special safeguards and care, including appropriate legal protection, both before as well as after birth." So in short, while the importance of prenatal care is recognized, the legal protection of children could include, but would not require, the prohibition of abortion.

The framers then mapped out the basic rights of the child. Following Thomas Hammarberg, we can divide these rights into the "three Ps": provision, protection, and participation.[26] The rights of provision refer to children's rights to be provided with basic welfare and nurturance. For example, children have the right to survival and development (article 6), basic economic welfare (article 27), health care (article 24), education (article 28), and play and recreation (article 31). They also have the right to a name, to acquire a nationality, and to know and be cared for by parents (article 7). The rights of protection refer to children's rights to be protected from harmful acts or practices. For example, children have the right to be protected from abuse and neglect (article 19), economic exploitation (article 32), sexual exploitation (article 34), and discrimination (article 2). Children in trouble with the law also have the right to protective treatment in the form of a separate and rehabilitative youth justice system (articles 37 and 40). Finally, rights of participation refer to children's rights to express an opinion in matters affecting them and to have that opinion heard (article 12). As part of participation, children have the right to freedom of expression and information (article 13); freedom of thought, conscience, and religion (article 14); and freedom of association and peaceful assembly (article 15).

The three Ps are rights that apply generally to all children. But the Convention also provides for rights concerning children in special circumstances or in particularly difficult situations. For example, children with special needs have a right to special care (article 23). Children who are orphans also have a right to special care (article 20). Refugee children have a right to special protection and assistance (article 22). And children of minority and Indigenous communities have the right to enjoy their own culture, practise their own religion, and use their own language (article 30).

The framers of the Convention recognized that given the many articles and broad language of the document, the interpretation and application of the Convention would not always be easy. For example, there could be conflict between the role of the family and the role of the state in providing for the welfare of children. There could be conflict between the wishes of parents and the wishes of children in making decisions. And there could be conflict over the relative priority of the rights of the child. It was necessary, then, that the framers include guiding principles in the Convention to serve as an aid in its interpretation and a guide to application and implementation. These principles would have to find appeal among the different parties and countries involved and find broad support for the Convention inside and outside the children's rights movement. The framers chose to highlight four general principles: the principle of the best interests of the child, where a primary consideration in all actions concerning children is their best interests; the principle of participation, where children have the right to be heard; the principle of non-discrimination, where children are to be protected against all forms of discrimination; and the principle of the right to life, survival, and development, where the child's fundamental physical and mental well-being are to be ensured to the maximum extent possible. The principles of non-discrimination and life, survival, and development are relatively straightforward. But the best interests principle and the principle of participation require elaboration because they appear to be in conflict.[27]

The best interests principle was given expression in article 3. This represented in some measure the position of child protectionists. According to article 3, "in *all* actions concerning children, whether undertaken by public or private social welfare institutions, courts of law, administrative authorities or legislative bodies, the best interests of the child shall be *a primary consideration*" (our emphasis). The principle is not as strong as many child protectionists and advocates had wanted.[28] For the principle is to be *a* primary consideration, not *the* primary consideration. This leaves the door open to the possibility of other considerations, such as parental interests or state interests, trumping the best interests principle in some instances. Nevertheless, making best interests a primary consideration puts the principle in a very strong position when read with other articles in the Convention. The principle is also very strong in that its scope includes *all* decisions concerning children, not only official decisions by the courts or administrative authorities. This means that parents also have a responsibility to make decisions in the best interests of the child. Under article 18, "the best interests of the child will be their basic concern."

The principle of participation is reflected in article 12. This was a unique and quite remarkable part of the Convention. Specific reference to this principle was not made in any previous international document on children's rights. The principle represented a compromise position between child liberationists and child protectionists on the issue of a child's evolving right to self-determination. According to article 12, "States Parties shall *assure* to the child who is capable of forming his or her own views the right to express those views freely in *all* matters affecting the child, the views of the child being given due weight in accordance with the *age and maturity* of the child" (our emphasis). In keeping with the position of child protectionists, a child does not have the absolute right to self-determination. Rather, recognition is given to the evolving capabilities of the child and to the age and maturity of the child. But in keeping with the spirit of the child liberationist position, although autonomy is not a right, participation is recognized as a right. Article 12 says that while decisions affecting the child may not be in accord with the views of the child, the state shall assure to the capable child the right to express views in all relevant matters. The views of the capable child need not be decisive, but they are to be listened to and taken seriously. In general, children have the right to participate in all matters affecting them. And in particular, as specified in the second paragraph of article 12, children have the right to be heard in judicial and administrative proceedings that affect them, either directly or through a representative.

What is the relation between the principles of best interests and participation? In the event of a conflict, does the right to participate trump consideration of best interests, or does the best interests principle come before participation? We may think of the case of a custody dispute in which a child wishes to express her view about who should have custody and her parents are concerned with shielding her from acrimonious proceedings. It would appear from the wording of the articles of the Convention, and from the documents and debates leading up to the Convention, that the framers intended participation to be an integral part of the best interests principle.[29] The framers regarded the ascertainment of the views of the child as a critical component in assessing the child's best interests. To exclude the views of the child in the dispute might well run contrary to the goal of determining her best interests in the outcome. Thus the principle of participation impinges on the best interests principle. But it is not a two-way street. The best interests principle does not impinge on the one of participation. The framers chose not to qualify participation by consideration of best interests. To do so would be overly paternalistic. The principle of participation was already qualified in article 12 in reference to the age and maturity of the child and to the fact that the right to be heard did not mean the right to decision-making power.

Finally, apart from general principles, the framers of the Convention highlighted the theme of the primary importance of the family to the child, a theme designed to gain the support of defenders of the institution of the family. It was given statement in many parts of the Convention. While the Convention did not recognize parental rights as fundamental rights—it is children who have fundamental rights—the framers did make the Convention very supportive of strong families and family values. Indeed, we may infer from the Convention that the child has a right to a family environment.[30] The framers purposefully did not provide a precise definition of "family" in order to allow for cross-cultural interpretations and the many different conceptions of family.[31] But they did strongly emphasize the importance to the child of a family environment supportive of the child. Thus the Preamble to the Convention states that "the child, for the full and harmonious development of his personality, should grow up in a family environment, in an atmosphere of happiness, love, and understanding." It also refers to "family" as "the fundamental group of society and the natural environment for the growth and wellbeing of all its members and particularly children." Respect for "family" is referred to many times in the articles of the Convention, especially in articles dealing with the rights of participation and the need for parents or guardians to provide children with guidance. For example, in article 13, in reference to the child's right to freedom of thought, conscience, and religion, the state shall respect the rights and duties of parents or guardians "to provide direction to the child in the exercise of his or her right in a manner consistent with the evolving capabilities of the child." Thus a child's family is recognized to be an important environment for guidance, support, and nurturance.

Family is so important to the child that the Convention establishes a duty for governments to preserve family relationships and to support families in providing for their children. For example, in article 7, the state shall implement the right of the child "to know and be cared for by his or her parents." In article 9, in the case of parental separation, the state shall respect the right of the child "to maintain personal relations and direct contact with both parents on a regular basis, except if it is contrary to the child's best interests." In the various articles on the rights of provision, the state shall provide assistance to parents in the raising of children should this be required. The state shall do this in general terms (article 18) and in the specific areas of child-care services (article 18), care for children with special needs (article 23), health care (article 24), and nutrition, clothing, and housing (article 27). The state is expected to assist parents but not to supplant them in the maintenance of a family environment supportive of children. The assumption is made that for the most part—except in cases of maltreatment or parental death or ill health—parents will provide for their children.

Thus the framers designed the Convention to incorporate the positions of child protectionists, liberationists, and defenders of families. They did so in a reasonable fashion, giving the different sides not all that they wanted but enough to strike a persuasive balance between the protection and autonomy of the child, and between children's rights and the importance of strong families. Not that the Convention is devoid of problems. For example, some have argued that it does not take into account major technological developments that have arisen since the 1980s, such as the Internet and social media and their problematic use by children.[32] However, the Convention is a major breakthrough in the setting of basic international standards.

## The Promise of Implementation

In signing and ratifying the Convention, Canada promised not only to recognize the inherent rights of children but also to ensure that children could actually enjoy the substance of these rights. We now review Canada's obligations under the Convention. We also examine major challenges in implementing the Convention, including enforcement, federalism, financial resources, and lack of public awareness of the rights of the child.

Under the Convention, Canada is obligated *in general terms* to put into effect the rights as described in the Convention. According to article 4, "States Parties shall undertake all appropriate legislative, administrative, and other measures for the implementation of the rights recognized in the present Convention." But like other countries, Canada is not necessarily required to implement all the rights. It may declare a reservation or statement of qualification with respect to a particular right or a particular aspect of the Convention.[33] It may do this as long as the reservation does not violate the overall purpose and spirit of the Convention and is agreed to by the United Nations. Canada declared two reservations. The first was in regard to youth justice. Canada stated that it could not promise to implement a section of the Convention that required children who are incarcerated by the legal system to be detained separately from adults. The second was in regard to adoption. Canada declared that out of respect for Indigenous cultural traditions and family practices, it could not apply a section that called for the state regulation of adoption.

Apart from these reservations, Canada is obligated to ensure that its laws, policies, and practices are consistent with the Convention and, where inconsistent or problematic, to implement changes. One means by which countries can apply the Convention is to make international treaties self-executing.[34] This means that upon ratification, treaties are immediately incorporated into domestic law and have automatic legal application. The Convention can thus be brought into play in a legal case and invoked in a court of law. But in countries such as Canada, international treaties are not of immediate application. If the Convention is to be brought into law and public policy, it has to be done through new legislation or amendments to existing legislation. So in line with Canadian tradition, although the Convention does not have immediate and wholesale application, Canada is obligated to ensure implementation over time through new legislation and policies.[35]

As part of implementation, Canada and other signatory states are to give account of their actions through a reporting and monitoring system established under articles 43, 44, and 45.[36] Accordingly, an expert committee based in Geneva—the Committee on the Rights of the Child—was created to review periodic reports made by states parties on measures taken and progress made in fulfilling Convention obligations. The Committee was to consist of ten members—now eighteen members—elected by secret ballot from a list of persons nominated by the states parties. The Committee was regarded as the highest international authority in interpreting the Convention and one responsible for prodding governments into more action where needed. Within two years of ratifying the Convention, Canada and other states parties were required to send an initial report to the Committee. A report was then to be sent to the Committee every five years after the first report, indicating the measures taken to comply with the Convention, the difficulties encountered, and the progress made. The role of the Committee was to review each report and provide feedback in its own report—called concluding observations—indicating positive developments and suggesting areas for improvement. As part of the review, the Committee could invite reports—called shadow reports—by other parties, including child advocacy groups, interested non-governmental organizations (NGOs), and specialized agencies dealing with children's issues. Such reports would be an important source of alternative information for the Committee and an aid in the evaluation. And as part of the implementation process, countries were expected to address the Committee's concerns and recommendations in their next report.

Through this system, Canada is obligated to report not only on measures it has taken on specific rights but also on initiatives in the area of public education about children's rights. The framers of the Convention saw public education as a critical part of implementation and enforcement.[37] If pressure was to be applied by child advocates, interested parties, and children themselves for government action, there must be public awareness about children's rights. For this reason, article 42 commits states parties to "make the principles and provisions of the Convention widely known, by appropriate and active means, to adults and children alike." And in article 44, states parties "shall make their reports widely available to the public in their own countries." The emphasis on "appropriate and active means" in article 42 implied that education should not simply mean that information be sent out in response to requests from children or the public. Rather, it implied a systematic, comprehensive, and effective program of public education. Indeed, the UN Committee urged Canada in 1995—and other countries during the 1990s—to incorporate children's rights into school curricula and to ensure education for professionals working with and for children.[38]

Canada made its first report to the UN Committee in 1994, explaining measures taken by the federal, provincial, and territorial governments. To assist in the review, a separate report was submitted by the Canadian Coalition for the Rights of Children, a large umbrella organization of child advocacy groups, highlighting gaps and shortcomings in Canada's effort.[39] The Committee reviewed both reports and replied to Canada in 1995, pointing out several problems, including high child poverty and youth suicide rates, the continuing practice of corporal punishment, and inadequate coordination among different levels of government.[40] Together with shadow reports from the Canadian Coalition, Canada made its second report in 2001 and its combined third and fourth report in 2009. The Committee replied in 2003 and 2012, respectively, repeating many of its earlier concerns and adding to the list other problems such as punitive elements in the youth justice system, the overrepresentation of Indigenous youth in the justice system, inadequate early childhood education, the lack of incorporation of the Convention into Canadian law, and the lack of public awareness and education on the rights of the child.[41]

Such a list of concerns suggests that implementation is far from a simple and easy task. Several obstacles stand in the way of Canadian governments meeting their obligations. One is the lack of a strong system of enforcement. As we discuss in Chapter 3, the Convention is not "hard law" in the sense that it can be enforced through a court of law or tribunal.[42] Rather, for Canada and many other countries, it is a system of "soft law" enforced indirectly over time through public opinion and international peer pressure. Without such pressure, compliance depends on the goodwill and political commitment of government authorities, which often is lacking.

Another obstacle is complacency. At the time of ratification of the Convention, the federal government had argued that the Convention already was incorporated into Canadian law through the *Charter*, federal and provincial human rights legislation, and other child-related federal and provincial legislation.[43] The government's position was that before it ratified the Convention, it consulted with the provinces and made the determination that Canadian laws already were largely in compliance with the Convention. This was necessary, said the federal government, because of the complexity of federalism, the fact that many children's rights issues cut across all jurisdictions, and the need to get provincial approval to move forward. Thus, apart from minor issues that may come up from time to time, there has been no need to incorporate the Convention into law or develop new laws consistent with the Convention.

Such reasoning is highly dubious. But it has been used to justify the unwillingness since 1991 by Canadian governments to incorporate the Convention, or parts of the Convention, into law. As we discuss in Chapter 4, no mention has been made of the Convention except in a few pieces of legislation, including the federal *Youth Criminal Justice Act*, federal legislation on child sexual exploitation, provincial adoption acts dealing with international adoptions, and child protection legislation in the territories and Ontario.[44] And because the Convention has seldom been referenced in legislation, Canadian judges do not often refer to it in decisions. The most that courts can do, in cases where the law is unclear or ambiguous, is to use the Convention as a guide to interpreting the law.[45] They justify this by saying that it can be presumed that Canadian Parliament and provincial legislatures would want to uphold the values enshrined in the Convention. However, in the absence of incorporation, the Convention at best has "persuasive force" rather than "obligatory force."[46]

Another difficulty is the complicated and sometimes contentious system of decentralized federalism.[47] Under Canada's constitution, the federal government has the authority to make international treaties, but it does not have the sole responsibility to put them into effect. When a matter falls under provincial jurisdiction, it is the provinces that have responsibility for implementation. This creates problems because not all provinces have the financial resources to fulfill all their responsibilities. Most rely on the federal government for fiscal transfers. The system has evolved such that many of the transfers are without conditions or with loose conditions, making strong uniform national programs difficult. Given all these complications and a history of federal–provincial friction, it is sometimes difficult to gain intergovernmental cooperation and to coordinate efforts for improving children's rights.

However, it is important to point out that although a complicated system of federalism presents a difficulty, it is not a legitimate excuse for inaction or failure. On the one hand, under Canadian constitutional law, it is well established that the federal government cannot enforce the implementation of an international treaty in areas under provincial jurisdiction.[48] But on the other hand, under the Vienna Convention on the Law of Treaties, to which Canada is bound, the internal law of a country and the lack of federal authority is not a legitimate defence for a country failing to live up to its international commitments. Once Canada has ratified a convention, the Canadian government must act in good faith to fulfill its obligations to the greatest degree possible. It has a legal obligation to ensure that other levels of government are aware of their responsibilities and that overall implementation of the convention takes place. Nonetheless, federalism does present difficulties because of the lack of a strict system of enforcing international treaties.

Further difficulties are financial resources and budgetary concerns. Implementing children's rights, especially social and economic rights such as health care, obviously takes money.[49] The Convention requires that social and economic rights be implemented progressively and with the maximum amount of available resources. Yet it is common in affluent countries such as Canada to claim the need for fiscal restraint or the lack of resources as a reason for inaction.[50] This problem was foreseen in 1990 at the World Summit for Children. It was agreed that countries (including Canada) would abide by the principle of "first call for children" where the needs of children would be given first priority in budgeting, regardless of economic conditions. Moreover, as noted by James Himes, the Convention and the principle of the best interests of the child do not allow countries to explain away their inaction through a cavalier reference to a lack of resources.[51] The onus is on them to demonstrate that they have done everything they could and have used *all* available resources to implement the rights of children.

Finally, another obstacle is the lack of public awareness of the Convention.[52] The system of implementing the Convention depends on moral and political pressure. But the building of this pressure is very difficult without public awareness. In Canada there still is little public awareness, little children's rights education in schools, little training of professionals, and even little awareness among politicians.[53] Among those who have opinions of children's rights, many have negative or ambivalent views based on what they see as too many rights for children, especially for youth in the justice system.[54] In the absence of full education, there is little public under-standing of the importance of the Convention and thus little pressure for its implementation. To the extent that there is public pressure to improve the situation of children, it is largely based on sympathy and old notions of charity and on the perception of children as vulnerable not-yets.

This leaves implementation largely dependent on the political will of politicians and government officials. This is a problem because amid the multiple demands on governments, in the absence of strong pressure, it is easy for children's rights to become ignored. Even when political leaders would like to take the initiative, they often want or need public pressure to justify what they do. Because the Convention is soft law rather than hard law, without pressure, it may be attractive to take the path of least resistance and ignore Canada's obligations.

## Hopes for a Child Rights–Respecting Canada

The period surrounding Canada's signing of the Convention was one of great excitement and optimism. Despite the many obstacles, child advocates were hopeful that the Convention would be a catalyst for inspiring serious efforts among governments to ensure that children more fully enjoy their rights to provision, protection, and participation.

First, there was optimism for progress in advancing children's provi-sion rights, particularly in regard to eliminating child poverty and enhan-cing child care and child health. Michelle Clarke, child advocate and social policy analyst, expressed hope that the Convention would spur efforts to reduce child poverty rates.[55] The Convention, she said, clearly states that all children have the right to a standard of living adequate for their develop-ment. But contradictory to this right, many children are living in poverty. A similar point was made by Martha Friendly, a child-care advocate and expert on early childhood education and care.[56] The Convention, she pointed out, obligates Canada to ensure that children benefit from quality services in child care. But Canada's system was greatly at odds with the Convention because of its patchwork services and lack of standards. The Convention would spur corrective action. In addition, said the Canadian Coalition for the Rights of Children, the Convention would inspire Canada to make a greater effort to promote children's health.[57] Much stronger action was required, said the Coalition, to tackle ongoing problems such as infant mor-tality and low birth weight, especially among Indigenous children.

Second, there was hope for a significant advance in children's protection rights, especially protection from abuse, exploitation, and violence. Legal analyst Anne Genereux expressed confidence that the Convention would be a catalyst to end the legal authorization of corporal punishment.[58] In her view, the Convention clearly commits Canada to protecting the child from all forms of violence, including corporal punishment. Also, according to legal expert Nicholas Bala, the Convention directs Canada to make greater efforts to protect children from sexual exploitation.[59] He pointed to two key problems: the lack of a federal law against child pornography and the lack of strong policies to support children caught up in the sex trade. He expressed hope that the Convention would inspire a new child pornography law and new policies to protect children and prevent their entry into prostitution. Moreover, as noted by the Canadian Coalition for the Rights of Children, the Convention calls on Canadian governments to build much stronger systems of child welfare to protect children from abuse and neglect.[60]

Third, there was hope for progress in advancing children's participation rights. According to youth delegates to meetings of the Canadian Coalition for the Rights of Children, Canada failed to assure children a voice in matters affecting them.[61] The Convention, they said, clearly states that children (or their representatives) should be provided the opportunity to be heard in decision-making and in judicial or administrative proceedings affecting the child. And as part of participation, children should be assured freedom of expression, freedom of thought and religion, and freedom of association and assembly, subject to reasonable limits. Yet, said the delegates, children's voices are too often silenced or restricted by the lack of structures and opportunities that facilitate participation. It was their expressed hope that the Convention would spur serious efforts in Canada to make children's participation rights a reality.

These were the hopes for a progressive Canada in 1991. In later chapters, we examine the degree to which these hopes have been realized. But first, we take a deeper look at the moral and legal status of children in Canada.

# CHAPTER 3

౨

# The Moral and
# Legal Status of Children

Although more than a quarter of a century has passed since Canada ratified the Convention, many people remain unaware of children's rights. Some believe parents have a right to rear their children as they see fit. Others question how international agreements apply in Canada, or how legal minors can raise rights claims. In this chapter, we distinguish moral rights from legal rights and explore the corresponding duties of parents and the state to safeguard and promote the independent welfare and developmental interests of children. We then address some legal implications of Canada's ratification of the Convention and some enduring problems associated with the ascription of legal rights to children.

## What Are Moral Rights?

Broadly speaking, moral rights are correlates of moral duties.[1] If Rajesh promises to do something for Kiran, his commitment gives rise to a corresponding expectation on Kiran's part that he will follow through. Kiran may remind Rajesh from time to time of his unfulfilled commitment until he follows through, and these reminders may take the form of a familiar moral claim: "But Rajesh, you promised!" If Andrea calls her friend Randy and offers to buy his motorbike for $1500, and he agrees, each has a moral duty to follow through on the deal. Should one renege, the other may claim the individual acted in bad faith or lied. Moral rights might be described as claims on the conscience of those who have voluntarily assumed moral duties. Whether between individuals or states, the idea that agreements must be kept—*pacta sunt servanda*—is a basic moral principle.

As persons, children have moral rights. These do not derive from the Convention, though the global consensus that gave rise to the Convention and its ratification by all UN member states (apart from the United States) clearly demonstrates that safeguarding and promoting the welfare and developmental interests of children is universally accepted as a sovereign duty—a state responsibility. Every child is born into a family of some sort and a community of some sort; this is not a matter of choice for the child and cannot give rise to any duties on the part of the child. Those who choose to bring a child into existence, on the other hand, assume some very serious moral duties. Immanuel Kant argued that parents "incur an obligation to make the child content with his conditions so far as they can."[2] John Stuart Mill made the claim even more forcefully: "To undertake this responsibility—to bestow a life which may be either a curse or a blessing—unless the being on whom it is to be bestowed will have at least the ordinary chances of a desirable existence, is a crime against that being."[3] By these influential accounts, parents have a moral duty to provide for the welfare and developmental interests of the dependent persons they have brought into existence, and both the child and the wider community have a corresponding expectation that these duties will be fulfilled. Mill went a step further, characterizing parental failure as a "moral crime both against the unfortunate offspring and against society" and holding that "if the parent does not fulfill this obligation, the State ought to see it fulfilled."[4]

## What Are Legal Rights?

With the above understanding of moral duties and rights in mind, let's go back to Andrea and Randy and the $1500 motorbike deal. If their agreement took the form of a signed contract, each might bring a legal claim against the other in court in the event of a breach. In making a formal contract, Andrea and Randy have duties and corresponding rights to one another that they know the state will recognize and enforce. As Mill observed, "When we call anything a person's right, we mean that he has a valid claim on society to protect him in the possession of it, either by the force of law, or by that of education and opinion."[5]

As we have seen, rights are associated with an expectation that duties will be fulfilled. While moral rights are claims on the conscience of one who has voluntarily assumed moral duties, legal rights are claims the state will recognize and enforce. In this sense, legal rights are *institutionally contingent*, as they require public structures within which rights claims may be raised, recognized, vindicated, and enforced.

Legal rights are also *proprietary*.[6] Most people tend to think of property in terms of tangible things like furniture or buildings, but property can be intangible as well. *Ballentine's Law Dictionary* defines *intangible property* as "rights not related to physical things, being merely relationships between persons, natural or corporate, which the law recognizes by attaching to them certain sanctions enforceable in the courts."[7]

In the absence of standing to raise rights claims in court, people have only interests, or claims on the conscience of others. This is a problem for children in Canada, because until they reach the age of majority, most cannot access the courts to make legal rights claims.[8] Most children must rely on their parents or the state to represent them when alleging a rights violation. Yet as we make clear throughout this book, when children's rights are violated, it is often by their parents or the state. Canada's failure to follow through on the commitments it made when it ratified the Convention is an obvious example. *Pacta sunt servanda*.

## Legal Standing

"The legal power to claim (performatively) one's right or the things to which one has a right seems to be essential to the very notion of a right," notes Joel Feinberg. "A right to which one could not make claim (i.e. not even for recognition) would be a very 'imperfect' right indeed!"[9] Because judges in the common-law provinces of Canada (all but Québec) have a *parens patriae* duty to prioritize the best interests of children in any matter before them, it could be argued that these interests need not be claimed.[10] But again, most children do not have access to courts in the first place.[11] In the absence of standing, fulfilling Canada's commitments under the Convention requires that all children have access to independent, publicly funded legal counsel to raise rights claims on their behalf.

Children in a number of European Union (EU) member states do have standing to make legal rights claims before the European Court of Human Rights and, in some jurisdictions, in civil courts as well. In Canada, only in Québec can a minor, "with the authorization of the court, institute alone an action relating to his status, to the exercise of parental authority or to an act that he may perform alone."[12] In *M.C. v. L.P.*, [2009] R.J.Q. 945, a 12-year-old in Québec sued her father after he refused to sign a parental consent form for a school trip, having grounded her for posting "inappropriate" pictures of herself online. In a decision upheld on appeal, the court found the father's punishment overly severe.[13] The prospect of children accessing the courts for judicial review of parental decision-making may be the stuff of nightmares for parental rights advocates, but the sky has yet to fall in Québec or the EU.[14]

## Rights as Social Guarantees

While legal rights are institutionally contingent, both moral and legal rights are *socially contingent*. As philosopher Henry Shue observes, "Enjoyment of the substance of a right is socially guaranteed ... only if all social institutions, *as well as individual persons*, avoid depriving people of the substance of the right and some provide, if necessary, aid to anyone who has nevertheless been deprived of the substance of the right."[15] Rights on paper cannot, in and of themselves, make much of a difference in the life or circumstances of any individual. Whether someone is actually able to enjoy the substance of their rights depends on what *others* do or fail to do. An everyday example may help to illustrate this point: In accordance with the *Smoke-Free Ontario Act*,[16] there are signs on every building of the local hospital complex indicating that smoking is not permitted within nine metres of any entrance. Yet the ground around some entrances is littered with cigarette butts. While the signs are evidence of a legal rule, the butts on the ground are evidence that some people routinely violate that rule (and that the environment is not, in fact, smoke-free). In order for everyone in and around every building to enjoy the substance of the statutory right to a smoke-free environment, social action is needed. Everyone needs to respect the no-smoking rule, and more people need to speak up when the no-smoking rule is violated.

By the same token, the Convention cannot, in and of itself, guarantee that everyone will abandon proprietary notions about children, or that all children will be able to enjoy the substance of their rights to provision, protection, and participation in every social and institutional context in which they find themselves, including—and perhaps especially—within families. Children's rights under the Convention have been guaranteed by the state, but the extent to which children actually exercise their rights depends on the attitude of their parents and guardians.[17] If Canada wishes to ensure that the substance of the rights outlined in the Convention are socially guaranteed, a cultural shift is required in terms of how people think about children. This is why article 42 of the Convention mandates children's rights education for children *and* for adults. This, in our view, remains one of the most important challenges of children's rights for Canada.

## Children as Legal Minors

According to article 1 of the Convention, "a child means every human being below the age of eighteen years unless under the law applicable to the child, majority is attained earlier." Included in this definition is a reference to the legal status of children and adults: An adult is someone who has reached the age of *majority*. A child is someone who has not reached the age of majority; in other words, a *minor*. The Convention recognizes that the age of majority may vary by jurisdiction. In Canada, the federal age of majority is eighteen, while the provincial age of majority is eighteen in Alberta, Manitoba, Ontario, Prince Edward Island, Québec, and Saskatchewan and nineteen in British Columbia, New Brunswick, Newfoundland and Labrador, Northwest Territories, Nunavut, Nova Scotia, and Yukon. Hence an eighteen-year-old would be considered a minor in British Columbia but would not be considered a child under the Convention.

The Convention also recognizes that there may be legal mechanisms in particular jurisdictions for the emancipation of minors, allowing them to be recognized as adults before reaching the statutory age of majority. For example, we sometimes hear of child stars in Hollywood filing emancipation petitions to manage their financial affairs without parental oversight. Québec permits emancipation petitions in some circumstances while Ontario does not.[18] The statutory age of majority also varies by activity or purpose. In Ontario, for example, young people may move out of their parents' homes and manage their own affairs at sixteen under the *Family Law Act*,[19] but they must continue attending school until they are eighteen under the *Education Act*.[20] In other words, they are legally free to withdraw from parental care and control at sixteen, but they are not legally free to withdraw from school until they are eighteen.

Provincial and federal laws impose both positive and negative duties on adults having care and control of legal minors. Under the compulsory schooling provisions of the Ontario *Education Act*, for example, "the parent or guardian of a person who is required to attend school ... shall cause the person to attend school ... unless the person is at least 16 years old and has withdrawn from parental control."[21] Anyone operating a motor vehicle in

Ontario is responsible for ensuring that passengers under sixteen years of age are wearing a seatbelt (positive duties).[22] In both these examples, the law starts holding sixteen-year-olds responsible, not their parents, should they choose not to attend school or wear a seatbelt. No retailer may sell alcohol or tobacco to a person under the age of nineteen, and no employer may hire a person under age sixteen to work during school hours (negative duties).[23] In both these examples, the law holds retailers and employers responsible should they fail to respect laws and regulations designed to protect minors. Because of their presumed immaturity and vulnerability, the law constrains or prohibits a wide range of activities involving children that would not generally be subject to regulation or restraint between consenting adults.

## Legal Competence

Obviously, people do not magically turn into fully mature and competent adults on the eve of their eighteenth birthday in Québec and their nineteenth birthday in Nova Scotia. Maturation is a lengthy process, and there may be considerable variation in levels of maturity among teenagers and young adults. Laws are by practical necessity categorical, as it would be impractical to make individualized judicial assessments in all circumstances. A statutorily defined age of majority reflects a shift in legal *presumptions* about competence. Someone who has reached the age of majority for particular purposes is *presumptively* mature, and hence legally competent for those purposes unless an individualized assessment determines otherwise. A person who has not reached the age of majority for particular legal purposes is *presumptively* immature, and hence legally incompetent for those purposes unless an individualized assessment determines otherwise. Unless and until a minor is legally competent, whether by reaching the statutory age of majority or by operation of law, he or she is not free to make certain kinds of decisions or to engage in certain kinds of activities without the permission and guidance of a parent or legal guardian.[24] This is consistent with the Convention. Under article 5, Canada has agreed to "respect the responsibilities, rights and duties of parents ... to provide, in a manner consistent with the evolving capacities of the child, appropriate direction and guidance in the exercise by the child of the rights recognized in the present Convention." Throughout Canada, the age of consent or competence for marriage is sixteen, but persons under the age of majority (eighteen or nineteen, depending on the province or territory in which they live) need the consent of a parent or a court. The age of consent or competence for enlisting in the military is eighteen, but seventeen-year-olds may volunteer with parental consent.[25] The age of consent or competence for engaging in sexual activities was raised from fourteen to sixteen by the federal government in 2008,[26] subject to a "close-in-age exception" allowing fourteen- and fifteen-year-olds to engage in consensual sex with persons no more than five years older. A notable exception to the shifting presumption rule is in the domain of medical treatment. Unlike the rest of Canada, Ontario has no statutory age of consent for medical treatment, so every patient is presumed competent unless a doctor has reasonable grounds to believe otherwise. In case of disagreement, individualized assessments are undertaken by a Consent and Capacity Board, taking into account the complexity of the proposed treatments and whether the patient can appreciate the foreseeable consequences of his or her choices.[27]

At common law, competent persons are those presumptively capable of safeguarding and promoting their own interests, of foreseeing and intending the consequences of their actions, and of governing themselves and their affairs in accordance with reason and reasonable laws.[28] Because competent persons can make decisions for themselves, they have an interest in doing so. Hence liberty interests are ascribed to adults, who are normally free to make decisions for themselves as a matter of right. Incompetent persons are those presumptively incapable (or not fully capable) of safeguarding and promoting their own interests; of foreseeing and intending the consequences of their actions; and of governing themselves and their affairs in accordance with reason and reasonable laws. Thus minors and other persons in Canada who are not fully competent are generally subject to some form of custody.[29] Custody is usually discussed in the context of separation agreements or divorce orders, but it is a much broader concept. It is the common-law mechanism by which competent persons exercise legal authority to make decisions on behalf of persons who are not fully capable of making decisions for themselves.[30] Consistent with the Convention, the Ontario *Children's Law Reform Act* provides that "a person entitled to custody of a child has the rights and responsibilities of a parent in respect of the person of the child and must exercise those rights and responsibilities in the best interests of the child."[31] As we will see in discussing authoritative or democratic parenting and teaching in Chapter 7, the exercise of custodial authority in a manner that respects the dignity and evolving capacities of the child while promoting his or her independent welfare and developmental interests is consistent with the Convention. In practice, respecting the evolving capacities of children means increasing opportunities for independent decision-making as they mature. While particular children may not be mature enough to make some decisions for themselves, they do have an interest in developing their capacity for self-governance and, as we shall see in Chapter 4, rights under both the Convention and the *Charter* to exercise their evolving capacities and capabilites.[32]

## The State as Parent

*Parens patriae* is the common-law doctrine by which "the state as parent" exercises substituted decision-making authority on behalf of minor children. This is public custodial authority in a very broad sense.[33] In cases involving children requiring life-saving medical treatments to which their parents have objected for religious or cultural reasons, for example, a judge may consent to the treatment on the child's behalf. In cases involving abused or neglected children, a judge may issue a wardship order limiting or suspending the custodial authority of the child's parents. In disputes between separating and divorcing spouses, a judge may issue a custody order. Public custodial authority is also reflected in legislation requiring parents to enrol their children in a provincially approved educational program of some sort.[34] An expansive conception of the *parens patriae* doctrine provided a primary legal basis for the establishment of juvenile justice and child welfare programs, the prohibition of child labour, and the enactment of compulsory schooling laws in the late nineteenth and into the early twentieth century. During this period, children came to be regarded as future adults and citizens with an interest in access to public knowledge and diverse formative influences. The state was expected to facilitate equality of opportunity and social mobility, so that no child's future options would be limited to what his or her parents alone might prefer.[35]

## The Evolving Status of Children

As we discussed in Chapter 2, the moral and legal status of children has evolved in three overlapping stages, from conceptions of children as the property of their parents (from colonial times to the mid-nineteenth century) to conceptions of children as not-yets (from the late nineteenth to the mid-twentieth century) to children as persons with inherent rights (after the Second World War). It is important to keep in mind that each of these conceptualizations did not give way to the next. The Convention, like all human rights instruments, is predicated on acceptance of the principle that children are persons, not property, and that all persons have inherent rights. Though this principle has been embraced in Canada, some people are still willing to assert or defend a view of children as parental property. In 2012, Steve Tourloukis, a dentist in Hamilton, Ontario, filed a lawsuit against the local school board because he wanted his children's teachers to give him advance notice before discussing family, marriage, and sexuality in the classroom. "My children are my own," he told reporters. "I own them. They don't belong to the school board."[36] Ultimately, in *E. T. v. Hamilton-Wentworth District School Board*, [2016] O.J. No. 5997, the court declined to issue the declaration sought by Tourloukis that he had final authority over the education of his children.

As we have already noted, the view of children as parental property—"I own them"—is sharply at odds with both the Convention and Canadian law. It is, moreover, both illiberal and immoral. "Liberals agree that liberty is important both to individual wellbeing and to civic life, and their sense of this importance is rooted above all in the experience of religious conflict and civil war during the Reformation," writes Randall Curren.[37] Enlightenment liberals rejected ascribed status and compulsory religion, holding that individuals are the sole bearers of rights and the appropriate centre of moral concern. According to Kantian moral principles, respect for human dignity requires that individuals be treated as ends in themselves and never as mere means to the ends of others.[38] To treat children as property is to deny their humanity, dignity, and moral worth. It is to deny they are persons with independent welfare and developmental interests. "The The United Nations says little in its declarations, covenants, conventions, and protocols about the grounds of human rights; it says simply that human rights derive from 'the inherent dignity of the human person,'" writes James Griffin, "but the most plausible interpretation of this use of 'dignity' is that it is still the Enlightenment use."[39] There is no plausible account of rights by which anyone could claim unlimited or absolute discretion in the upbringing of a child.[40]

## The Interests of Children

We have already noted that rights are widely understood as correlates of duties. Within this framework, there are two competing theories on the nature of rights.[41] According to the will theory, rights are associated with an individual's capacity to choose whether to enforce or waive correlative duties on others. According to the interest theory, rights protect interests "of sufficient importance to impose on others certain duties whose discharge ensures the enjoyment ... of the interest in question."[42] In other words, "where an interest is sufficient to ground a responsibility in others to protect that interest, a right is created."[43] All human rights instruments, including the Convention, are predicated on the idea that all human beings have interests and corresponding rights as persons, along with the foundational liberal principle that individuals are the sole and proper objects of fundamental moral concern.[44] "Not all people or cultures accept or even acknowledge that children have rights. And the very notion of rights has arguably problematic roots in Western [liberal] individualism," writes philosopher John Wall. "But one would be hard pressed to find another social framework today that has gained such universal standing."[45]

Children have welfare interests in common with all persons, but as minors they also have developmental interests, including an interest in continuing to acquire the capacities that will enable them to become self-governing adults, free to make all decisions for themselves in accordance with reason. All persons who are not fully competent have an interest in becoming fully competent. The Convention recognizes the conceptualization of children as persons "entitled to special care and assistance" for the duration of their minority. The Convention thus endorses the view of child protectionists, who believe that eliminating minority status and the additional legal protections associated with it would make children more vulnerable to abuse, exploitation, and other social toxins. To the extent that minority status helps to ensure every child's right to provision, protection, and participation, conceptualizations of the child as not fully competent remain relevant.

Children and adults have welfare interests in common, because welfare interests correspond to basic human needs including food, shelter, security, love, and a sense of identity and belonging. Welfare interests do not vary with age or status; they refer to the very things all people need to survive and thrive. Thus children have welfare interests as persons, along with corresponding welfare rights, in the present.

As we noted earlier, children also have an interest in acquiring the capacities associated with the competence that will be ascribed to them when they reach the age of majority. Thus children have developmental interests that competent adults do not have. Developmental interests refer to the need for education and access to diverse formative influences, including the guidance and support of parents and guardians, teachers and other health and human service professionals, and the state. Children, then, have developmental interests that evolve as they mature, along with corresponding developmental rights in the present.[46]

Liberty interests have long been associated with agency, or a fully developed capacity for rational decision-making and self-governance in accordance with reason. People who are capable of making decisions for themselves have a strong interest in doing so; this is the very core of human dignity.[47] According to the capability approach developed by Amartya Sen and elaborated by Martha Nussbaum, laws and policies should be evaluated according to their impact on people's capabilities, not just their present functioning. They hold that capabilities are ends, and ends are what ultimately matter to well-being and quality of life.[48] Self-determination theory strongly supports the view that people who make their own decisions tend to be happier than those whose lives are controlled by others.[49] We tend to become angry or offended if others try to impose their will on us, or to second-guess our decisions, because this sort of behaviour constitutes an indignity.

Do children have liberty interests? In the past, philosophers thought they did not. "This doctrine [of liberty] is meant to apply to human beings in the maturity of their faculties," wrote John Stuart Mill. "We are not speaking of children or of young persons below the age which the law may fix as that of manhood or womanhood. Those who are still in a state to require being taken care of by others must be protected against their own actions as well as against external injury."[50] Following Mill, Kenneth Strike observes, "Where people have not actualized their capacity for moral agency, these rights do not serve their point."[51] Many people likewise forget that while the presumptions associated with legal status are categorical, competence and moral agency are not. As we noted earlier, children do not become fully competent on the eve of their eighteenth birthday in Ontario or their nineteenth birthday in New Brunswick. Competence and moral agency are not completely absent in minors and completely present in adults. We know that competence for particular kinds of decision-making evolves as young people mature, and that both adults and children can be more or less mature or more or less competent. It seems reasonable to assume that if the capacities associated with competence to make decisions independently develop over time, an individual's interest in exercising those capacities increases over time. In other words, children have liberty interests that increase as they mature, along with corresponding liberty rights in the present.[52]

Joel Feinberg has characterized the liberty rights of minors as "rights-in-trust," rights to be safeguarded by competent adults while children are young so that they may be exercised in the future. By his account, "Respect for the child's future autonomy, as an adult, often requires preventing his free choice now."[53] As noted earlier, it is unacceptable for adults to substitute their judgment or impose their views on other adults; that kind of paternalism is offensive. But whether paternalism is acceptable for a particular child depends on the child's level of maturity. "The primary point of paternalism is to prevent the immature from making choices, taking on commitments and relationships, or choosing directions for their lives when they cannot grasp their significance," says Strike.[54] If children become competent to make more and more decisions for themselves as they mature, then paternalism becomes less necessary over time. Of course, there may be sharp differences of opinion between parents and adolescents in particular circumstances, making disagreements with parents and teachers a hallmark of the transition to adulthood. The *wishes* of a child (what children say they want) may be quite different from the *best interests* of a child, which are largely determined by others. Any parent will say their children tend to be quite clear on what they want, but children do not have a right to do whatever they want. No one does.

Children have rights corresponding to their independent welfare and developmental interests, and parents, guardians, and other caregivers have a corresponding duty to promote those interests through substituted decision-making, modelling, and guidance. Eight-year-old Yvonne might prefer to eat cheeseburgers every day, but her parents know that this would lead to poor health outcomes, especially if she eats cheeseburgers every day as a teenager (when guidance from parents is less welcome). In accordance with the democratic parenting model, they would structure Yvonne's options while she is young by allowing her to choose from a variety of healthy dinner options, making similar choices themselves, and explaining why some food choices are healthier than others. Described by R.S. Peters as "the intentional bringing about of a desirable state of mind,"[55] initiation into healthy eating habits is best undertaken at home rather than a fast-food restaurant. Structuring Yvonne's options and preferences might include limiting her access to fast-food advertisements and preparing meals at home as often as possible.

In this chapter, we have discussed the moral and legal status of children and the nature of their independent welfare interests, developmental interests, and liberty interests. Welfare interests are applicable to both adults and children because all persons have an interest in living well. Developmental interests are applicable to children because they have an interest in developing their capacity for self-governance in accordance with reason. Liberty interests are ascribed to children as they mature, because persons capable of governing themselves have an interest in doing so. While legal presumptions about competence are categorical, competence itself is not. Because many people continue to regard the liberty interests of children as categorical, it is difficult for children to enjoy the substance of their rights under the Convention.[56] In the next chapter, we will examine decisions by the Supreme Court of Canada in which children's rights under the Convention and the *Charter* have been recognized.

## CHAPTER 4

# The Supreme Court of Canada and the Convention

In the absence of federal or provincial implementing legislation, Canadian courts could not immediately recognize the Convention as a basis for legal rights claims when it was ratified by Parliament in 1991. But at the time of ratification, Canada was in the midst of a legal revolution that began when the *Charter of Rights and Freedoms* came into full force and effect in 1985. Over the past quarter century since its ratification, the Convention has been invoked in twenty decisions by the Supreme Court of Canada to interpret the rights of children under the *Charter* and federal or provincial legislation.[1] These decisions illustrate the effects of judicial recognition of the Convention in the absence of implementing legislation, the effect of incorporating the Convention by reference into the Preamble of the *Youth Criminal Justice Act* in 2002,[2] and more broadly how children's rights and freedoms under the *Charter* have been reconciled with the doctrine of *parens patriae*. In this chapter, we begin with a look at international law and the rapidly changing legal and political context in Canada in 1991. We then review fourteen of the twenty Supreme Court decisions to date in which the Convention has been invoked in support of the best interests of the child principle.

## International Law

International law is different from domestic law in a number of ways. The subjects of international law are sovereign states such as Canada, India, and Japan; non-governmental organizations (NGOs) such as Save the Children, Oxfam, and Amnesty International; and intergovernmental organizations

(IGOs) such as the United Nations, the World Bank, and the North Atlantic Treaty Organization. Individual persons, including *natural persons* (such as the authors of this book) and *legal persons* (such as the publisher of this book) do not have standing at international law and are not generally subject to it. International law consists of formal agreements—including conventions, treaties, covenants, and pacts—between the various international actors noted above. The Convention is an agreement between member states of the United Nations, and this is why it refers to its signatories as *states parties*.

The UN is an intergovernmental organization made up of 193 member states. Thus the name United Nations is somewhat misleading, as it is not an association of *nations* (groups of people with a shared history, culture, or language) but of *states* (politically organized territorial entities with a central government). The UN succeeded the defunct League of Nations when it was founded on October 24, 1945, in the wake of the Second World War (when, of course, the name United States was already taken). On December 10, 1948, the UN General Assembly adopted the Universal Declaration of Human Rights (UDHR), which recognizes "the inherent dignity and … the equal and inalienable rights of all members of the human family."[3] As we noted in previous chapters, the dominant conception of children had by this point started to shift from not-yets to persons with inherent rights, in keeping with the hopeful spirit of the times. Forty-eight states voted in favour of the UDHR and none voted against it, with eight abstentions. In 1959, the United Nations General Assembly adopted the Declaration of the Rights of the Child, the first major international consensus on the fundamental principles of children's rights since the Geneva Convention on the Rights of the Child adopted by the League of Nations in 1924 acknowledged five welfare and developmental interests for children and corresponding duties on the part of the "men and women of all nations" to provide for those interests.[4]

The International Bill of Human Rights (IBHR) consists of the UDHR, the International Covenant on Economic, Social and Cultural Rights, and the International Covenant on Civil and Political Rights, along with two Optional Protocols adopted by the UN General Assembly in 1966. Ten years later, after it was ratified by 35 member states, the IBHR became binding on all states at international law, setting an international "standard of achievement for all peoples and all nations."[5] Since 1976, the IBHR has been routinely cited as a basis for an array of human rights agreements, including the Convention. These agreements and declarations have inspired states around the world to draft new constitutions enshrining human rights and freedoms. Canada was no exception; as we noted earlier, the *Charter* was entrenched into our newly patriated *Constitution Act* in 1982. The equality provisions under section 15 came into full force and effect three years later.

## Adopting the Convention

When it ratified the Convention in 1991, Canada made a commitment to recognize the rights of children outlined within its provisions. Because states are sovereign unto themselves, because individuals lack standing at international law, and because enforcement mechanisms against sovereign states at international law are limited, it would have been overly simplistic at that point to say that children in Canada had rights because the Convention said so. When it was first made available for signature, the Convention represented a moral commitment by states to safeguard and promote the welfare and developmental interests of children, but signatory states were essentially making that commitment to one another, not to children per se. As we saw in Chapter 3, moral rights are correlates of moral duties, including duties assumed by states.[6] But *legal* rights are institutionally contingent in ways that moral rights are not. There must be an institutional structure—courts of law—within which legal claims may be raised, recognized, and enforced.[7]

In the absence of federal or provincial implementing legislation, Canadian courts could not immediately recognize the Convention as a source of legal rights for children following its ratification.[8] Moreover, neither children nor their parents had standing at international law or recourse to the UN except through the Canadian government. What would have happened if a well-informed twelve-year-old who did not want to be taken to church by her parents each week insisted that she had religious freedoms under the Convention in 1991? Her parents might have laughed. They might have been angered. Either way, they probably would not have taken her rights claim seriously. As it happens, article 14(1) of the Convention requires signatory states to "respect the right of the child to freedom of thought, conscience and religion." But neither this right nor the corresponding obligations for Canada are unqualified. Under article 14(2), Canada also promised to "respect the rights and duties of the parents ... to provide direction to the child in the exercise of his or her right in a manner consistent with the evolving capacities of the child." The duties associated with the Convention are those of the state, not those of the parents of our precocious twelve-year-old, and Canada had promised to recognize and balance children's rights with the responsibilities of their parents and guardians. And as a minor, our twelve-year-old would have few avenues for legal recourse other than through her parents.

In the previous chapter, we noted that if Randy and Andrea had signed a formal agreement for the purchase and sale of a motorbike and Randy reneged, Andrea could enforce her contractual rights in the courts. But if a signatory state reneges on its commitments under the Convention, there is no international court in which another signatory state or intergovernmental organization could sue Canada. Moreover, other states are unlikely to impose penalties through trade sanctions or restrictions on capital mobility should a state party fall short on its commitments under the Convention. According to legal philosopher H. L. A. Hart, "rules are conceived and spoken of as imposing obligations when the general demand for conformity is insistent and the social pressure brought to bear upon those who deviate or threaten to deviate is great."[9] Perhaps this is why, under article 42, Canada and other signatory states have agreed "to make the principles and provisions of the Convention widely known, by appropriate and active means, to adults and children alike."

As we noted in Chapter 2, article 43 of the Convention establishes a Committee on the Rights of the Child to review reports of states parties in implementing the Convention and make recommendations for progress. Although the Committee cannot require full implementation, it can bring pressure for change. The reports are publicly available and highlight short-comings in implementation. Thus while there is no enforcement mechanism as such, there are mechanisms for "naming and shaming" states that have failed to fulfill their commitments under the Convention.[10] Of course, the situation is much different in the United States, where the Convention has been signed but has yet to be ratified.

## The United States and the Convention

For some Americans, the fact that the United States remains the *only* UN member state not to have ratified the Convention is shameful. Why hasn't the United States ratified the Convention? Many Americans do not seem to have much knowledge of international affairs. Many seem to be deeply suspicious of the United Nations, or at least deeply committed to the idea of American exceptionalism.[11] There are serious constitutional obstacles to ratification because decisions by the US Supreme Court from *Wisconsin v.*

*Yoder,* [1972] 406 U.S. 205 to *Reno v. Flores,* [1993] 507 U.S. 292 to *Troxel v. Granville* [2000] 530 U.S. 57 have prioritized parental rights and interests over those of their children, putting American jurisprudence sharply at odds with Convention principles.[12] "So long as certain minimum requirements of child care are met, the interests of the child may be subordinated to the interests of other children, or indeed even to the interests of parents or guardians themselves," wrote Justice Antonin Scalia in *Reno* (p. 305). "Whether for good or for ill, adults not only influence but may indoctrinate children, and a choice about a child's social companions is not essentially different from the designation of the adults who will influence a child in school," wrote Justice David Souter in *Troxel* (pp. 78–79). As a practical matter, the ratification of an international treaty or convention requires the approval of two-thirds of the US Senate. Given that the US Senate tends to be closely split between Democrats and Republicans, and that Republicans tend to be aligned with conservative groups and the parental rights movement, the prospects for US ratification of the Convention remain dim.

## Enforcing the Convention

As we noted in Chapter 3, in order to have a *legal* right, one must have standing to raise a valid claim in court. Rights to which one cannot make a claim are imperfect at best,[13] and rights claims that are not enforceable in the courts are mere interests, hopes, or wishes. In order for the Convention to be enforceable in Canadian courts, its terms had to become part of domestic law. This happens automatically when some countries sign treaties, but in Canada and other parliamentary democracies on the Westminster model, ratification of treaties and conventions is generally done with a bill before Parliament explicitly implementing the treaty or convention, or by a bill incorporating some or all of its provisions into existing legislation by reference.

Because the government is usually made up of members of a single party or coalition holding a majority of seats in the House of Commons, most treaties and conventions that are signed are subsequently ratified. Canada ratified the Convention on December 13, 1991, with reservations on adoption and separation of young offenders.[14] Parliament did not adopt an implementing statute for the Convention because the *Constitution Act* of 1867 calls for a separation of powers between the provinces and the federal government. While the federal government is responsible for international relations, immigration, criminal law, and divorce, the provinces are individually responsible for social welfare, marriage, health, and education.[15] Because the Convention deals with so many areas that fall within provincial jurisdiction, each province and territory needed to consent to its ratification and to incorporate its provisions into its own legislation if children across the country were to have comparable legal rights to provision, protection, and participation.[16] As we discuss in later chapters, Canada still has a long way to go in this respect.

## The *Charter* and the Convention

When Canada ratified the Convention in 1991, a legal revolution was already underway. Before the *Charter*, "Canadian law was primarily concerned with the regulation of economic, commercial and property affairs, and with the control of deviant personal behaviour by means of the criminal law," observed Nicholas Bala. With the advent of the *Charter*, "the role of law in Canadian society has changed dramatically. Law has become an important social policy tool, affecting virtually every aspect of Canadian public policy." For the first time, Canadians found themselves in "an increasingly 'rights-based' society … in which individuals [could] look to the courts to address a broad range of concerns."[17] Among these concerns were the limits of the *parens patriae* doctrine, historically exercised to safeguard the welfare and developmental interests of children. In a new rights-based legal landscape in which all persons were constitutionally entitled to equality before and under the law, could Canadian courts continue to prioritize the best interests of children? Where would Canadian courts look for guidance in interpreting *Charter* rights and freedoms? The United States had ample experience with its own Bill of Rights, but as noted above, American constitutional jurisprudence since 1972 had prioritized the interests of parents over the interests of children.

The Supreme Court of Canada began using international agreements to interpret the *Charter* almost immediately after it came into full force and effect. In *Re Public Service Employee Relations Act*, [1987] 1 S.C.R. 313, Chief Justice Brian Dickson observed that "the similarity between the policies and provisions of the *Charter* and those of international human rights documents attaches considerable relevance to interpretations of those documents by adjudicative bodies." In 1993, two years after Canada ratified the Convention, a pair of custody disputes made their way to the Supreme Court of Canada from British Columbia and Québec. Decided concurrently, the cases involved *Charter* challenges to the application of the best interests of the child principle. For the very first time, the Supreme Court turned to the Convention as an interpretive aid.

The Supreme Court of Canada is the highest court in the land. It hears appeals from all the provincial, territorial, and federal courts of appeal. Its majority decisions must be followed by courts across Canada as authoritative and definitive statements of the law. When the Supreme Court finds federal or provincial legislation unconstitutional or inadequate, the legislation must be revised. Dissenting opinions may have no formal legal weight, but they often influence future majority decisions.[18] Thus, as we shall see, the invocation of the Convention by the Supreme Court of Canada has, in a slow and piecemeal way, helped turn children's rights under the Convention into social guarantees for Canadian children.

In *Young v. Young*, [1993] 4 S.C.R. 3, the British Columbia Supreme Court granted Irene Young custody of her three daughters, while James Young was granted access subject to the condition that he not discuss his faith with the children, take them to religious services, or include them in door-to-door canvassing activities. This was largely because the two older children did not share their father's identity as a Jehovah's Witness. At the Supreme Court, James Young claimed *his* freedom of religion, *his* freedom of expression, *his* freedom of association, and *his* equality rights under sections 2(a), (b), (d) and section 15 of the *Charter* had been infringed by the conditions imposed by the Court. He also claimed that the best interests of the child standard was unconstitutionally vague.

Five of the seven Supreme Court justices who heard the appeal issued separate opinions agreeing in whole or in part with one another—a clear sign of the difficulty of balancing parental and state authority and the interests of children under the *Charter*. One point on which there was general agreement was Justice Claire L'Heureux-Dubé's characterization of custody as the right of the *child*: "The power of the custodial parent is not a 'right' with independent value granted by courts for the benefit of the parent," she wrote. "Rather, the child has a right to a parent who will look after his or her best interests and the custodial parent a duty to ensure, protect and promote the child's best interests." Unless separating spouses made reasonable arrangements in the best interests of their children, the courts, acting in a *parens patriae* capacity, would continue to do so. "[I]n those rare cases where parents cross the line and engage in … 'indoctrination, enlistment or harassment,' courts have a duty to intervene in the best interests of children," she concluded. In her view, parents were not the only parties whose freedom of religion and expression were at stake in custodial disputes: "Freedom of religion is not an absolute value. Here, powerful competing interests must also be recognized, not the least of which, in addition to the best interests of the children, are the freedoms of expression and religion of the children themselves."

Justice L'Heureux-Dubé found that the best interests of the child principle was "completely consonant with the articulated values and underlying concerns of the *Charter*, as it aims to protect a vulnerable segment of society by ensuring that the interests and needs of the child take precedence over any competing considerations in custody and access decisions" (para. 83). She strongly denied that the best interests principle was unconstitutionally vague. "[T]he need to make the best interests of the child [a] primary consideration in all actions concerning children, including legal proceedings, is specifically recognized in international human rights documents such as the United Nations Convention on the Rights of the Child" (para. 910).

*P. (D.) v. S. (C.)*, [1993] 4 S.C.R. 141, decided concurrently with the *Young* case, involved a couple who had lived together for three years following birth of their child. They then signed a separation agreement ratified by the Québec Superior Court giving the mother [C.S.] custody and the father [D.P.] access privileges. After D.P. became a Jehovah's Witness, C.S. asked the Court to bar him from discussing his faith or engaging in door-to-door proselytizing during his access visits. The Superior Court recognized D.P.'s "religious fanaticism" as a source of anxiety for the child and granted C.S.'s application. Although *parens patriae* doctrine does not apply in Québec, the *Civil Code* permits courts within the province to exercise comparably broad discretion in the best interests of the child. The Québec Court of Appeals upheld the ruling.[19]

For a unanimous Supreme Court, Justice L'Heureux-Dubé again defended the best interests of the child standard under the *Charter* and the Convention. "The right to custody of a very young child includes that of educating and instructing it in accordance with its best interests having regard to its moral, intellectual and physical development," she wrote. "A court has a clear duty to observe and apply this principle, and this has nothing to do with a violation of judicial neutrality or failure to respect the constitutional guarantee of freedom of religion." As in the *Young* case, Justice L'Heureux-Dubé invoked the Convention as clear evidence that the best interests of the child standard was anything but vague: "This criterion has also been applied for decades by courts in Québec and abroad, giving rise to a large body of case law. This indicates the universal and lasting value of the criterion, as well as the fact that its content is significant" (para. 101).

Three years later, the Supreme Court heard a third custody dispute. *Gordon v. Goertz*, [1996] 2 S.C.R. 27 involved Janet Gordon, a custodial parent who planned to move from Saskatchewan to Australia with her child. Robin Goertz sought custody or an order barring the move. The Saskatchewan courts had dismissed his application and varied his access order to allow for visits in Australia only. The Supreme Court unanimously agreed that as the custodial parent, Janet Gordon could relocate as she saw fit. Robin Goertz could have access visits in both Canada and Australia. While there was no presumption in favour of the custodial parent seeking to relocate, her views and those of the child were to be taken into account. Writing for a majority on the Court, Justice Beverley McLachlin described the best interests principle as "an eloquent expression of Parliament's view that the ultimate and only issue when it comes to custody and access is the welfare of the child whose future is at stake" (para. 20). Concurring on this point, Justice L'Heureux-Dubé found that under the *Divorce Act*, "All decisions as to custody and access must be made in the best interests of children, assessed from a child-centred perspective" (para. 143) and in accordance with the Convention: "International awareness of children's rights is illustrated by various international documents [including] the United Nations Convention on the Rights of the Child … which recognizes the need to make the best interests of the child the primary consideration in all actions concerning children, including legal proceedings" (para. 87).

As the highest court in the land, the Supreme Court of Canada agrees to hear appeals from across the country in all areas of law, especially where there is uncertainty or inconsistency in the interpretation or application of law among the lower courts. In the same year as *Young v. Young* and *P. (D.) v. S. (C.)*, the Supreme Court agreed to hear an appeal from Manitoba on the constitutionality of section 715.1 of the *Criminal Code*, which permits videotaped testimony from child victims of sexual assault to protect them from the trauma of testifying in open court and in full view of their abusers. In *R. v. L. (D.O.)*, [1993] 4 S.C.R. 419, a man charged with sexually assaulting a nine-year-old girl argued that videotaped testimony violated *his* rights under sections 7 and 11(d) of the *Charter*. Citing the Convention, Justice L'Heureux-Dubé concurred with her colleagues in rejecting these claims. "I find that the inclusion of all children up to the age of 18 under the protections afforded by s. 715.1 of the *Criminal Code* is required by the continued need for such protection and is in conformity with international and domestic instruments," she concluded (para. 69).

A watershed for judicial recognition of the Convention occurred six years later in *Baker v. Canada* [1999] 2 S.C.R. 817, a case involving Mavis Baker, a Jamaican citizen who had arrived in Canada on a tourist visa in 1981. A deportation order was issued against her in 1992. The following year, she sought a ministerial exemption to apply for permanent residency from within Canada on humanitarian and compassionate grounds, arguing that she and her four Canadian-born children would suffer emotional hardship if they were separated. Significantly, she also argued that the Convention required immigration officials to prioritize the best interests of her children when making a decision in her case.

At the Federal Court, Trial Division, Justice Sandra Simpson dismissed Baker's application for judicial review and denied her Convention claim. In her view, the Convention was not part of domestic law, so it could not give rise to a legitimate expectation on Baker's part that her children's interests would be a primary consideration in the circumstances. The Federal Court of Appeal agreed and referred the following question to the Supreme Court: "Given that the *Immigration Act* does not expressly incorporate the language of Canada's international obligations with respect to the Convention on the Rights of the Child, must federal immigration authorities treat the best interests of the Canadian child as a primary consideration in assessing an applicant under s. 114(2) of the *Immigration Act?*"

At the Supreme Court, Justices Frank Iacobucci and Peter Cory agreed with the lower courts, answering the question from the Federal Court of Appeal in the negative. "It is a matter of well-settled law that an international convention ratified by the executive branch of government is of no force or effect within the Canadian legal system until such time as its provisions have been incorporated into domestic law by way of implementing legislation," wrote Justice Iacobucci. "I do not agree with the approach adopted by my colleague, wherein reference is made to the underlying values of an unimplemented international treaty in the course of the contextual approach to statutory interpretation and administrative law," he continued, "because such an approach is not in accordance with the Court's jurisprudence concerning the status of international law within the domestic legal system" (para. 79).

Justice Iacobucci was referring to the approach taken by Justice L'Heureux-Dubé, whose decision in *Baker* was supported by a majority on the Court. She answered the question from the Federal Court of Appeal in the affirmative. "Another indicator of the importance of considering the interests of children when making a compassionate and humanitarian decision is the ratification by Canada of the Convention on the Rights of the Child," she wrote, "and the recognition of the importance of children's rights and the best interests of children in other international instruments ratified by Canada." She acknowledged that the Convention had not been implemented by statute. Nevertheless, she concluded that "the values reflected in international human rights law may help inform the contextual approach to statutory interpretation and judicial review" (paras. 69–70), citing a tenet of statutory interpretation that "the legislature is presumed to respect the values and principles enshrined in international law, both customary and conventional.... In so far as possible, therefore, interpretations that reflect these values and principles are preferred."[20]

"Because the reasons for this decision do not indicate that it was made in a manner which was alive, attentive, or sensitive to the interests of Ms. Baker's children, and did not consider them as an important factor in making the decision," concluded Justice L'Heureux-Dubé, "it was an unreasonable exercise of the power conferred by the legislation, and must, therefore, be overturned." Mavis Baker would be allowed to remain in Canada with her children and apply for permanent residency.

This was a victory for Mavis Baker and her children, but also for the Convention as a touchstone for children's rights in Canada. Following *Baker*, the federal government amended the *Immigration and Refugee Protection Act*, requiring officials to consider the best interests of a child directly affected by decisions made on humanitarian and compassionate grounds under section 25(1).[21] Consistent with article 3 of the Convention, which, as we have previously noted, stipulates that the best interests of the child shall be *a* primary consideration rather than *the* primary consideration, the federal government maintains that "the best interests of a child is only one of many important factors that the decision-maker needs to consider when making an H&C [humanitarian and compassionate] decision that directly affects a child."[22]

The following year, the Supreme Court upheld the constitutionality of provisions within the *Manitoba Child and Family Services Act* allowing for the warrantless apprehension of a child in a non-emergency situation.

*Winnipeg Child and Family Services v. K.L.W.* [2000] 2 S.C.R. 519 involved a woman whose two older children had been taken into care due to parental neglect and intoxication. Having reasonable and probable grounds to believe her newborn third child was also in need of protection, social workers apprehended the baby. K.L.W. alleged this violated *her* section 7 *Charter* right to "life, liberty and security of the person and the right not to be deprived thereof except in accordance with the principles of fundamental justice." Writing for a majority on the Supreme Court, Justice L'Heureux-Dubé observed, "From the child's perspective, state action in the form of apprehension seeks to ensure the protection, and indeed the very survival, of another interest of fundamental importance: the child's life and health." Citing the protection of children from harm as "a universally accepted goal" under the Convention (para. 73), and "because children are vulnerable and cannot exercise their rights independently, particularly at a young age, and because child abuse and neglect have long-term effects ... the State has assumed both the duty and the power to intervene to protect children's welfare" (para. 75).

In a notorious case from the British Columbia Court of Appeal the following year, a majority on the Supreme Court recognized certain types of pornographic writings as forms of expression protected under section 2(b) of the *Charter*. In *R. v. Sharpe*, [2001] 1 S.C.R. 45, which we discuss in greater detail in Chapter 6, the criminal charges associated with John Sharpe's possession of *written* child pornography were dismissed, while the charges associated with his possession of *graphic* child pornography would stand. In a searing dissent, Justice L'Heureux-Dubé objected to the protection of *any* form of child pornography under the *Charter*, citing articles 2, 19, 9, 16, 32, 33, 35, 37, and 34 of the Convention, which had at that time been signed by 191 states (para. 171), and the Optional Protocol to the Convention on the Sale of Children, Child Prostitution and Child Pornography, which at that time been signed by 69 states (para. 178). "The possession of child pornography has no social value; it has only a tenuous connection to the value of self-fulfillment underlying the right to free expression," she concluded. "As such, it warrants only attenuated protection. Hence, increased deference should be accorded to Parliament's decision to prohibit it" (para. 186).

Another setback for children's rights and the Convention occurred three years later, when the Supreme Court agreed to hear an appeal from Ontario on the constitutionality of Canada's so-called spanking law in *Canadian Foundation for Children, Youth and the Law v. Canada*, [2004] 1 S.C.R. 76.

Striking another person is a form of assault. Section 43 is a statutory defence that may be invoked by parents and schoolteachers charged with assault under the *Criminal Code*. Section 43 of the *Criminal Code* provides as follows: "Every schoolteacher, parent or person standing in the place of a parent is justified in using force by way of correction toward a pupil or child, as the case may be, who is under his care, if the force does not exceed what is reasonable under the circumstances."[23] It is important to note that while teachers who use corporal punishment may invoke section 43 if they are charged with criminal assault, it is of absolutely no use to them if they are sued for battery in a civil proceeding, or if they are stripped of their licence for violating professional standards of conduct and school policies.

As we note in Chapter 6, the Canadian Foundation for Children, Youth and the Law argued that corporal punishment violates children's section 7 (security of the person), 12 (cruel and unusual punishment), and 15 (equal protection) rights under the *Charter*, along with Canada's commitments under the Convention, including article 3 (best interests of the child), article 19 (protection from all forms of physical or mental violence by parents or others in positions of authority), article 28 (school discipline and human dignity), and article 37 (degrading treatment). The Attorney General for Canada successfully defended section 43 of the *Criminal Code* with the assistance of a number of well-financed intervenors, mostly US-based parental rights organizations (including Focus on the Family and the Home School Legal Defense Association). The section 43 defence had been invoked successfully in numerous cases involving corporal punishment against children of all ages by parents and teachers by 2004, and in its report on Canada's compliance with the Convention the preceding year, the UN Committee on the Rights of the Child expressed "deep concern" that Canada had taken "no action to remove section 43 of the *Criminal Code*."[24]

Writing for a majority on the Supreme Court, Chief Justice Beverley McLachlin found that section 43 of the *Criminal Code* did *not* violate children's section 7 *Charter* rights. In her view, the best interests of the child is not a principle of fundamental justice, and laws affecting children need not be in their best interests. Noting that children's interests are represented in criminal trials by the Crown as *parens patriae*, she found there were adequate procedural safeguards for children under section 43. Whether corrective force is "reasonable in the circumstances," according to the Chief Justice, should be understood in light of Canada's international treaty obligations (paras. 31–32). But by her account, "[n]either the Convention on the Rights of the Child nor the International Covenant on Civil and Political Rights explicitly require state parties to ban all corporal punishment of children" (para. 33). "Without s. 43, Canada's broad assault law would criminalize force falling far short of what we think of as corporal punishment," she concluded. "The decision not to criminalize such conduct is not grounded in devaluation of the child, but in a concern that to do so risks ruining lives and breaking up families—a burden that in large part would be borne by children and outweigh any benefit derived from applying the criminal process" (para. 62).

In a vigorous dissent, Justice Louise Arbour accused the Chief Justice of rewriting section 43 in order to validate its constitutionality (para. 139). In her view, section 43 violated the *Charter* rights of children because, among other things, the reasonable in the circumstances criterion had been interpreted differently across the country in dozens of cases. Thus section 43 violated the principle of fundamental justice that laws be clear. "A vague law violates the principles of fundamental justice because it does not provide 'fair warning' to individuals as to the legality of their actions," she noted (para. 177). In addition, she found that the degree of protection to which children are entitled under the *Charter* had to be informed by the rights of protection under the Convention (para. 186).

Justice Marie Deschamps penned a separate dissenting opinion finding that section 43 violates children's rights under both the *Charter* and the Convention. "[Children] have been recognized as a vulnerable group time and again by legislatures and courts. Historically, their vulnerability was entrenched by the traditional legal treatment of children as the property or chattel of their parents or guardians," she wrote. "Fortunately, this attitude has changed in modern times with a recognition that children, as individuals, have rights, including the right to have their security and safety protected by their parents, families and society at large" (para. 225). However, she continued, "s. 43 appears to be a throwback to old notions of children as property."

Given Chief Justice Beverley McLachlin's defence of section 43 of the *Criminal Code* and its reasonable in the circumstances standard in 2004, her opinion in a youth justice case from Nova Scotia the following year was somewhat surprising. *R. v. R.C.* [2005] 3 S.C.R. 99 involved a youth who stabbed his mother in the foot with a pen and punched her in the face after she yelled at him to get out of bed and go to school. R.C. pleaded guilty to assault with a weapon. Under section 487.051(1)(a) of the *Criminal Code*, courts must authorize the taking of DNA samples from persons accused of assault unless the accused person establishes that the impact of such an order on his or her privacy and security interests under section 7 of the *Charter* "would be grossly disproportionate to the public interest in the protection of society and the proper administration of justice."

Writing for the majority, the Chief Justice found that "[t]he taking and retention of a DNA sample constitutes a grave intrusion on a person's right to personal and informational privacy" (para. 39). "While no specific provision of the youth criminal justice legislation modifies s. 487.051, Parliament clearly intended that this legislation would be respected whenever young persons are brought within the criminal justice system." Citing the Convention, she added, "Parliament has recognized their heightened vulnerability and has sought to extend enhanced procedural protections to them, and to interfere with their personal freedom as little as possible" (para. 41). In her view, the trial court's decision not to order a DNA test was reasonable in the circumstances and should not have been set aside by the Court of Appeal (para. 70).

It may have been difficult for observers to understand how spanking a child for corrective purposes could be considered reasonable in the circumstances and constitutional in *Canadian Foundation for Children, Youth and the Law*, while the taking of DNA with a mouth swab could be considered unreasonable in the circumstances and unconstitutional in *R. v. R.C.* The Chief Justice's apparent about-face may have been related to the coming into force on April 1, 2003, of the *Youth Criminal Justice Act* (YCJA), replacing the *Young Offenders Act.*[25] Hailed as "the most systematic attempt in Canadian history to structure judicial discretion regarding the sentencing of juveniles,"[26] the YCJA was a significant piece of legislation because, for the first time, Parliament explicitly incorporated Canada's commitments under the Convention into its Preamble by reference: "WHEREAS Canada is a party to the United Nations Convention on the Rights of the Child and recognizes that young persons have rights and freedoms, including those stated in the Canadian Charter of Rights and Freedoms and the Canadian Bill of Rights, and have special guarantees of their rights and freedoms ..."

The effects were readily apparent in the next two decisions from the Supreme Court of Canada. The first concerned a consolidated 2006 appeal from Manitoba and British Columbia; the second concerned a separate 2008 appeal from Ontario. In *R. v. B.W.P. and R. v. B.V.N.*, [2006] 1 S.C.R. 941, fifteen-year-old B.W.P. killed 22-year-old Chya Saleh by hitting him over the head with a pool ball in a sock and pleaded guilty to manslaughter. The sentencing judge held that general deterrence was not applicable under the YCJA and sentenced B.W.P. to one day in open custody and 15 months under conditional supervision in the community. The Manitoba Court of Appeal affirmed this decision. Sixteen-year-old B.V.N. punched and kicked a 42-year-old heroin addict and pleaded guilty to aggravated assault. The sentencing judge issued a nine-month closed custody and supervision order to ensure his participation in rehabilitation programs. The British Columbia Court of Appeal upheld the sentence, affirming that while general deterrence was a permissible factor under the YCJA, it had not increased the length of B.V.N.'s sentence.

General deterrence is a principle by which lengthier sentences may be imposed to deter other people from committing similar crimes, essentially using the convicted person as an example. "It is quite clear in considering the Preamble and the statute as a whole that Parliament's goal in enacting the new youth sentencing regime was to reserve the most serious interventions for the most serious crimes and thereby reduce the over-reliance on incarceration for non-violent young persons," wrote Justice Louise Charron in her opinion for a unanimous Supreme Court (para. 35). Finding that "Parliament's goal in enacting the new youth sentencing regime was to reserve the most serious interventions for the most serious crimes and thereby reduce the over-reliance on incarceration for non-violent young persons," in keeping with the Convention, she stated that "Parliament deliberately excluded general deterrence as a factor of youth sentencing" (para. 34).

In *R. v. D.B.*, [2008] 2 S.C.R. 3, seventeen-year-old D.B. got into a fight with a friend at the mall who later died from his injuries. D.B. pleaded guilty to manslaughter. Under the YCJA, an adult sentence was presumptively applied in offences including manslaughter, with the onus on the accused to convince the Court to apply a youth sentence. D.B. argued that this reverse onus violated his section 7 *Charter* rights.

Writing for a majority on the Supreme Court, Justice Rosalie Abella agreed with D.B. "The presumption of an adult sentence in the onus provisions is inconsistent with the principle of fundamental justice that young people are entitled to a presumption of diminished moral culpability throughout any proceedings against them," she wrote (para. 69). "The legislative history of the youth criminal justice system in Canada confirms that the presumption of diminished moral culpability for young persons is a longstanding legal principle [that] ... also finds expression in Canada's international commitments, in particular the UN Convention on the Rights of the Child" (paras. 59–60).

In Chapter 3, we discussed legal competence as an evolving capacity. While the statutory age of majority for particular purposes in each province or territory is categorical, marking the point at which legal presumptions of competence shift, competence itself evolves over time as a child matures. Thus children have an interest in making more and more choices for themselves as they mature. In the next decision by the Supreme Court of Canada, in *A.C. v. Manitoba*, [2009] 2 S.C.R. 181, this approach was found to be consistent with children's rights under the Convention. Fourteen-year-old A.C. was admitted to hospital with gastrointestinal bleeding due to Crohn's disease. In keeping with her family's beliefs as Jehovah's Witnesses, she had earlier signed a directive declining blood transfusions. Child and Family Services apprehended her as a child in need of protection, and sought a treatment order under section 25(8) of the Manitoba *Child and Family Services Act* (CFSA). A judge ordered the transfusions, concluding that for a child under sixteen, *parens patriae* authority could be exercised in the best interests of the child. A.C. and her parents argued this infringed her rights under sections 2(a), 7, and 15 of the *Charter*. The Manitoba Court of Appeal upheld the constitutionality of the CFSA and of the blood transfusion order.

"The extent to which [input from the child] affects the 'best interests' assessment is as variable as the child's circumstances, but one thing that can be said with certainty is that the input becomes increasingly determinative as the child matures," wrote Justice Abella in her concurring majority opinion. "This is true not only when considering the child's best interests in the placement context, but also when deciding whether to accede to a child's wishes in medical treatment situations" (para. 92). "The Convention … describes 'the best interests of the child' as a primary consideration in all actions concerning children (article 3)," she continued. "It then sets out a framework under which the child's own input will inform the content of the 'best interests' standard, with the weight accorded to these views increasing in relation to the child's developing maturity" (para. 93).[27] Because sufficiently mature children under sixteen can rebut the statutory presumption of incompetence to make medical treatment decisions, Justice Abella found the Manitoba CFSA did not violate section 7. Nor did it violate section 15 of the *Charter*, because capacity to consent to medical treatment is a function of *maturity*, not age.

Three years later, in an appeal from Nova Scotia concerning a pervasive social toxin for young people across Canada, the Supreme Court found that the privacy interests of children are a function of age, not maturity. In *A.B. v. Bragg Communications*, [2012] 2 S.C.R. 567, the issue was whether the privacy interests of a victim of cyberbullying trumped freedom of the press. Through her father, fifteen-year-old A.B. had asked the Nova Scotia courts to compel her Internet service provider to release the IP address and identity of the person who had created a fake Facebook profile with A.B.'s photo, negative comments about her appearance, and some sexually explicit references. Bragg Communications was not opposed to disclosing the information. However, the *Halifax Herald* and Global Television opposed A.B.'s request to proceed anonymously and for a publication ban on the proceedings, arguing that this would impair freedom of the press. The trial court agreed with the media companies and awarded costs against A.B. The Court of Appeal upheld the decision, primarily because A.B. had not shown real and substantial harm to her that would justify a publication ban.

For a unanimous Supreme Court, Justice Rosalie Abella granted the appeal. "[A.B.'s] privacy interests in this case are tied both to her age and to the nature of the victimization she seeks protection from. It is not merely a question of her privacy, but of her privacy from the relentlessly intrusive humiliation of sexualized online bullying" (para. 14). In her view, the protection of children from cyberbullying outweighed both open court and free press principles. The lower courts should have recognized that as a child, A.B. was inherently vulnerable: "Recognition of the inherent vulnerability of children has consistent and deep roots in Canadian law. This results in protection for young people's privacy under the *Criminal Code*, the *Youth Criminal Justice Act* and child welfare legislation, not to mention international protections such as the Convention ... all based on age, not the sensitivity of the particular child," wrote Justice Abella (para. 17). "As a result, in an application involving sexualized cyberbullying, there is no need for a particular child to demonstrate that she personally conforms to this legal paradigm. The law attributes the heightened vulnerability based on chronology, not temperament."

In the most recent case of those examined in this chapter, the Supreme Court heard an appeal from the Federal Court of Appeal that was similar in some respects to the groundbreaking *Baker* case in 1999. The legal landscape had changed, however, as the best interests of the child principle was incorporated into section 25(1) of the *Immigration and Refugee Protection*

*Act* in the wake of *Baker*. As we noted earlier, this created a statutory obligation to take into account the best interests of any child directly affected by an Immigration and Refugee Board of Canada (IRB) decision, in accordance with Canada's commitments under the Convention. In *Kanthasamy v. Canada*, [2015] 3 S.C.R. 909, sixteen-year-old Jeyakannan Kanthasamy claimed refugee protection based on his fear that he would be arrested if returned to Sri Lanka. The IRB denied his claim. The following year, Kanthasamy filed an application for humanitarian and compassionate relief under section 25(1). Although Kanthasamy was diagnosed with post-traumatic stress disorder and depression, the IRB determined that his return to Sri Lanka would not result in "unusual and undeserved or disproportionate" hardship, and the Federal Court of Appeal upheld that decision.

For a majority on the Supreme Court, Justice Rosalie Abella granted the appeal. In her view, because children were "rarely, if ever, deserving of any hardship, the concept of unusual or undeserved hardship was presumptively inapplicable to the assessment" of a child's application for humanitarian and compassionate relief (para. 41). Kanthasamy's status as a child under the Convention should have triggered the requirement that his best interests be taken into account (para. 59). "It is difficult to see how a child can be more directly affected than where he or she is the applicant," concluded Justice Abella (para. 41). Kanthasamy would be allowed to remain in Canada and to apply for permanent residency.

Taken together, these decisions illustrate the effects of judicial recognition of the Convention in the absence of implementing legislation, the effect of incorporating the Convention by reference into the Preamble of the *Youth Criminal Justice Act* in 2002, and more broadly how children's rights and freedoms under the *Charter* have been reconciled with the doctrine of *parens patriae*. Many of these decisions marked important steps forward that would not otherwise have occurred in the absence of a federal implementing statute or incorporation of the Convention by reference into legislation affecting children in Canada. The slow and piecemeal incorporation of Convention principles and provisions into federal and provincial legislation has been helpful, but much remains to be done if children in Canada are actually to enjoy the substance of their rights under the Convention.

## CHAPTER 5

ॐ

# The Rights of Provision

Many years have passed since Canada ratified the Convention in 1991. How well has Canada performed in implementing children's rights of provision? Has significant progress been made in actualizing the rights of the child to economic welfare, health care, and early education and child care, in line with the hopes of child advocates? We will address these questions by reviewing Canada's record in each of these areas. Finding major deficits in the record, we then explain why it is imperative that Canada fulfill its obligations under the Convention to take more seriously the rights of provision.

## Provision of Economic Welfare

Canada is given clear direction under the Convention to provide for the child's right to basic economic well-being and security. Article 6 directs Canada to "ensure to the maximum extent possible the survival and development of the child." Article 27 calls on Canada to recognize and implement "the right of every child to a standard of living adequate for the child's physical, mental, spiritual, moral, and social development." And article 4 obligates Canada to undertake appropriate measures for the child's basic economic rights to the "maximum extent" of its available resources, in accordance with national conditions and within its means. In ratifying the Convention, Canada promised to ensure that children do not live in conditions of poverty and deprivation. As the Convention recognizes that parents have primary responsibility for children, Canada agreed to assist parents and others responsible for the child in providing for the child's economic needs. But where necessary, Canada also has a direct responsibility to provide for the economic needs of children.

As we noted in Chapter 2, the Convention states that the child's best interests shall be a primary consideration in all actions concerning children under article 3. Best interests are not given full substantive definition in the Convention or in the comments of the UN Committee on the Rights of the Child. But from the words of the Convention and the comments of the Committee, it can be seen that the best interests principle refers to the process of making decisions consistent with the rights of the child, the healthy development of children, the creation of conditions necessary for the enjoyment of children's rights, and the findings of child impact assessments and research on measures or conditions that promote the well-being of children.[1] A wide body of research has established that living in poverty, especially in the early childhood years, is associated with unfavourable health, educational, and other outcomes for children. This is clearly at odds with the best interests of the child.

Canadian federal, provincial, and territorial governments have taken a number of positive steps to reduce the number of children living in poverty. In 1989, as the Convention was adopted by the United Nations General Assembly, the House of Commons unanimously passed an all-party resolution to eliminate child poverty in Canada by the year 2000.[2] This reflected growing national attention and increasing concern across the country about the negative effects of poverty on children. Then, in 1990, as a follow-up to the signing of the Convention, Prime Minister Brian Mulroney co-chaired the World Summit for Children, where he and the leaders of 71 countries developed a global plan of action for the survival, protection, and development of children.[3] Countries were to design their own plans, make resources available for children's needs, and recognize the important principle of "first call for children." This principle boldly stated that the basic needs of children should be given high priority in the allocation of a state's resources, in hard times as well as good times. The recognition of this principle was very much in keeping with the directive of article 4 of the Convention that state parties undertake measures for children "to the maximum extent of their available resources."

Canada's expression of commitment was followed by action. In 1992, in response to the World Summit for Children, the federal government published a document called *Brighter Futures* that described an action plan to better provide for the rights and needs of children.[4] The federal government would work with other levels of government to improve employment conditions for low-income parents and bolster programs of income support. It would also enhance child benefits to assist parents with the costs of raising children. Although a variety of measures would be undertaken by various levels of government to help counter poverty—for example, subsidies for child care, supports for housing, increases in the minimum wage, stronger enforcement of child support orders—the chief policy instrument for reducing child poverty rates would be child benefits.[5]

Canada's program of child benefits evolved in the following steps.[6] First, in 1993, the federal government introduced a new single, tax-free, income-tested Child Tax Benefit. Monthly payments were based on family income. As part of the system, the provinces and territories delivered their own child benefits to families on social assistance. Second, in 1998, the federal, provincial, and territorial governments launched the new National Child Benefit reform, which expanded benefits and coordinated action among the different levels of government. The central feature of the National Child Benefit was the Canada Child Tax Benefit, which had two components: a basic tax-free payment to low- and moderate-income families, and the National Child Benefit Supplement, a benefit targeted to low-income families. Under the system, the federal government gave benefits directly to eligible families—proportionately more to working-poor families—and to the provinces and territories for welfare-poor families. The provinces and territories in turn used the extra amount in ways they saw fit, whether for child care or more social assistance or a separate benefit. Third, in 2006, the Harper Conservative government scaled back the Canada Child Tax Benefit and added a new Universal Child Care Benefit, a modest new benefit for all families but subject to income tax (except for single parents) and not indexed to inflation. Although the term *child care* was used in the new benefit, it was really a child benefit because parents could use it for any purpose related to children, not necessarily for child care.

Child benefits rose substantially over time. Federal expenditures roughly tripled from 1993 to 2015, increasing from $5.1 billion to over $15 billion (the Canada Child Tax Benefit and the Universal Child Care Benefit combined).[7] And during the same period, the maximum annual benefit for one child rose from $2575 in 1993 to almost $5700 in 2015 (in constant 2015 dollars). In 2016, the Justin Trudeau Liberal government increased the benefit even more. Under the new Canada Child Benefit—which combined the previous benefits—the maximum rose to $6400 per child under age six and to $5400 for children between ages six and seventeen. In addition, the Trudeau government announced it would adjust benefit levels to increases in the cost of living. However, despite the increasing generosity of the benefits over time, child poverty rates have remained unacceptably high.[8]

Child poverty can be measured in a number of ways.[9] It can be measured in absolute terms as the lack of a certain fixed amount of goods and services. Or it can be measured in relative terms as the percentage of children living in households under a certain minimum income. The relative measure is the most commonly used in Canada. Although it tells us little about absolute deprivation, it describes inequality of material conditions and the difference between the lives of children in poverty and their more affluent peers, which has important implications for health, education, and well-being. The relative measure is also useful for comparative purposes. Particularly helpful is the low-income measure, which has been used extensively in international comparisons by organizations like the Organisation for Economic Co-operation and Development (OECD) and UNICEF, and by Canadian child advocacy groups such as Campaign 2000, formed to measure and monitor rates of child poverty in Canada. In the low-income measure, child poverty is defined as the proportion of children growing up in households with incomes less than 50 percent of the national mean. The rate of child poverty is the percentage of children growing up in such households in comparison to the overall number of children.

As noted by Campaign 2000, in 1989, the year the Convention on the Rights of the Child was approved by the United Nations, the child poverty rate in Canada—measured by the low-income measure after tax—was 15.8 percent.[10] Then, ironically, despite the House of Commons resolution and despite Canada's ratification of the Convention, the rate increased during the 1990s and early 2000s, reaching 22.3 percent in 2000 and 22.6 percent in 2004. By 2015, the rate declined to 17.4 percent but was higher than in 1989 when the Convention was approved by the United Nations. This clearly shows that despite the growth in child benefits, there has been a lack of substantial progress in advancing the child's right to economic welfare. Analysis by Campaign 2000 also shows that some groups of children are much more likely to live in poverty than others.[11] Among the groups disproportionately at risk of poverty are children who are Indigenous (an astonishing 60 percent on reserves live in poverty), immigrants, refugees, children who have special needs, and children living in female-headed, single-parent families. Among the provinces and territories, the highest rates of poverty are in Nunavut, Manitoba, and Saskatchewan. The lowest rates are in Yukon and Québec. The number of children living in poverty is reflected in rising food bank use. As noted by Food Banks Canada in 2016, 36 percent of food bank use was by children, with the greatest usage in Saskatchewan, Manitoba, and the territories.[12]

International comparisons show that efforts by Canada to reduce child poverty rates have been weaker than those of most other developed countries. In UNICEF's 2016 report *Fairness for Children*, the world's wealthiest nations were compared on the basis of outcomes in health, education, and economic well-being.[13] Canada ranked a mediocre twenty-ninth out of forty-one nations. The lowest rates were in the Nordic countries. Canada's rate of child poverty, although lower than in the United States, was over three times the rates of countries like Denmark, Norway, and Finland.

In accounting for child poverty rates, international reports and analyses point to a combination of three general factors: (1) economic and employment conditions such as unemployment, underemployment, and low-wage jobs; (2) social trends such as family breakdown and the rise of single-parent families; and (3) the strength of government policies and programs in providing for income support.[14] It is important to keep in mind that virtually all of the world's wealthiest nations in recent decades have been challenged by global economic pressures, unfavourable employment and labour market conditions, and social problems such as family breakdown. It also is important to note that all nations have made efforts to tackle child and family poverty. But some countries have made more of an effort than others. Canada, for example, has established a relatively generous program of child benefits. When we combine child benefits with other family programs, Canada's efforts to reduce the number of children living in poverty have been much stronger than those of the United States.[15] However, compared to northern and western European countries, Canada's policies have been much weaker. As reported by the OECD in 2014, where the Nordic countries and many countries in western Europe have spent between 3 and 4 percent of GDP on family income programs, Canada's family spending was under 1.5 percent.[16] Although Canada's spending was more than that of the United States, spending in Sweden, France, Finland, and Norway was over double that of Canada and spending in Denmark was over four times the amount. Overall, Canada's spending has been well below the OECD average.

What accounts for the differences? In Urie Bronfenbrenner's description of social environments surrounding the child, beyond the family and local community and beyond government policies and programs, there is the context of culture and political culture.[17] Political culture—the prevailing political values and beliefs of a country—has a major role to play in the nature and strength of government policies, including child and family policies. In the Nordic countries and in many western European nations, there is a strong cultural belief in social responsibility.[18] It is assumed that it takes a village to raise a child, that children are the responsibility of the family and the state, and that the state has an obligation to assist parents and ensure that children have their basic material needs met. Such a belief is a driver of relatively strong policies of income support. But in North America and especially the United States, there is an enduring belief in individual responsibility.[19] Individuals are responsible for themselves, and parents are primarily responsible for the raising of children. Although the state should step in to assist parents, it should do so only in exceptional cases and only to a limited degree. The continuation of such a belief helps explain relatively weak policies of income support and the relatively modest efforts made so far to support families and to reduce the number of children living in poverty.

## Problems Associated with Living in Poverty

There is no question that being raised in poverty takes a heavy toll on children, in sharp contrast to their best interests. Poverty that occurs early in the child's life and that is persistent has a more profound impact than does poverty that occurs later and is temporary. This means that we can make predictions about the impact of poverty on a child born into a poor family with some degree of accuracy. We do not, however, anticipate the same outcomes for a child who experiences temporary poverty later, for example during a post-divorce family reorganization period. In this section, we describe the effects of living in poverty when it is experienced early and persists for at least the first four years of the child's life. We examine the mechanisms by which poverty exerts its effects. We then summarize the research findings on the impact of poverty on children's development. Three primary means by which early and persistent poverty affects child development have been identified in the research literature: the chronic stress that children experience, inadequate parental resources, and high levels of family stress.

Exposure to chronic stress affects the child's brain structure and functioning through its impact on stress hormones.[20] The areas affected are those associated with self-regulation and executive function.[21] *Executive function* is the term used to describe what is essentially the control network that is in the prefrontal cortex. The control network is responsible for abilities such as thinking, reasoning, planning, remembering, constraining impulses, and focusing attention. How strong or effective the control network is varies with the child's early environment.[22]

Poverty in the first four years of life has been shown to have a significant effect on reducing self-regulation and executive function skills.[23] It is an effect that, in the absence of early intervention, seems to be constant through childhood and adolescence.[24] Poor executive function skills in turn are associated with academic difficulties and poor decisions about health and social behaviours.[25] It may be that the high rates of drinking, smoking, poor diet, and physical inactivity that are so often seen in deprived populations stem from the effects of early and persistent poverty on brain structure and functioning.[26]

As described above, efforts to support parents and parenting in Canada have been inadequate. As a result, parenting can be particularly difficult for those living in poverty. Inadequate parental resources, both personal and material, often mean that parents have less to invest in their infant's and child's healthy development. Investment in the child varies with parents' income, education level, and parenting capacity.[27] As we noted in Chapter 1, when parents' incomes and education levels are low, they tend to have more difficulty parenting effectively, and invest less in the child. This includes investing in the child's cognitive development by providing the child with appropriately stimulating environments—educational toys and books, sports, and recreational and cultural activities.[28]

Parents in poverty face multiple challenges that are very stressful. They are often lone parents, their housing may be inadequate, their income may be insufficient to cover basic needs, and they are often coping with social isolation.[29] The resulting stress, not surprisingly, makes parenting less satisfying and more frustrating.[30] In turn, parenting behaviours and the child–parent relationships are negatively affected.[31] Low-income parents tend to engage in harsher discipline practices and to give less attention and support to their children's needs.[32] Findings from the Canadian Incidence Study of Reported Child Abuse and Neglect underscore the pernicious effect of poverty on parenting.[33] Parents who maltreat infants typically are struggling with poverty. Similarly, the Ontario Child Health Study found poverty in childhood to be associated with an increased risk of physical and sexual abuse.[34]

A family's socioeconomic status plays a critical role in the development of children's physical health and well-being.[35] As found in a study of families in Ontario, low-income families have difficulty providing nutritious foods, adequate health care, and appropriate housing.[36] These challenging environments pose a significant risk to children's health. Deprivation in early childhood can lead to high blood pressure, dysregulated metabolic activity, obesity, compromised immune systems, and many chronic diseases.[37] Disadvantaged children in urban neighbourhoods, for example, may live close to industrial zones with high concentrations of pollutants.[38] They may also be exposed to noise, overcrowding, allergens, heavy traffic, and crime, with few safe play places or parks.[39] A number of researchers have shown that the lower the family's socioeconomic status, the higher the incidence of child accidental poisoning, injuries, traffic accidents, and death.[40]

Consistent links have also been found between socioeconomic status and children's mental health. In a review of studies of socioeconomic inequality and children's mental health that was conducted in Australia, Europe, and North America, children from low-income homes consistently were found to have greater vulnerability to mental health problems.[41] Compared with their more affluent peers, children living in poverty overall were two to three times more likely to have behaviour problems. Being raised in poverty is a major predictor of internalizing problems, or problems that affect the self, such as anxiety, depression, and social withdrawal. Poverty also is a major predictor of externalizing problems, or problems that affect others, such as aggression, hyperactivity, and non-compliance.[42] For example, Casey Holtz and his colleagues examined the incidence of both positive and negative behaviour of children under the age of five whose families were living in poverty and found a very high and age-inappropriate rate of hitting, tantrums, and bothering others.[43] Such problems are not unusual. In their examination of research evidence, researchers from the Simon Fraser University Children's Health Policy Centre conclude that behaviour disorders may be the leading cause of mental health problems for Canadian children.[44] They estimate that at any given time there are 678,000 children (12.6 percent) between the ages of four and seventeen years with one or more behaviour disorders.

In addition to mental and physical health challenges, children who spend the first few years of life in low-income families show significant delays in cognitive development.[45] These delays have a profound impact on their academic achievement. Their vocabularies and test scores, already lower than those of their peers at age three, are almost 20 percentile ranks lower by age seven.[46] Lacking basic competencies in language, literacy, and numeracy skills, they are ill-prepared for formal schooling.[47] The challenges they face in adapting to the school environment stem from material deprivation (lack of books, educational toys, and experiences) and from poor performance on executive control function tasks as described above. For example, difficulties with attention control interfere significantly with school success.[48] Attention control—the ability to focus on a given task despite distractions—is needed to succeed in the classroom environment. The early disadvantage persists. Learning tends to be cumulative, and starting school with delays in cognitive development is predictive of later poor performance in language, reading, and math.[49] Catch-up is rare.[50] Neither interventions nor grade retention has been found particularly effective.[51] Not surprisingly, the achievement gap by socioeconomic status that is evident early most often widens as children progress through grade levels.[52]

Behaviour problems interfere with learning and educational success.[53] Effective emotion regulation skills and impulse control are needed when children start school to allow coping with frustrations and inhibiting aggressive responses. Aggressive and disruptive behaviours at school have been identified as a significant problem for children in low-income families.[54] Children who have difficulty controlling their impulses and their aggression may struggle with group learning activities and attract a lot of negative attention. As they enter adolescence, the behaviour problems tend to escalate into more serious conduct disorders that can result in being suspended or expelled from school.[55] Difficulty controlling aggression in primary school also is strongly associated with voluntary early school leaving. Canadian researchers have reported an early school leaving rate among children with a history of disruptive behaviour as six times higher than the average.[56]

Persistent and early poverty poses a barrier to healthy development and educational achievement that is very difficult for the child to overcome. The effects of poverty are evident early, substantial, and persistent through adulthood. Poor physical and mental health and school failure perpetuate a cycle of poverty. Reduced education is strongly associated with unemployment, poorer mental and physical health, and involvement in the criminal justice system.[57] And the next generation is at risk of repeating the cycle. All of this is, of course, contrary to the best interests of the child.

## Provision of Health Care

According to article 24 of the Convention, a child has the right to "the enjoyment of the highest attainable standard of health." In implementing this right, article 24 says that Canada and other states parties have the obligation to take appropriate measures to diminish infant and child mortality, to ensure the provision of necessary medical assistance and health care to children, to combat disease and malnutrition, and to ensure appropriate prenatal and postnatal health care for mothers. There is an obligation also to develop preventive health care for children and to ensure that parents, children, and others are informed, have access to education, and are supported in the use of basic knowledge of child health and nutrition. In the Convention the term *health* is understood to mean not merely the absence of disease but a state of positive well-being, including mental and emotional well-being as well as physical well-being.[58]

Since Canada's ratification of the Convention, a variety of progressive measures have been taken by federal, provincial, and territorial governments to improve health care and health outcomes for children. In line with Canada's action plan announced in *Brighter Futures*, the federal government established the Child Development Initiative in 1992, consisting of programs to address risks that threaten the health of children, especially young children up to six years of age. This was followed by a series of other programs, including the Community Action Program for Children (1993), the Canada Prenatal and Nutrition Program (1995), Aboriginal Head Start (1995), the Fetal Alcohol Spectrum Disorder Initiative (2008), and the Mental Health Strategy for Canada (2012), a follow-up to the creation of the Mental Health Commission of Canada (2007). At the provincial and territorial levels, a variety of healthy pregnancy, healthy infant, early years, and child health programs were established, including Saskatchewan's Action Plan for Children (1993), Ontario's Healthy Babies, Healthy Children program (1998), British Columbia's Healthy Start Initiative (2011), and Yukon's Wellness Plan for Children and Families (2014). Finally, beginning in the early 2000s, to improve access to health care for children as well as adults living in remote rural, northern, and Indigenous communities, programs such as Telehealth were developed by federal, provincial, and territorial governments. Through videoconferencing and other technology, Telehealth was designed to address geographical isolation and compensate for the shortage of health-care professionals and services in remote areas.[59]

Through these and other efforts, important progress has been made in improving child health. For example, rates of infant mortality—one of the primary indicators of child health—declined. Although the rates (measured as infant deaths in the first year of life per 1000 live births) had been declining since the 1970s, they decreased further, falling from 6.1 in 1992 to 5.1 in 2008 to 4.7 in 2014.[60] The rates also declined where they had been the highest, such as among infants who are Indigenous and those in the territories. Furthermore, rates of sudden infant death syndrome (SIDS) declined.[61] The rates (measured as infant death due to SIDS per 1000 live births) had been falling since the 1980s. But they decreased further thanks to a decline in risk factors such as maternal tobacco use during pregnancy and to health education about the proper positioning of a baby during sleep. In 1990, the rate was 1.0. By 1995, it fell to 0.5 and by 2009, to 0.3. And as in the more general case of infant mortality, the rates fell where they had been highest such as among Indigenous infants and in the North.[62]

However, other risk factors have not shown the same progress. First, rates of low birth weight—another leading indicator of child health and a major risk factor for poor health—have remained the same or slightly increased over time.[63] Measured as a weight below 2500 grams at birth, the low-birth-weight rate rose from 5.7 percent in 1994 to 6.0 percent in 2008 and to 6.1 percent in 2011. Second, rates of immunization against serious diseases—another leading health indicator—have fallen since the mid-2000s.[64] In 2002, 95 percent of two-year-olds were vaccinated against measles and 94 percent against mumps. But by 2013, the rates for both fell to 89 percent, due in part to false rumours that vaccines were linked to autism. Third, rates of youth suicide—a key indicator of mental health—have remained a serious problem, especially among males and among youth living in the northern territories. As reported by Statistics Canada, from 1974 to 2012, the suicide rate for youth ages fifteen to nineteen has persisted at nine to ten per one hundred thousand of the population.[65] The rate is particularly high among Indigenous youth who experience strong feelings of hopelessness.[66] This has been noted as a major issue of concern by the UN Committee on the Rights of the Child. Fourth, rates of childhood obesity—associated with a wide range of health problems—have increased. In 1976, the rate for children and youth ages three to nineteen was 5 percent; by 2013, the rate had reached 13 percent.[67] Finally, major health inequalities have persisted based on income and ethnicity. As discussed earlier, children in higher-income households in general (as well as adults) have continued to have better health outcomes than children in lower-income households.[68] And despite improvement in some areas, children who are Indigenous have continued to have significantly higher rates of infant mortality, SIDS, low birth weight, suicide, substance abuse, obesity, and fetal alcohol spectrum disorder (FASD). This difference is in contradiction to the Convention principles of best interests and non-discrimination.[69]

International comparisons show that Canadian efforts have been weaker than what they could have been. In UNICEF's *Fairness for Children* report (2016), Canada ranked twenty-fourth out of thirty-five countries on child health as measured by children's self-reported health symptoms.[70] And in a previous report by UNICEF (2013), Canada ranked an embarrassing twenty-seventh out of twenty-nine for child health outcomes.[71] UNICEF examined data on four leading indicators: infant mortality, low birth weight, national immunization rates (average coverage for measles, polio, and diphtheria), and child and youth mortality. Although Canada's ranking was average for low birth weight, it was very poor for infant mortality and immunization, contributing to its low overall rating. Canada did not supply data for child and youth mortality. But from findings reported in 2014 in the *Lancet*, Canada was given a ranking of fifth worst for child mortality (18.8 child deaths per 10,000) among high-income nations.[72] It might be tempting to think that Canada's low rating was related simply to inadequate government spending on health care. But according to data from the OECD (2016), health-care spending per capita in Canada has been above average among OECD nations.[73] What would seem to be more important, as in the case of children living in poverty, is a lack of commitment specifically to children and to the concept of social responsibility for children.

Of further concern have been efforts in the area of prenatal health care. Although in Canada there always has been attention to the importance of healthy pregnancies, concern increased since the 1990s with expanding knowledge of the linkage between maternal use of alcohol, tobacco, solvents, or drugs during pregnancy and risks to healthy child development. The problem of FASD, for example, has been highlighted as never before. It was because of awareness of the importance of prenatal care that the Convention requires states parties to ensure appropriate prenatal as well as postnatal care as part of overall child health care. However, a major problem for child health has been that children have virtually no legal protection against damage to their health caused during pregnancy. Health Canada and provincial departments of health have launched educational programs to inform parents and the public about healthy pregnancies. These programs have been valuable but they have not been followed up by regulations or laws making prenatal health care a parental legal duty.

That prenatal care was not a legal duty became crystal clear in three important court rulings during the 1990s. In *R. v. Drummond*, [1997] O.J. No. 6390, an Ontario woman fired a pellet gun into her vagina toward the end of her pregnancy. Shortly after Jonathan was born, he developed life-threatening meningitis. Doctors performed surgery to remove the pellet only after Drummond disclosed what she had done. She could not be charged with attempted murder because a fetus is not a person until birth; hence Drummond received a suspended sentence and thirty-month probation for failure to provide the necessaries of life after Jonathan's birth.[74] The Ontario government decided not to appeal, mindful that in *R. v. Morgentaler*, [1988] 1 S.C.R. 30, the Supreme Court of Canada had struck down provisions in the *Criminal Code* regulating abortion on the grounds that a fetus is a part of a woman's body until birth. Accordingly, abortion laws violated a woman's section 7 *Charter* right to security of the person.

In *Winnipeg Child and Family Services v. G.(D.F.)*, [1997] 3 S.C.R. 925, a woman addicted to glue sniffing who had previously given birth to three children with brain damage was detained in a rehab facility to protect her unborn child. The Supreme Court ruled that Winnipeg Child and Family Services could not exercise *parens patriae* authority in this way. "Under the law as it presently stands, the fetus on whose behalf the agency purported to act in seeking the order for the respondent's detention was not a legal person and possessed no legal rights," wrote Justice Beverley McLachlin in her majority decision (para. 16). She rejected the claim by Child and Family Services that because some Canadian courts had begun allowing negligence suits for injuries sustained in utero, a fetus could sue the mother, noting that a fetus is legally part of a woman's body until birth. "To permit an unborn child to sue its pregnant mother-to-be would introduce a radically new conception into the law; the unborn child and its mother as separate juristic persons in a mutually separable and antagonistic relation," she wrote (para. 29). Accordingly, D.F.G.'s detention by Winnipeg Child and Family Services violated her section 7 *Charter* rights to liberty and security of the person.

The implications of these rulings are disturbing. They affirm that a mother is within her legal rights to put her unborn child at risk of injury or brain damage through negligence, assault, substance abuse, or misuse of drugs or alcohol. The Supreme Court did not rule out the possibility of legal protection of the unborn, but this would be a matter for legislatures, not the courts.

In the D.F.G. case, Justice John Major wrote a minority opinion holding that *parens patriae* authority could be exercised to detain a pregnant woman addicted to glue sniffing who had refused an abortion and medical treatment and who had decided to carry her child to term. He was unwilling to sustain a legal distinction between children before and after birth, describing the born-alive rule as a legal anachronism rooted in the rudimentary medical knowledge of the past. While he acknowledged that confinement would interfere with the mother's liberty interests, her interests had to give way "where devastating harm and a life of suffering can so easily be prevented" (para. 93). If D.F.G. wished to avoid confinement in the interests of her unborn child, she could terminate her pregnancy and with it, the state interest. In other words, once a mother has chosen to bring a fetus to term, exercising her right to autonomy and choice under the *Charter*, she then has a duty to provide optimal conditions for the health and well-being of the unborn child. If she puts her unborn child at risk through negligence or abuse, the state should have the legal means of intervening and protecting the unborn.

Under the Convention, Canada has an obligation to ensure appropriate prenatal and postnatal care. As we discussed in Chapter 3, the state has a responsibility as *parens patriae* to act in the best interests of the child. The health and well-being of the child after birth is inseparable from the health and well-being of the child before birth.

## The Imperative of Prenatal Care

The development of the child is a joint function of genetic endowment and environmental conditions, including the prenatal environment. A prenatal environment that exposes the fetus to toxins can profoundly compromise the physical and neurological status of the newborn, and as a result, the healthy development of the child. The postnatal environment is limited in the extent to which it can undo damage experienced in the prenatal environment. If we are to be proactive in providing for children's rights, we know that we must pay attention to the health of the child's gestational environment. Yet prenatal environmental health risks continue. Perhaps most egregious among them are continued gestational exposure to alcohol and second-hand smoke.

Fetal alcohol syndrome was first described in Seattle in 1973 to account for the effects seen in children whose mothers had consumed alcohol while pregnant. At that time, drinking through pregnancy was common.[75] Fewer women now drink during pregnancy, but despite all the consistent evidence of its potential to do harm, fetal alcohol exposure remains the leading preventable cause of developmental disability in Canada.[76] The early research showed a link between drinking during pregnancy and the child's intel-ligence and attention skills through adolescence.[77] Since then, mounting evidence has confirmed that prenatal exposure to alcohol has the potential to produce lifelong social and cognitive disabilities. Researchers have shown that any prenatal alcohol exposure has the potential to disrupt healthy fetal growth and to damage the development of the physical and central nervous systems.[78] But not all children are affected equally. For example, some chil-dren have major learning problems, whereas others may have few if any cog-nitive deficits but have serious behaviour problems. The nature and extent of damage varies with the dose and pattern of alcohol consumption, the gestational time of exposure, the health of the mother, whether the mother is using other substances, and genetics.[79] To account for the diversity of out-comes, it is now common to describe the effects of prenatal alcohol exposure with the umbrella term fetal alcohol spectrum disorder. The term describes a continuum of alcohol-related developmental damage from fetal alcohol syn-drome (the most severe and debilitating) to alcohol-related neurodevelop-mental disorder.[80]

The core characteristics of FASD are facial abnormalities and organ and central nervous system dysfunction. The neurodevelopmental deficits associated with FASD increase the risk of adverse health and social con-sequences.[81] Affected children will display some level of learning, mem-ory, attention, problem-solving, and social and mental health difficulties throughout their lives.[82] They typically show poor judgment, distractibil-ity, impulsivity, and gullibility. The consequences are seen in poor health, educational failure, difficulty with social relationships, and, importantly, a high likelihood of involvement in the juvenile justice system. A number of researchers in Canada and the United States have reported that adolescents with FASD are nineteen times more likely than their non-affected peers to be arrested.[83] Canada does not keep statistics on rates of FASD-affected youth in the juvenile justice system (or even on the prevalence of the disor-der), but estimates are that on any given day in Canada there are around 280 youth with FASD in custody.[84] If we include those over the age of eighteen, then the estimate jumps to 4000. These are all individuals whose fundamen-tal right to health was denied prior to birth.

Although we have no national data on the numbers of children or adults whose ability to enjoy the substance of their rights has been compromised by fetal alcohol exposure, 2014 estimates are 350,000 Canadians, with between 3000 and 4000 new cases added each year.[85] The overall prevalence rates are estimated to be 9 to 10 alcohol-affected individuals per 1000. Not surprisingly, given the historical context of colonization, intergenerational trauma, high poverty rates, and social isolation, the prevalence in Canada's northern communities is estimated to be about twenty times higher than the general population.[86] Studies of Indigenous communities in Canada show a prevalence rate that ranges from 34 to 62 percent.[87] In a study of 248 Inuit women in northern Québec, for example, reports of alcohol use were very high, with 60 percent of the women saying they drank alcohol during pregnancy. The researchers estimated an FASD rate of 47 per 1000 births. A major problem identified in this sample was the extent of binge drinking, with ten alcoholic drinks on one occasion being common. A key problem with binge drinking is its link with unplanned pregnancy.

When a pregnancy is unplanned or unintended, the likelihood is high that the woman will consume alcohol before knowing she is pregnant. Fetal alcohol exposure may be particularly damaging in the first trimester of pregnancy, when the cells are dividing and migrating to areas that will form the brain.[88] Unfortunately, Statistics Canada data show that rates of binge drinking—defined as five or more drinks on one occasion twelve or more times in the previous year—are highest among eighteen- to twenty-four-year-olds (47 percent).[89] This is the age range in which unplanned pregnancy occurs most frequently and is strongly predicted by alcohol use.[90] Interestingly, the highest percentage of binge drinking is found in the Atlantic provinces and northern Canada.[91] Similarly, the highest rate of unplanned pregnancy is in the Atlantic provinces and the North.[92]

Recognizing the problem of high rates of FASD in the North, alcohol warning labels are mandated in Nunavut and the Northwest Territories.[93] Alcohol warning labels are being tested in the Yukon.[94] In the rest of Canada, health-related information is on all food and beverage labels with the exception of alcohol.[95] Back in 1992, a House of Commons committee recommended requiring warning labels on alcohol bottles. The then health minister Benoit Bouchard rejected the recommendation, saying it "would not be useful to require the warnings because women usually drink out of a glass and may not see the bottle or its label." Since then there have been numerous efforts in Canada to require warning labels on all bottles of alcohol. In 2005, for example, Ontario's Paul Szabo introduced a private member's bill in Parliament, C206. And Manitoba MP Judy Wasylycia worked tirelessly to convince her colleagues to support warning labels.[96] In addition to these efforts by individuals, four standing committees of Parliament, including the Royal Commission on New Reproductive Technologies, have recommended warning labels to reduce the incidence of FASD. None has been successful. Perhaps in response to opposition from the industry, there has been continued insistence that warning labels would not be useful and that women don't always see the alcohol container.[97] It is true that warning labels do not always change behaviour. But they do serve a useful educative function, and they are used in more than twenty other countries.[98] Moreover, we have learned from warning labels on tobacco that appropriately designed labels can be effective in modifying behaviour.[99]

Tobacco also poses an avoidable threat to healthy fetal and child development. Nicotine crosses the placental barrier, reducing the supply of oxygen and nutrients to the developing fetus and increasing carbon monoxide in the gestational environment.[100] A wide range of adverse outcomes are associated with prenatal nicotine exposure. Poor health outcomes include reduced birth weight, preterm birth, and childhood asthma.[101] There are also a number of neurocognitive deficits that affect the child's intellectual ability and behaviour, including attention-deficit/hyperactivity disorder.[102] The effects are dose-dependent: The more cigarettes the mother smokes per day during her pregnancy, the more adverse the outcomes for the child.[103] Children are at particular risk of developmental difficulties when pregnant women both smoke and drink. The two behaviours often coexist.[104] For example, the Inuit women in northern Québec—again, living in very challenging circumstances—whose drinking habits were described earlier, also were heavy smokers. An astonishing 92 percent reported smoking tobacco through the pregnancy.[105] The combined effects of drinking and smoking are more damaging than the sum of the effects of the individual behaviours.[106] Not surprisingly, the worst outcomes are seen in children prenatally exposed to alcohol, tobacco, and other drugs.[107] Nonetheless, nicotine alone profoundly affects the developing fetus.

Montreal researcher Caroline Fitzpatrick and her colleagues used data from the Québec Longitudinal Study of Child Development to examine the effects of nicotine alone on children whose mothers smoked during the pregnancy. Their focus was on children's impulsive behaviour at age ten.[108] Compared with children whose mothers did not smoke during pregnancy, those whose mothers smoked ten or more cigarettes each day were more impulsive, less focused on tasks, and less compliant at school. The implication of these findings is that these children are at increased risk of poor health-related behaviours, academic underachievement, and poor psychosocial adjustment. What was particularly interesting in their find-ings is that these differences in impulsivity by maternal smoking were not affected by factors such as the mother's school involvement, socioeconomic status, and mental health, or whether the child also had been exposed to alcohol or illicit drugs in utero.

Fortunately, the Public Health Agency of Canada reports that the rate of maternal smoking during pregnancy has declined steadily.[109] However, rates remain high among pregnant women ages fifteen to twenty-four. Almost half of women who smoke continue to do so during pregnancy.[110] Of those who stop smoking when they find out they are pregnant, almost half relapse before the child's first birthday. Their children, like all others exposed to second-hand smoke, are at elevated risk of ear and respiratory tract infections, asthma, behaviour disorders, cognitive deficits, and learn-ing disabilities. The effects, like those of prenatal exposure, will be lifelong.

## Provision of Early Childhood Education and Care

The framers of the Convention understood the need not only for child-care services among contemporary families but also for standards and quality in these services, consistent with the best interests of the child. They therefore inserted into the Convention provisions on child care, later referred to in international terminology as *early childhood education and care*. Thus, under article 18, states parties are obligated to take measures to ensure that chil-dren of working parents have the right to benefit from early childhood edu-cation services. And under article 3, as part of the best interests of the child, states parties are required to ensure basic standards for child-care services and facilities, especially in the areas of safety, health, and the number and suitability of staff. In this section, we examine Canada's record in providing for early childhood education. But first, we review the types of care and the complications of Canada's federal system in providing care for children.

The term *early childhood education and care* refers here to a broad range of services, arrangements, facilities, and programs that provide early educa-tion and non-parental care for young children.[111] The purpose of these servi-ces is twofold: to enhance child development and well-being, and to provide support for parents.[112] Within the broad umbrella of early childhood edu-cation and care are two basic forms: One is general programs of daycare and before- and after-school care available for all children, which may be publicly funded and operated, publicly subsidized, or privately funded and operated. The other is specialized enrichment programs targeted for children at risk, which are typically publicly funded or subsidized.[113] Both forms are available in Canada. Enrichment programs are designed, among other things, to improve school readiness and educational performance among socially disadvantaged children. A prime example is Aboriginal Head Start, modelled in part after Head Start in the United States.[114] In Canada, more than half of families now use one of three main types of daycare services.[115] The most common is unregulated in-home care by relatives, neighbours, or hired caregivers. The second most common is regulated institutional care provided in workplaces, schools, or community centres. The third most common is regulated in-home care provided in private residences.

Canada's system of providing for early childhood education and care has been greatly complicated by federalism. The provinces and territories have primary responsibility for the administration and delivery of early education. They are responsible for licensing, for regulation (e.g., health and safety, staff qualifications, staff child ratios), and—to the extent that they can—for the funding of services and programs. Because the provinces have flexibility in what they do and because of variation in resources, there have been major differences across the country in terms of costs, fees, regulations, and types of services. The outcome, as often said, has been an uneven and patchwork system.[116] But the federal government also has important roles to perform. The federal government has responsibility for child care in Indigenous communities and for military families. And because of its taxing and spending powers, the federal government has the ability to provide parents with income tax deductions for child-care expenses, provide parents directly with financial payments for the costs of care, and assist the provinces and territories with funding for services and programs. Historically, up to the signing of the Convention, although the federal government provided certain tax deductions for parents and financial assistance to the provinces and territories, it made little progress to overcome the patchwork and to establish a strong and accessible system of early care.[117]

After the signing of the Convention, Canadian governments at all levels made more serious efforts to expand and improve early childhood education. They did so not so much for principled reasons but because of growing social and political pressures to act. Social pressures arose because of important demographic trends: the rising number of women in the workforce, the growing number of dual-earner and single-parent families with a need for early care, and the increasing number of children four years of age and younger in Canada's population.[118] With this demographic change and with the shortages and high costs of child care came a rising demand among parents for governments to act. Growing numbers of parents called on governments to make child care more available and more affordable. Accompanying this call were pressures by women's organizations and child-care advocacy groups. They argued for a strong, universal, and affordable system of early childhood education. Most of their arguments focused on child care as a means to advance equality for women, provide support for working parents, and counter family poverty. But some of the advocates also gave attention to children, arguing that quality child care was a means of advancing the rights and best interests of the child.[119] However, it must be noted that not all groups urged a strong universal system. Conservative groups such as Real Women of Canada argued against such a system, calling on governments to assist parents directly for their child-care needs and to support parental choice in child-care arrangements.[120]

In response to the growing pressures, Canadian governments began to take stronger action during the late 1990s and early 2000s.[121] At the provincial level, in 1997 Québec introduced the most ambitious and accessible program of early childhood education and care in North America. For $5.00 per day—increased to $7.00 in 2004 and $7.30 in 2014—parents could enrol their four-year-olds in child-care services (full-day kindergarten was available for five-year-olds). Coverage later was extended to all children under age four and the number of regulated spaces was expanded significantly. At the federal level, in 1995, the government established two major programs for children who are Indigenous: the First Nations/Inuit Child Care Initiative, created to improve access to affordable care among Indigenous families, and Aboriginal Head Start, designed as an enrichment program for children who are Indigenous and living in urban and northern communities. A key aim of Aboriginal Head Start was to increase school readiness and enhance child development. In 1998, the program was extended to cover children living on reserves. Finally, at the joint federal, provincial, and territorial level, after many years of setbacks and failures, the Multilateral Framework on Early Learning and Child Care was announced in 2003. It involved a commitment to the significant funding and development of regulated early care programs, particularly for children under age six. Through agreements between the federal government and each of the provinces and territories, the primary objective was to provide support for parents by improving access to affordable and quality care. To this end, in the 2005 federal budget, an unprecedented $5 billion would be spent over five years.

The movement for improved child care suffered a significant reversal in 2006.[122] The Harper Conservative government abruptly cancelled agreements under the Multilateral Framework and replaced the program with its own Universal Child Care Benefit program and the Child Care Spaces Initiative. Influenced by interest groups urging more parental choice in child care, the Harper government set up the Universal Benefit in 2006 to give money directly to parents through monthly payments of $100 for each child under age six (the payment was increased to $160 in 2015). As we noted earlier, it was not really a child-care benefit: Parents could use the money for children in any way they saw fit, whether for regulated child care or care at home by parents, or something else. This said, the Conservative government continued to assist the provinces and territories in providing funding for regulated care. But funding levels were modest. Under the Child Care Spaces Initiative, announced in 2006, $250 million a year would be invested by the federal government in child care for five years, starting in 2007–08. This amount was not insignificant. But it was a major step back from the funding commitments made under the Multilateral Framework. Disappointingly, the result has been a child-care situation not very different from previous decades: a patchwork of services, shortages of spaces, waiting lists, high costs for parents (except in Québec), lack of standards and quality care, and wide use of unregulated, informal care, disproportionately affecting low-income families.[123]

International comparisons reveal that the measures taken by Canada to improve early childhood education and care have been weaker than the measures taken by most other developed countries. According to the Economist Intelligence Unit (2012), in examining the record of forty-five countries in meeting benchmarks on early childhood education such as affordability, availability, and quality, Canada ranked a mediocre twenty-sixth.[124] As with child poverty rates and child health indices, the Nordic nations and European countries were dominant in the higher rankings. And as reported by the OECD (2008), in examining public spending on child care and early education services in thirty-seven developed countries (as a percentage of GDP), Canada ranked thirty-sixth, ahead only of Greece.[125] While Denmark's spending was almost 1.4 percent of GDP, Canada's spending was less than 0.2 percent. It comes as no surprise, then, that given Canada's poor record, the UN Committee on the Rights of the Child (2012) expressed strong criticism of Canada for its failure to invest in and strengthen its early childhood education and care services.[126] Such failure has been antithetical to the hopes of Canadian child advocates at the time of the signing of the Convention, and very much contrary to the rights and best interests of the child.

Why has Canada been a laggard in providing for early childhood education and care? Part of the answer may be federalism and the lack of coordinated efforts among different levels of government.[127] But, as with persistently high child poverty rates, a deeper reason is the pervasiveness of a belief in individual responsibility rather than social responsibility. Québec has been an exception with its progressive social programs in recent decades, including early childhood education. Such developments in Québec have been due in part to a social democratic culture resembling those in the Nordic countries, featuring a collective belief in social responsibility and government action to support children and families.[128] But in the rest of Canada, as in the United States, although a belief in social responsibility has been growing, individual responsibility continues to inform the thinking of many interest groups, citizens, and policy-makers. It is a belief that says individual parents should be primarily responsible for the care of their children, not governments. Governments may help at the margins, but the lion's share of responsibility is with those choosing to have children. This belief remains ingrained in the political culture, accounting for reluctance among governments in Canada, other than in Québec, to make a serious effort to build a strong system of early childhood education and care. The Harper Conservative government is an obvious example of such reluctance at the national level. But Liberal governments have failed to take substantive action as well.

### The Imperative of Quality Child Care

The proliferation of child-care use over the past few decades has been accompanied by two controversial questions: Does daycare harm children? Should mothers stay home to raise their children? Because child care has grown to serve the needs of women in the workforce, research findings showing problems associated with child-rearing outside the home have often been dismissed as attempts to block the equality of women in the workplace. Visions of women in twinsets and pearls have often clouded objective assessments of data. In 1986, psychologist Jay Belsky reviewed studies of the effects of non-parental care and concluded that children entering care in infancy are at risk for disrupted relationships with parents and peers, and for heightened aggression.[129] His conclusion engendered much controversy. Little has changed. Substantial criticism and debate continue. More than thirty years after Belsky's conclusions, evaluations of the Québec child-care initiative showed an increase in reported child behaviour problems.[130] Researchers at Queen's University in Ontario summarized the early findings as indicative of a wide range of undesirable family, health, and developmental outcomes resulting from participation in Québec child care.[131] Subsequent discussions of using the Québec system as a model for the rest of Canada resulted in outrage in the popular press. The criticism was well summarized by *Globe and Mail* columnist Margaret Wente. She pointed to concerns of peer socialization replacing parental nurturance and guidance.[132] Tasha Kheiriddin, writing in the *National Post*, argued that governments should enable parents to take care of their children themselves rather than "outsource" child care.[133] And the editors of *Maclean's* magazine pointed out that daycare in Québec was making children "sick and angry" and posed the question, "If you were reborn as an infant tomorrow, would you choose to leave home for school when you turned two?"[134] The research data would best answer with "It depends." What type of care? How many hours a week? Is it a high-quality situation? What is the home situation?

*Type of Care.* With a shortage of regulated daycare spaces, many parents must rely on unlicensed home care. Such situations can be adequate or even excellent, but parents must be vigilant. Across Canada, there are few regulations for unlicensed home care other than the number of children. And most home daycares are not inspected unless there are complaints. Waiting for problems, child injuries, or child deaths clearly is contrary to the child's best interests. The consequences, as noted by a number of advocates, are serious. Writing in the *Canadian Medical Journal*, Adam Miller points to the many threats to children's safety found in unlicensed care facilities.[135] Inspectors of unlicensed home daycares, he notes, have found expired and rotting food, unclean kitchen utensils and toys, pets that are not properly cleaned up after, and frequently more children than is allowed. The Ontario Coalition for Better Child Care and the Canadian Broadcasting Company have highlighted a number of cases of neglect, injury, and deaths of young children while in unlicensed care.[136] For example, four children died during a seven-month period in the Greater Toronto region alone, including two-year-old Eva Ravikovich. After Eva's death in 2013, twenty-nine children and fourteen dogs were found in the home. Ontario now allows unlicensed care providers a maximum of five children under the age of thirteen under the *Child Care and Early Years Act* (including their own children under age six, with no more than two children under age two).

An equally egregious oversight is the lack of screening or requirements for caregivers. In 2014, Christine Allen of Kitchener, Ontario, was convicted of poisoning two of the children in her care. Her lawyer explained that Ms. Allen was a mentally ill drug addict who used her child-care earnings to pay for drugs. These problems are not unique to Ontario. Child deaths and injuries while in unlicensed home care have been recorded across the country. Generally, due to regulations, centre child care may be considered to be safer than unlicensed home care. Nonetheless, we cannot be complacent and assume all child-care centres are in the best interests of the child. As will be discussed subsequently, there are wide variations in their quality and child outcomes.

In addition to the use of unlicensed home care, many parents—particularly those who work long hours or part time—find themselves needing to use multiple types of care. Children may attend centre care on some days and receive home-based care on others, or even both through the day. The resulting instability is associated with an increase in problem behaviours and a decrease in prosocial behaviours among two- and three-year-old children.[137] Changing caregivers, peers, and settings is stressful for children, especially when the expectations for behaviour vary between settings. And that stress can interfere with the child's eating and sleeping routines, attachment relationships, and capacity for self-regulation.[138]

*Hours Spent in Care.* One of the perhaps unintended consequences of the Québec daycare model has been a large increase not only in the number of children in care, but also the number of hours spent in care. The low cost and long hours provided by Québec have created a strong incentive for parents to place their children in care at an early age for long hours.[139] Québec provides year-round care for ten to twelve hours a day. This is a very long day for a preschool child. Many studies of the effects of daycare have found that more than twenty hours a week of non-parental care is associated with negative developmental outcomes.[140]

There have been a number of large national studies in the United States, as well as numerous smaller studies in various locations, showing that children who have spent long hours in care in the first few years of life are rated by their teachers as more aggressive and defiant, and having poorer self-regulation skills and peer relationships than others.[141] There is also some evidence that the early effects are sustained and manifest in more risk-taking and impulsive behaviours during adolescence.[142] Interestingly, the link between hours in care and behaviour problems is stronger when those hours are spent in centre-based care. It should, therefore, not be surprising to learn that following the implementation of child care in Québec, reported behaviour problems among children increased more in Québec than in any other province in Canada.[143] But why centre care?

Through the first years of life, children do best with committed and continuous individual care. It is not necessary that the caregiver be biologically related to the child. It is not necessary that the caregiver be female. But it is necessary that the caregiver be sensitive to the child's needs, be responsive and overtly affectionate, and provide guidance through the setting of age-appropriate demands and limits. Young children need routines, caregiver time, hugs, and comfort. They need to play, to have stories read, and to have accomplishments noticed and praised. It is difficult for centre-based caregivers to meet these developmental needs. Usually in centre care children spend more time interacting with peers than adults, and typically group sizes are large. As Aletha Huston and her colleagues explain, young children in groups use aggression to obtain resources, toys, and equipment.[144] It pays to be belligerent. Social interactions in groups are less positive and more aggressive, particularly if there are insufficient toys or equipment for the numbers of children. And in centre care there can be a lack of emotionally supportive adult–child interactions. Of course, there are high-quality child-care centres in which toys are plentiful, group sizes are small, and adults are supportive. Here the negative outcomes associated with long hours are lessened.[145] It is these high-quality centres that are consistent with children's rights.

*Quality of Care.* The quality of a daycare setting has two components that are associated with developmental outcomes: one that describes process variables, and one that describes the structural factors.[146] The process variables are those that pertain directly to the child's experiences, such as social interactions and relationships, play, and health and safety behaviours. The structural variables include caregiver training and stability, group size, and caregiver-to-child ratio. The two components typically coexist. A high-quality setting is characterized by positive peer interactions; supportive, well-trained adults who are stable caregivers; appropriate toys and play opportunities; attention to health and safety; small group sizes; and a small number of children per adult. Unfortunately, much of the research indicates that high-quality care is rare.

It turns out that the negative outcomes associated with the Québec system were a result of the majority of care centres being of adequate to poor quality—in essence, many children were spending long hours in sub-standard care.[147] This was particularly the case for vulnerable children from low-income families. As a result, not only was Québec's goal of increasing school readiness among low-income children not realized, but there were also negative effects on the cognitive development of four- and five-year-old children from low-income families.[148] Negative developmental effects of daycare have been associated with a lack of emotionally supportive adult–child interactions and difficult peer interactions that produce stress in the child.[149] Increased stress levels generally are found in children attending poor-quality daycare; both psychosocial and cognitive development are compromised as a result.[150]

Health and safety issues in poor-quality daycare centres also place the child's physical development at risk. Studies in Ontario find a lack of oral health care policy and insufficient physical activity in centre-based care—the latter being a particular concern with rising rates of childhood obesity.[151] The Canadian Paediatric Society points to a number of health and safety issues in child-care centres.[152] Daycare attendance, they find, is associated with increased rates of respiratory and gastrointestinal illnesses, as well as vaccine-preventable illnesses such as measles and mumps. Moreover, child-care centres are not required to have policies on the management of sick children. Preventable injuries—falls, cuts, burns, and so forth—occur when child supervision is inadequate. Hospital records show a thousand injuries incurred in children under the age of five while at daycare in a little over a one-year period.

The child outcomes associated with high-quality child care are quite different. In addition to more attention to child health and safety, high-quality child-care centres consistently have been found to promote social and cognitive development. The social and emotional support provided by adults in high-quality centres is associated with fewer behaviour problems and high levels of social competence.[153] And compared with children in poor-quality centres, those in high-quality centres show superior levels of literacy and numeracy.[154] These children are well prepared for the transition to formal schooling. It is no surprise, then, that the higher than average levels of achievement in reading and math these children show in early childhood are sustained through school and into adulthood.[155]

*The Home Situation.* High-quality child care is disproportionately beneficial for children whose home situation is characterized by poverty and its correlates described earlier in this chapter. In essence, an environment that is positive, consistent, and developmentally appropriate can compensate for poverty and family dysfunction.[156] In fact, even when vulnerable children spend long hours at a centre-based daycare, if it is of high quality they benefit both behaviourally and cognitively.[157]

Evaluations in Québec, for example, show that behaviour problems are reduced in disadvantaged children who attend child care, while behaviour problems among their parent-reared peers increase.[158] Nonetheless, it is critical that the care be of high quality for it to be beneficial for vulnerable children; this is particularly so for their cognitive development and school readiness.[159] Time in high-quality care improves disadvantaged children's cognitive development and school readiness. In high-quality care, the children are provided age-appropriate and stimulating educational toys and learning materials, and they interact with well-trained, responsive, and supportive caregivers. These experiences promote cognitive development and the acquisition of skills and knowledge necessary for successful transition to formal schooling.[160]

So, perhaps the naysayers to expanding the Québec approach across the country were not entirely wrong. Certainly the provision of accessible and affordable child care is consistent with the Convention, but unless every centre is also of high quality, it is not in the best interests of the child.

# CHAPTER 6

஭

# The Rights of Protection

What is Canada's record in providing for children's rights of protection? Has appropriate action been taken against the toxins of violence, exploitation, and maltreatment, in line with the Convention and the early hopes of child advocates? We now review developments in the areas of the corporal or physical punishment of children, sexual exploitation, and the protection of children from abuse, neglect, and maltreatment. Finding serious shortcomings in Canada's record, we explain why it is necessary that Canada, in meeting its obligations under the Convention, abolish corporal punishment, strengthen measures against sexual exploitation, and establish a proactive child protection system that works to prevent the incidence of child abuse and neglect, rather than reacting to cases after the fact.

## Protection from Violence

The UN Convention clearly calls for the protection of children from violence and from assault on their physical integrity and dignity. Article 19 directs states parties to take all appropriate legislative, administrative, and educational measures to protect children from all forms of physical or mental violence, and from injury or abuse by parents or other caregivers, and to provide for programs of support, prevention, and treatment in cases of violence and child maltreatment. In the area of school discipline, article 28 calls on Canada to ensure that school discipline is administered in a manner consistent with the child's human dignity. Under article 37, children are not to be subject to cruel or degrading treatment. And once again, article 3 comes into play, making the best interests of the child a primary consideration.

Allowing for violence in the form of corporal punishment would be in violation of the best interests principle.

The Convention does not directly address the issue of corporal punishment except to say that school discipline is to be consistent with the child's dignity. However, the UN Committee on the Rights of the Child has considered the issue and has interpreted the Convention to mean that corporal punishment is a type of violence, a form of cruel or degrading punishment, and a practice contrary to the dignity and best interests of the child.[1] It cannot be justified on grounds such as religious freedom or children's best interests. Therefore, countries that permit corporal punishment are obligated to take measures to eliminate the practice, whether it takes place in homes, schools, or elsewhere. This requires not only that laws be established to prohibit corporal punishment, but also that educational measures be taken to raise public awareness of the law and the importance of non-violent discipline. With this in mind, the Committee urged Canada and other states parties during the 1990s and early 2000s to take legal and educational measures to end corporal punishment.[2]

Historically, like many other countries, Canada has permitted the widespread practice of corporal punishment in homes, schools, and other institutions. The practice was justified on various grounds: religious views ("spare the rod, spoil the child"), parental rights, or idiosyncratic understandings of "the child's own good."[3] In the 1870s, government-sponsored residential schools were established for the purpose of "civilizing" Indigenous children and assimilating them into mainstream Canadian society. In these schools, corporal punishment was frequently used to "correct" undesired behaviour, including a child's use of his or her Indigenous language.[4]

Corporal punishment was widely accepted in Canadian society in the late nineteenth century. In 1892, corporal punishment became a statutory defence to assault under section 43 of the *Criminal Code*, which still states that "every schoolteacher, parent or person standing in the place of a parent is justified in using force by way of correction toward a pupil or child, as the case may be, who was under his care if the force does not exceed what is reasonable under the circumstances."

By the 1990s, corporal punishment in Canada had been prohibited by law in most institutional settings other than by parents in homes: in all licensed daycare facilities (except in New Brunswick), all youth justice facilities, most foster care and alternative care settings, and most schools and school districts (except in Alberta and Manitoba).[5] The practice also ended in residential schools when the last was closed down in 1996. But lawmakers took no action to ban the practice in homes beyond a number of private members' bills in Parliament that failed. However, with the ratification of the Convention, together with the *Charter*, child advocates saw the possibility of launching a successful legal challenge against section 43 and putting an end to the use of corporal punishment in homes as well as in all schools. The Canadian Foundation for Children, Youth, and the Law therefore challenged the law in the courts, first in Ontario (which was unsuccessful) and then before the Supreme Court of Canada in 2004.[6] As we discussed in Chapter 4, the federal government chose not to repeal section 43 but to defend it in the courts with the support of a number of conservative interest groups including the Coalition for Family Autonomy.

The Foundation's argument before the Supreme Court was that section 43 violates three sections of the *Charter*: the child's right to security of person contrary to the principle of fundamental justice (section 7), the right against cruel and unusual treatment (section 12), and the right to equal treatment without discrimination based on age, because the law denies children the legal protection against assault that is given to adults (section 15).[7] Section 43 is unconstitutional, said the Foundation, because it contravenes these rights and cannot be upheld as a reasonable limit on the rights of children since it is vague, overly broad, and at odds with the best interests of the child, a principle of fundamental justice affirmed in the *Charter*. The Foundation further argued that section 43 violates four articles of the Convention: the principle of the best interests of the child (article 3), the responsibility of parents to provide for the child's best interests (article 18), the requirement that children be protected from all forms of violence (article 19), and the requirement that school discipline be consistent with the child's dignity (article 28). Children's best interests are compromised because corporal punishment is a form of abuse and violence and an affront to the dignity of children.

As explained in Chapter 4, the Supreme Court ruled against the Foundation, saying that the law permitting corporal punishment was constitutional. However, the Court did establish some limitations on the use of physical punishment beyond "for the purpose of correction": Corporal punishment can be used only with children between the ages of two and twelve; physical objects may not be used; children are not to be hit out of anger or frustration; blows to the head are not allowed; and teachers are not to use physical force except to restrain students during a conflict.

Since 2004, despite pressures by child advocacy groups to repeal section 43, the federal government has not acted. The most significant development was in the recommendations of the Truth and Reconciliation Commission of Canada (TRC), established in 2008 to examine the impact and legacy of residential schools. In 2015, the TRC released its final report.[8] Among the 94 recommendations was a call to repeal section 43 and end the practice of corporal punishment not only in schools but also in homes. In the words of the TRC, "corporal punishment is a relic of a discredited past and has no place in Canadian schools or homes."[9] In responding to the recommendations, Prime Minister Justin Trudeau announced his government would implement all the recommendations.[10] But it remains to be seen if the government will follow through on repealing section 43.

Regardless of the outcome, public education on the issue and on the law will likely remain a problem. In *R. v. T.F. and T.A.F.*, [2016] B.C.J. No. 129, a high-profile case in British Columbia, two parents were convicted for assaulting their fourteen-year-old daughter with a plastic hockey stick and a skipping rope after she had "sexted" nude photos of herself to a friend. The father testified (para. 27) that he had "no clue that the law does not allow corporal punishment, and that he was breaking the law when he spanked his daughter." Clearly, child welfare authorities in British Columbia and across the country need to do more to educate parents on the state of the law.

In international comparisons, Canada has been a laggard in the global movement to ban corporal punishment in all settings.[11] In Europe, most countries now have legal bans on all corporal punishment of children or have committed to do so. By the end of 2017, thirty-two states had full prohibitions in all settings. Sweden pioneered the movement in 1979, instituting a legal ban on all physical punishment, accompanied by a major public education campaign showing the benefits of alternative forms of discipline.[12] Other Nordic countries followed suit: Finland in 1984, Denmark in 1986, Norway in 1987, and Iceland in 2003. With the Nordic countries as leaders, and with pressure by international child advocates and the UN Committee on the Rights of the Child, other countries in Europe and other parts of the world also established prohibitions on all corporal punishment. By 2017, fifty-three countries worldwide had instituted bans and another fifty-six expressed a commitment to follow suit.

Canada, along with the United States, the United Kingdom, and a number of other countries, has been hesitant to ban all corporal punishment. Part of the explanation again lies in a political culture resistant to social responsibility. Whereas a country such as Sweden strongly supports the principle of social responsibility for children, Canada continues to endorse a belief that it is the individual responsibility of parents—not state officials—to care for and discipline their children in ways they see appropriate, subject to reasonable limits. This view was reflected in the decision of the Supreme Court not to overturn section 43. It also was reflected in court arguments by the federal government and conservative interest groups in opposing the repeal of section 43. The persisting strength of the belief in individual responsibility continues to serve as a brake on change.

## The Importance of Non-Violent Socialization

Raising children is difficult. As well as physical care and supervision, children need to be taught how to behave so that they can internalize values, enjoy positive relationships with others, and function well in society. Too many parents choose reactive means of responding to non-compliant or defiant behaviours with physical punishment. As we summarize here, this approach is ineffective and associated with a wide range of unintended negative outcomes. The use of corporal punishment is a social toxin that is particularly damaging to the child's social and emotional development.

Physical punishment does not make children more compliant, other than sometimes in the very short term. In fact, the opposite occurs. Children respond best to parents with whom they have a warm and trusting relationship. Numerous studies have shown that the quality of the parent–child relationship is eroded when the parent uses physical punishment.[13] It is difficult for children to trust those who hurt them either physically or psychologically, and so they tend to avoid their parents and the relationship becomes more distant. The outcome is children who are more difficult to socialize.[14] The more the child associates the parent with pain or distress, the more the child avoids and distrusts the parent, and the less compliant the child becomes.[15] Children's relationships with their peers and siblings also suffer.

Among the most consistent findings in the research literature, across time and countries with vastly different social systems, is that physical punishment is associated with more antisocial and aggressive behaviour.[16] Children experiencing physical punishment show heightened aggression and bullying in their interactions with their peers and siblings, and as they grow, with their dating partners and spouses.[17] And the relation is causal. It is not the case that children who are aggressive are more likely to elicit parental use of physical discipline.[18] We know this because there is strong evidence of a dose-dependent association. For example, with a large group of parents and children, Catherine Taylor and her colleagues assessed levels of aggression and mothers' use of physical punishment with their children, when the children were ages three and five.[19] The findings clearly showed that the more frequently the mothers used physical punishment with the child at age three, the more aggressively the child behaved at age five. The children had learned to be aggressive.

Internalizing behaviour problems are also associated with physical discipline.[20] As researchers Joan Durrant and Ron Ensom conclude, a wide range of mental health problems and psychological maladjustment across childhood and adulthood are associated with corporal punishment.[21] While being spanked, children feel both depression and anxiety.[22] These negative feelings continue long after the punishment ends.[23] The extent to which these feelings are sustained is exemplified in a study of young adult students at the University of Manitoba.[24] An astonishing 54 percent of the students surveyed reported that they had been physically punished when they were ten years old. This group of students reported significantly higher levels of depression and anxiety than their peers whose parents had not hit them, and significantly lower levels of self-esteem. The link may be explained at the neural level.

Young adults who report chronic physical punishment as children, as with the Manitoba sample, are found to have reduced grey matter volume in an area of the prefrontal cortex.[25] The brain region most affected by physical punishment has been implicated in a number of mental health problems including depression and vulnerability to substance abuse.[26] The evidence that physical punishment affects brain structure in ways that are contrary to children's rights and best interests is growing rapidly at this time, and it is becoming increasingly robust.[27]

Being proactive in parenting is both more effective and more consistent with children's best interests. Proactive parenting practices involve anticipatory strategies designed to pre-empt incidents of unwanted behaviours.[28] For example, in situations that are likely to elicit conflict or be boring for the child, the parent will anticipate the child's response and be prepared with action he or she knows will engage the child. The strategies may vary with age, but include monitoring, involvement, redirection of attention, teaching, discussion, and modelling.[29] In addition, proactive parents provide support and direction to the child as needed, while respecting the child's autonomy.[30] These parenting strategies result in much more positive interactions between parent and child than do reactive disciplinary responses. And early positive interactions are of key importance in preventing problem behaviours.[31]

The developmental outcomes associated with proactive parenting are overwhelmingly positive. Young children are more compliant, show fewer behaviour problems, and have a greater ability to delay gratification than their peers who have been socialized in a more reactive manner.[32] Proactive parenting is also associated with children's self-regulation skills.[33] And there is growing evidence that proactive parenting prevents problem behaviours through adolescence. Proactive parenting has been described as an asset to the health and well-being of adolescents.[34] In their study of parenting practices of relevance to health, Vaughn Rickert and his colleagues found proactive parents, compared with others, had significantly more discussions with their adolescents about a wide range of health topics, and encouraged their children to discuss mental and physical health issues with their doctor. In consequence, their children engaged in more healthy behaviours.[35] And like other researchers, Rickert and his colleagues found that teens with proactive parents were likely to delay initiation into alcohol and marijuana experimentation or use.[36]

The more positive interactions and relationships experienced by children with proactive parents means they are likely to internalize the values they have been taught both directly through parental use of discussion and reasoning, and indirectly through parental respect for autonomy and parental modelling. The internalization of positive parental values itself can promote prosocial behaviour and lessen the likelihood of the child engaging in antisocial behaviour.[37] Proactive and democratic parenting teaches children to be aware of and respond to the needs and rights of others.[38]

In essence, when children are raised by parents who respect their rights and make their best interests a priority, there is intergenerational transmission of prosocial behaviours, an ethic of compassion, and concern for the rights of others. This, of course, is in sharp contrast to the intergenerational transmission of violence that stems from the use of physical punishment. And it is much more desirable.

## Protection from Sexual Exploitation

According to article 34 of the Convention, states parties have the responsibility to protect children from all forms of sexual exploitation and sexual abuse. In contrast to article 19, which is focused more generally on child abuse, including sexual abuse, the purpose of article 34 is to combat commercial sexual exploitation, specifically in the areas of child pornography, child prostitution, and the trafficking of children for sexual purposes.[39] Thus Canada and other states parties are directed to take measures to prevent the use of children in pornography and the sex trade, and the coercion or luring of children into unlawful sexual activities. In addition, Canada has the responsibility to counter sexual exploitation under the Optional Protocol on the Sale of Children, Child Prostitution and Child Pornography, which Canada ratified in 2005.

Since ratifying the Convention, Canadian governments have taken a number of positive steps to combat child sexual exploitation.[40] As a first step, to address child pornography, the federal government amended the *Criminal Code* in 1993 (s. 163.1), banning the production, distribution, and sale of child pornography, defined as (1) visual representations of sexual activity with persons under age eighteen or depicted as such, (2) other visual representations of children for a sexual purpose, and (3) written or visual material that advocates or counsels illegal sexual activity with children, unless the material has educational, scientific, or medical value, or "artistic merit."[41] This was a very progressive step. However, the exemption for artistic merit became a problem. As we discussed in Chapter 4, John Robin Sharpe was convicted for possessing child pornography, including graphic sex stories he had written himself. At the Supreme Court, he argued that his section 2(b) freedoms under the *Charter* included writing sex stories for his personal use. The Supreme Court ruled that although the child pornography law was constitutional, the exemption for artistic merit must be interpreted broadly and include works of the imagination.[42] Thus, said the Court, it is not illegal to possess artistic materials such as stories, drawings, or poems that are products of the imagination and used only by the creator of the material. This ruling drew strong criticism.

To address the issue of artistic merit and other concerns, the federal government amended the *Criminal Code* again in 2005.[43] It replaced the exemption of artistic merit with material that has a "legitimate purpose" and does not pose an undue risk to children. It was hoped that with this tighter wording, children would be more fully protected by the courts. The amendment also made it illegal to advertise child pornography materials, to produce or possess pornographic audio materials (as well as visual and written materials), and to engage in sexual voyeurism, defined as the surreptitious observation by any means of persons (including children) in situations of nudity or explicit sexual activity. In the case of voyeurism, the amendment made it illegal to knowingly distribute or possess voyeuristic material, punishable by up to five years in prison. Furthermore, in 2015, tougher penalties were imposed than had existed in the original legislation.[44] For making or distributing child pornography, the punishment was increased from a maximum of ten years in prison to fourteen years, and, for its possession, from a maximum of five years to ten years. For luring a child into illegal sexual activity, the punishment was increased from ten years to fourteen years.

The spread of child pornography through the Internet and digital technologies became a growing concern during the 1990s and early 2000s. In 2002, to address the problem, the federal government amended the *Criminal Code* to make it illegal to knowingly access child pornography online, distribute child pornography through the Internet, and lure children on the Internet for illegal sexual activity.[45] For any of these offences, perpetrators could face up to ten years in prison. In addition, in 2008, the *Criminal Code* was amended to make it a legal duty to report Internet child pornography by any person who became aware of its presence. And in 2011, this duty was extended to providers of Internet services who were advised of an Internet address where child pornography may be available. However, despite the expansion of child pornography laws, enforcement has been problematic. As noted by Anne McGillivray, although prosecutions have increased and tip lines have greatly assisted with prosecutions, policing the Internet has been difficult, and sentences for offenders often have been light and thus inadequate to deter perpetrators.[46] That Canada has been a leading country in the Internet production of child pornography shows the difficulty authorities have had in tackling the problem. In a 2009 study by Cybertip.ca of more than sixty countries worldwide hosting child pornography websites, Canada ranked third behind only the United States and Russia.[47] It remains to be seen whether the duty to report child pornography, together with tougher penalties and improved detection, can make a difference in closing websites and reducing access to child pornography.

Canadian governments also have undertaken important measures to address the problem of children in the sex trade. At the federal level, in 1997, the *Criminal Code* was amended to create a new criminal offence of aggravated procurement that made it illegal for pimps to coerce persons under age eighteen into the sex trade through intimidation, threats, or violence, punishable by five to fourteen years in prison.[48] The amendment also made it easier for youth to testify against pimps in court (through the use of screens or video) and made it illegal for customers to obtain or attempt to obtain sex from a person under age eighteen or believed to be under age eighteen, punishable by up to five years in prison. In the same amendment, and in response to mounting pressures to deal with the problem of child sex tourism, the *Criminal Code* was changed to allow for the prosecution of Canadian citizens and permanent residents for offences of sexual exploitation of children abroad.[49] Building on this amendment, in 2002, the law was changed to make the prosecution of sex tourists easier.[50] Previously, the Canadian government could not proceed with prosecution unless requested to do so by the country where the offence had taken place.

Such action by Canada has been very welcome and in line with the Convention and Optional Protocol. However, as in other areas, enforcement remains an issue. A key problem has been the difficulty of collecting the necessary evidence in other countries, given obstacles such as long distances, different languages and culture, and lack of cooperation of witnesses and authorities. As a result, there have been very few prosecutions or convictions.

At the provincial level, efforts also have been made against sexual exploitation. In Alberta, the *Sexually Exploited Children Protection Act* was created in 1998 to include children involved in the sex trade within the definition of sexually exploited children.[51] The legislation allowed the police and child protection workers to place the children involved in protective safe houses for counselling and treatment for up to three days. The objective was to help the children break free from the destructive life of the sex trade. The approach taken in this law was progressive in that it treated children as persons in need of care and protection rather than as criminals.[52] However, the law was declared unconstitutional by an Alberta court in 2000 because it violated children's legal rights under the *Charter*, such as the right to a lawyer. Alberta subsequently revised its law in 2001, incorporating children's legal rights and lengthening the time in safe houses from three to five days to allow more counselling and support. The law also allowed authorities to apply for two additional detention periods for up to twenty-one days each if more support was needed.

Unfortunately, there has not yet been a long-term comprehensive and independent evaluation of Alberta's law. Alberta's Children's Services did conduct a short-term review that showed the safe houses to be beneficial for at least some of the children apprehended.[53] They were helped in terms of safety, medical treatment, and assessment of drug abuse problems. However, many of the children had been apprehended multiple times. Although the review showed that the number of children apprehended had fallen in the short term, there was no way of knowing whether the sex trade simply had moved from the streets to underground activities such as escort services. Most importantly, Alberta's law did not address the underlying problems that brought children into the sex trade in the first place. Many of the apprehended children had been victims of abuse, were living in poverty, were addicted to drugs, or were living with mental health problems such as undiagnosed FASD prior to involvement in the sex trade.[54]

Other provinces have decided not to follow Alberta's lead, given these limitations and given concerns over coercing children into detention against their will. However, Alberta's approach of treating the children as victims rather than criminals has been widely adopted.[55] Using this approach, new programs have been implemented in several provinces to provide child victims with counselling and support. For example, in Saskatchewan and Ontario, laws have been changed to make it easier to restrain those who sexually exploit children, and in Manitoba, legal changes have been made to allow child victims to sue those who have exploited them.[56]

Federal and provincial measures to protect children involved in the sex trade have been progressive, in line with the Convention and the hopes of child advocates. However, these measures have been largely in response to incidents of sexual exploitation after the fact. It must be kept in mind that article 34 of the Convention calls on governments to take measures to *prevent* the involvement of children in the sex trade. Prevention may be assisted in some degree by laws. Laws can be of educational value and can serve as a deterrent to offenders. But laws do little to prevent children from involvement in the sex trade in the first place. Moreover, the difficulties of prosecution underscore the importance of early identification of and intervention with children who are vulnerable.

## The Toxicity of Sexual Exploitation

Sexual exploitation is among the most socially toxic and developmentally damaging experiences for children. We are able to identify which children are most vulnerable to sexual exploitation by looking at their early family environments and parenting. Similar family factors predict children's vulnerability to online luring, coercion into the sex trade, and involvement in the production and distribution of pornography.

Children's home environments are the key predictor of their level of vulnerability. Proactive parenting and warm family relationships are strong protective factors against sexual exploitation.[57] In contrast, poor parent–child relationships, dysfunctional families, family violence, and parental substance abuse consistently are found in the family histories of children who have been sexually exploited.[58] Many children who are sexually exploited have a family history of maltreatment, neglect, physical abuse, and/or sexual abuse.[59] In one study of 361 children in street situations in Vancouver, for example, almost all reported some form of serious childhood maltreatment.[60]

In addition to family factors, there are associated individual factors that predict vulnerability to sexual exploitation: these, of course, do not apply to infants and very young children who are sexually exploited. Mental health issues are prominent among these factors. Low self-esteem, depression, anxiety, loss of hope for the future, and suicidal thoughts tend to be present.[61] In addition, children who identify as LGBTQ2, as well as those who are questioning their sexual orientation, are particularly vulnerable.[62] And Indigenous children are disproportionately represented among sexually exploited youth. In fact, to date, Indigenous children remain the only identifiable group trafficked for sexual purposes from city to city across Canada.[63]

The toxic outcomes associated with sexual exploitation pose challenges that can and do last a lifetime. And there are increasing numbers of children affected. The sexual exploitation of children is an extensive problem in Canada.[64] It is facilitated by the widespread use of social media as a basis for communication and relationships. Unprecedented opportunities now exist for child luring and for the production and distribution of child sex abuse images. The effects on children are profound. The tragic case of Amanda Todd exemplifies the process and harm potential of Internet luring.

Amanda was a twelve-year-old British Columbia student in grade seven "when she made a mistake that would haunt her until her death, three years later."[65] Amanda used video chat to meet new people. Chat rooms enable pedophiles to adopt the identity they need to interact with their targeted victim and build trust. Adolescent girls are their most frequent victims.[66] Amanda thought she was chatting with a peer. As it turned out she was chatting with a thirty-five-year-old Dutch man, Aydin Coban, who subsequently was charged with Internet luring and the possession and distribution of child pornography. Over time, he was able to win Amanda's trust. Pedophiles troll the Internet for vulnerable children, and with the eventual aim of involving the child in some sex act, they build a relationship of trust.[67] Trust is developed by flattery, attention, and empathy.[68] Once a trusting relationship has been established, sexual content is introduced into the chats.[69] Coban asked Amanda to bare her breasts during a video chat. Because she trusted him and believed him to be a friend, she complied, and he took a photo using screen capture. He then had leverage for future control over Amanda. It is not at all unusual for pedophiles to demand further sexual activity using the threat of distribution of the existing image.[70] Coban threatened Amanda that if she did not comply with further sexual activity he would distribute the photo to her friends. And indeed he did. Such images are not erasable and become widely distributed very quickly. The end result was Amanda's suicide at age fifteen. Before she died, Amanda told her story online.[71] And she told of the panic disorder, anxiety, depression, and unendurable bullying that her one mistake had led to.

The Office of the Federal Ombudsman for Victims of Crime reports that tens of thousands of new images or videos of child pornography are put on the Internet every week. It is estimated that there are now available over five million unique child sexual abuse images.[72] These images are mostly of children under the age of twelve, with almost two-thirds being age five or younger. And they are becoming increasingly graphic and violent. For the most part, these images are produced by family members or adults known to the child. Sex abuse images also can be widely distributed globally as live-action webcam feeds; some allow subscribers to provide verbal direction to the streamed abuse as it occurs.[73] Overall, in response to demand, the images are becoming increasingly violent and sadistic and the victims increasingly young; it is no longer unusual to see the violent sexual abuse of infants.[74]

A rapidly growing body of research suggests that the children who are abused in making the images will experience significant distress and trauma; the distress is compounded by the permanence of the images.[75] As described in one victim impact statement,

> I know that these pictures will never end and that my "virtual abuse" will go on forever. Usually when someone is raped and abused, the criminal goes to prison and the abuse ends. But since (he) put these pictures on the Internet, my abuse is still going on. Anyone can see them. I have been told that my pictures are the most popular on the Internet. How can so many people delight in the horrible things that happened to me?[76]

Jennifer Martin explains it this way.[77] Any sexual abuse is traumatic for a child and is associated with fear, shame, anger, anxiety, post-traumatic stress disorder, and self-destructive behaviour. For children whose sexual abuse is recorded and disseminated through the Internet, the humiliation, shame, and distress are intensified. As Amanda Todd discovered, child victims are powerless to change or stop public access to, or distribution of, the images. And they must deal with the knowledge that law enforcement databases store and share their images. Victims of online sexual abuse must live with the knowledge that anyone anywhere anytime can view their abuse, and that people are getting pleasure from so doing. The damaging effects on the way these children think, feel, and behave are profound and lifelong. Their histories of maltreatment and stress also make children who have been sexually exploited online at risk for later involvement in the sex trade—exchange of sexual activities for drugs, money, or shelter.[78]

A child's exchange of sexual activity for any commodity is considered to be a form of sexual exploitation. Mostly associated with children in street situations, this type of sexual exploitation is also found in children living at home. Studies in Québec and British Columbia find that 2 to 4 percent of students from grades seven through twelve exchange sex for money, drugs, or gifts.[79] For children in street situations, however, sexual activity is often a means of survival.

As we noted in Chapter 1, the greatest predictors for street involvement are a history of sexual abuse and a home environment characterized by violence, neglect, and instability.[80] Many children in street situations start at or about age sixteen, when they lose child protection services in many provinces and the legal age at which parents can tell the child to leave. Some are less than age thirteen.[81] Children in street situations are easy targets for recruitment into the sex trade.[82] They are approached at bus stops, train stations, and fast-food restaurants, offered friendship and gifts, and then introduced to a pimp. Over time, the seduction is replaced with coercion as the pimp hooks the child on drugs and threatens violence if the child does not engage in sex trade work. Others engage in survival sex, exchanging sex for food, shelter, money, or drugs. Children who identify as LGBTQ2 are at greater risk than others of engaging in survival sex. They are less likely to use condoms with their partners and to have more partners than their heterosexual peers.[83]

Children describe sex trade work as traumatic.[84] Children in street situations in Toronto, for example, talk about being regularly manipulated and assaulted, and of losing their friends to drug overdoses, suicide, or homicide.[85] They are at high risk of a variety of mental and physical health adverse outcomes including depression, suicide, violence, and sexually transmitted infections. Breaking away from the sex trade and the streets is very difficult. After two years on the streets, few are able to leave.[86] Children who are sexually exploited in this way tend to lose all hope for their future. They tend to be kept isolated by their pimps and by their own sense of shame and humiliation. Rather than being understood as children with an extensive history of rights violations, too often they are shunned as "bad kids."[87]

## Protection from Maltreatment

Under article 19, the Convention calls on states parties to take measures to protect the child from "all forms of physical or mental violence, injury or abuse, neglect or negligent treatment, maltreatment or exploitation, including sexual abuse." The article further requires that protective measures include providing supports for children and families, prevention programs, and procedures for the "identification, reporting, referral, investigation, treatment and follow-up of instances of child maltreatment." This article goes beyond the commercial sexual exploitation of article 37 and refers to *all* forms of abuse, neglect, and violence that occur in families, institutions, and other settings involving children.[88] In addition, under article 20, if children are removed from their home, they are entitled to special protection and alternative care by the state. We use the umbrella term *maltreatment* to cover the types of harm to children mentioned in article 19. It is important to note that maltreatment violates not only article 19; it also violates the Convention's principle of the right to life, survival, and development of the child (article 6) and the principle of the best interests of the child (article 3).

In its General Comment 13 (2011), the UN Committee on the Rights of the Child clarified the measures that should be taken by states parties in protecting children from maltreatment.[89] The Committee emphasized that child protection is not simply a matter of establishing laws in which government agencies react to instances of child maltreatment, safeguard children, and punish perpetrators. Although such laws are important, the approach is too narrow. Article 19, said the Committee, requires a more comprehensive approach in which prevention is to be primary. It is in children's best interests that they are not in an environment that makes them vulnerable to maltreatment in the first place. To promote a positive environment and to optimize the well-being of children, strong social programs and supports are required within and beyond the child welfare system. These include programs for reducing poverty and improving child health, prenatal and postnatal services, home visitation and quality early childhood education programs, and education on child rights and best practices in parenting. In short, child protection measures need to be much more than legal responses after maltreatment has occurred. The approach must be holistic, focused on prevention, and consistent with all the rights of the child described in the Convention.

After ratifying the Convention, Canadian governments have made certain progress in strengthening laws to protect children from maltreatment. But before we analyze the measures taken, it may be helpful to review the two basic means by which governments provide protection. First, there is protection afforded through the federal *Criminal Code* and criminal prosecution.[90] Over the years, the *Criminal Code* has evolved to protect children from such criminal offences as physical assault, sexual assault, criminal negligence, child abandonment, deprivation of the necessities of life, sexual interference, invitation to sexual touching, and sexual exploitation of a young person. As with all applications of criminal law, a basic difficulty is the demanding standard of showing proof beyond reasonable doubt. Given this demanding standard, many cases of suspected child maltreatment cannot be pursued successfully through the route of criminal law.

Second, partly because of this difficulty, there is protection afforded through provincial and territorial child protection (or child welfare) legislation.[91] This is the route of the majority of maltreatment cases. The legislation rests on the less demanding civil law standard of proof based on the balance of probabilities, which makes it easier to proceed with cases. Under this legislation—which is in the provincial (and territorial) jurisdiction since child welfare is a provincial constitutional responsibility—child protection agencies have been given the authority to investigate suspected cases of maltreatment (including physical abuse, neglect, sexual abuse, and emotional abuse) to determine if a child is "in need of protection." If a child is so determined, the agency may respond by providing support and counselling to the family, or go to family court and get a court order to have the child removed from the home (temporarily or permanently). If the child is removed from the home, the agency arranges alternative care in forms such as foster care, group homes, or adoptive homes. The basic principle governing decisions is the best interests of the child. As part of the system, child abuse registries are in place to store information on past abusers and official child advocacy offices are responsible for monitoring the system. The child welfare system is funded in part by the federal government through—since 2003—a block transfer program called the Canada Social Transfer and, in part, by provincial or territorial governments.

Since the 1990s, certain improvements have been made in both criminal and child protection law. In criminal law, in 1995, a reform gave judges the power to issue warrants for collecting DNA samples from those suspected of sex crimes, including against children.[92] In 2000, to further assist police investigation, a national DNA data bank was created to store the DNA of serious offenders, including those convicted of sex offences against children. This was followed by the establishment of a national sex offender registry in 2004 to provide police with rapid access to information on offenders and to assist them in preventing or investigating criminal sex offences, including against children. Finally, in 2005, the *Criminal Code* was amended to increase maximum sentences and to impose new minimum sentences for sexual interference, invitation to sexual touching, and sexual exploitation. In addition, the amendment made it easier for children to testify in court.

Progressive measures also were taken in child protection legislation. First, the types of child maltreatment were enlarged. From physical abuse, neglect, and sexual abuse, coverage was expanded to include emotional abuse and exposure of children to family violence.[93] Second, definitions of child maltreatment were enlarged to include not only harm to a child but also risk of harm.[94] In Nova Scotia's legislation, for example, reference was made to "substantial risk." Third, the functions of child abuse registries were widened and a new registry was created in Québec in 2009.[95] These registries now functioned not only to store information on past abusers but also to assist in determining whether a child is in need of protection and to screen prospective foster, adoptive parents, and others wishing to work with children. Fourth, the number of Indigenous child welfare agencies was increased.[96] Before the 1990s, there had been a movement among Indigenous communities to establish their own Child and Family Services. In 1991, this movement received a major boost when the federal government introduced a program called Directive 20–1 to fund First Nations Child and Family Services on reserves. Although the program did not apply in Ontario (where a previous funding agreement existed) or to other Indigenous communities, it did substantially increase the number of services on reserves.

Despite progress in these and other areas, Canada's child protection system remains flawed on many fronts. One flaw is variation in the legal protections afforded children. Although the provinces and territories have developed similar child protection legislation, because of federalism and the different approaches taken by different jurisdictions, there is considerable variation from one jurisdiction to another.[97] The outcome has been uneven protection for children. There are many examples of this. In some jurisdictions, a child in need of protection is defined as under age nineteen; in others, under age eighteen; and in others, under age sixteen. This means some children are left unprotected and "age out" of the system sooner than others. In some jurisdictions, abuse and neglect have broad and detailed definitions; in others, definitions are narrower. In some jurisdictions, the penalty for failing to report child abuse is substantial (a large fine and/or time in prison); in others, it is much smaller. In some jurisdictions, child abuse registries have a broad mandate; in others, they do not even exist. These are but a few examples. Although some of the variations are minor, when taken together, they spell significant unevenness in child protection across the country.

Another defect in the system is the patchwork of services for Indigenous children.[98] Although there has been growth in the number of First Nations Child and Family Services, Indigenous children continue to experience a highly fragmented system of child welfare. For many such children, especially those living off reserve, the provinces make legislation and policy, regulate services, and provide funding. For other children, the provincial and/or federal governments grant specific powers to Indigenous agencies for particular purposes but retain overall authority. Finally, for a minority of children, there is both Indigenous service delivery and a measure of Indigenous control over funding and policy. Referred to as the self-government model of child welfare, it is one that most Indigenous communities prefer. Apart from fragmentation, a significant problem has been major underfunding. In 2007, a complaint was made by the Assembly of First Nations and the First Nations Child and Family Caring Society to the Canadian Human Rights Commission that the federal government practised discrimination against First Nations children living on reserves.[99] The complaint was that the federal government provided significantly less funding—about 38 percent less—for children living on reserves than the provinces provided for Indigenous children living off reserves. After federal resistance and a long battle, the complaint was finally upheld in 2016 by a human rights tribunal.[100] It remains to be seen how far the federal government will go to provide equitable and adequate funding.

Another flaw is the lack of a consistent focus on the well-being of individual children. Nothing is more basic to the well-being of children than their safety and security. Yet into the 1990s and beyond, a perspective that put children's safety in jeopardy has had great influence. According to this perspective, often referred to as the family preservation model, the best interests of children are to remain in the home with their parent(s) even when the parenting is questionable, except in extreme cases of abuse or neglect.[101] This is considered better for children than their removal from the home and placement in alternative care. Therefore, according to the model, in reported incidents of child maltreatment, child protection agencies should use the least intrusive means of intervention. Rather than removing the child from the home, they should make every effort to provide the parent(s) with counselling and support. If the child has to be removed from the home, it should be done only as a last resort, on a temporary basis, and with ongoing contact between the child and parent so as to facilitate reunification. This perspective was most influential in Alberta and Ontario, where legislation made family autonomy a central principle and made it very difficult for agencies to remove children from the home. In other jurisdictions, although less explicit in the legislation, policies also became ones of preserving the family unit as much as possible.

During the 1990s, a series of horrific and highly publicized child deaths became a catalyst for change.[102] As leading examples, in 1992, five-year-old Matthew Vaudreuil was severely beaten and strangled to death by his mother in Vancouver; in 1996, two-year-old Jacqueline Brewer died of neglect and dehydration at the hands of her parents in Saint John; and in 1997, infant Jordan Heikamp was allowed to starve to death by his mother in Toronto. In all these cases, the family situation was well known to child protection officials. Yet, operating under the philosophy of family preservation, they failed to act for the safety of the children. This led to public outrage and to a number of public inquiries and reviews. Following the Gove inquiry in British Columbia, a child death review of the Brewer case in New Brunswick, and the Hatton inquiry in Ontario, child protection legislation in these provinces was amended to give priority to the safety of children. The legislation now essentially says that in the event of a conflict between protecting children and supporting parents, protecting children comes first. To accomplish this, a number of reforms were put into place. Structured and standardized risk assessment tools were introduced into child welfare practice to better determine the likelihood of future maltreatment in cases of abuse or neglect.

Legal procedural changes made it easier for child protection workers to remove children from homes when the likelihood of future maltreatment was high. These reforms, together with the principle that child safety comes first, influenced other child welfare systems across Canada.

This shift toward a more child-centred approach has been progressive. However, the focus on child well-being has not been consistent. One reflection of this has been a failure to fully implement the principle that child safety comes first. During the 2000s, despite the reforms in British Columbia, Ontario, and New Brunswick, child abuse deaths and system failures have continued to be reported in the media.[103] And as noted by Statistics Canada, from the 1990s into the 2000s, the rate of homicides against children by parents did not decrease substantially.[104] One possible reason for this—when child deaths involve the child welfare system—is difficulty in determining risk and applying risk assessment tools. In many rural and northern areas, for example, the use of standardized risk assessment is seen as inappropriate.[105] Another factor may be that in the current context of large caseloads, overworked child protection workers, and inadequate resources, mistakes are bound to occur. But another reason is the persisting influence of the family preservation model. The training and culture of child welfare practitioners remains based on the belief that the main clients of agencies are parents, not children, and that the best interests of children are tied up with the well-being of their parents and with agency support for their parents. Thus in the annual reports of provincial child advocates, agency failures have continued to be linked to child abuse deaths. As one example, in a 2015 report by Saskatchewan's Advocate for Children and Youth, the deaths of two young children named Sarah and Michael were associated with a failure by the agency to adequately investigate suspected child abuse.[106] Despite multiple reports of problems in the family, agency workers erred on the side of preserving the family rather than assuring child safety.

Another reflection of the inconsistent focus on child well-being is the failure to implement permanency planning. Based on the belief that the well-being of children involves not only their safety but also their stability, permanency planning refers to a practice of maximizing stability in the living conditions for vulnerable children brought to the attention of child welfare authorities.[107] The concept essentially means that early in the decision-making process, authorities should make a plan for the permanent home situation of a child, whether the child is to remain in the current home with supports or to be placed in a new home such as with adoptive parents. Failure to do so, say advocates of the concept, means that many children are left in limbo, drifting between foster care and parents or among multiple foster homes or group homes, contrary to their emotional health and well-being. As pointed out by Charlotte Waddell and her colleagues, the research findings suggest that permanency planning is in the best interests of children.[108] However, despite wide support for the concept, permanency planning has not been put into effect in Canada. This is because a central aim of child welfare systems—influenced by the family preservation model—has remained family reunification.[109] If children have to be removed from the home, the aim has been to place them in *short-term* foster care or other care and then return them to their parents. Thus permanency planning has not been a serious option.

Finally, another flaw in the system is a continuing lack of attention to prevention.[110] Although prevention has been recognized as important, and although prevention and intervention programs such as family counselling, parenting education, and home visitation have become incorporated into systems across Canada, implementation has been minimal. Part of the problem remains inadequate funding of child welfare. Since the late 1990s, with major federal cuts to the Canada Health and Social Transfer (after 1995) and to the Canada Social Transfer (after 2003), and with less funding by provincial and territorial governments in relation to growing caseloads, child welfare authorities have given most attention to protection services.[111] Prevention has had to take a back seat. But a deeper problem has been the failure to appreciate that prevention requires comprehensive measures outside the formal child protection system. It requires serious efforts to build a healthy social environment for children and reduce vulnerability through measures such as reducing child poverty rates, improving child health, improving head start programs, and establishing strong programs of early childhood education and care. Compared to many countries in Europe, Canadian efforts have been weak.

In international studies of child welfare, Neil Gilbert and his colleagues divide child welfare systems in North America and Europe into three types.[112] First is the legalistic child protection orientation, most visible in the United States, the United Kingdom, and Canada. Here, the problem of maltreatment is assumed largely to be one of faulty parents or caregivers who abuse or neglect their children. The appropriate response is to react in a legalistic way, one that allows for removing children from their homes when necessary. But removal is to be done as a last resort, keeping the family unit together as much as possible. Second is the family service orientation, in place in much of Europe. Here, the problem is assumed to be one of social conditions creating stress or pressures within families such that abuse or neglect is the outcome. To guard against such an outcome, the proper approach is to employ a proactive policy that provides supports for families at risk, including parenting education, information and referral services, and counselling and therapeutic services. Gilbert and his colleagues point out that no country has a system that is purely reactive or proactive. Rather, the systems are best described as *orientations* in which elements of each are present. Third is the emerging child-focused orientation, most visible in countries such as Norway and Finland. Its focus is less on the family as a whole (as in the family service model) and more on the individual child. The concern is not simply one of protecting the child from maltreatment (as in the child protection model), but also of advancing the child's overall development and well-being. This requires that the state provide legal protection to abused children and supports to families at risk, as well as strong policies and programs of prevention, early intervention, and child development. A major influence behind this orientation is a belief in children's rights and in the need to implement the Convention.[113] According to this belief, children should be protected from maltreatment not because they are in need of protection, pity, or charity, but because they have inherent rights. And in line with the General Comment of the UN Committee on the Rights of the Child, protection means more than a legal response to an incident of maltreatment. It means comprehensive action to promote the healthy development of children through strong social policies and programs.

Canada's system of child welfare contains certain elements of the family service and child-focused orientation. But it remains largely one of reactive child protection.[114] Contrary to the early hopes of child advocates, relatively little attention has been given to prevention and comprehensive action to advance child development and the rights of the child. Why this is so is related once again to political culture and the persisting belief in individual responsibility. A part of this belief is the view that although governments should support parents to a degree, parents are primarily responsible for raising their children. In cases of suspected maltreatment, child protection agencies should intervene when necessary. But they should do so only as a last resort when parents have failed in their responsibilities, and usually with the purpose of reuniting families. A degree of social responsibility for children is accepted. Child protection legislation has been put into place, and, to an extent, family supports and prevention programs have been established to reduce the risks. But the concept that it takes a village to raise a child has yet to be seriously entertained.

## Maltreatment and the Problem of Reactive Intervention

Although there seems to be widespread agreement that child maltreatment is a significant public health problem in Canada, its prevalence remains understudied compared with the United States, Mexico, and parts of Europe.[115] Nonetheless, there are consistent findings on the effects of maltreatment and the inadequacies of responses to it. We can estimate the scope of child maltreatment by looking at criminal investigations, child welfare investigations, and community samples.

Statistics Canada provides an analysis of data from the Incident-Based Uniform Crime Reporting Survey and the Homicide Survey of violent criminal acts against children and youth.[116] The analysis shows a disturbing picture of police-reported child maltreatment by family members, mostly parents. In 2013, the violent victimization rate for children was 848.8 per 100,000. The rate was slightly lower than that for adults—995.3 per 100,000. But it is widely assumed that family violence against children is vastly under-reported. Most children are too young or too afraid to report parental maltreatment, and children who are younger than fifteen do not participate in the General Social Survey on Victimization. Even so, the data tell us that it is infants and young children who are the most frequent victims of family violence. Seventy-one percent are under the age of four years. Infants in the first year of life are the most frequent child victims of family violence. Infants are also the most likely to be victims of homicide, usually motivated by parental frustration. In fact, overall, 60 percent of child homicides are committed by family members—a figure that is double that of adult victims of familial homicide.

Despite such statistics, charges are laid in fewer than half of all family violence incidents against children. Charges are laid in 71 percent of intimate partner violence incidents and in 59 percent of cases of adult victims of family violence. But charges are laid only in 45 percent of cases when the victim is a child. We can only speculate on whether that stems from insufficient evidence, an antipathy to criminalizing parents, a false belief in the endless resilience of children, or a lack of value placed on children.

The Canadian Incidence Study (CIS), conducted by the Public Health Agency of Canada, provides information about victims of maltreatment who come to the attention of child protection agencies. Again, it is assumed that these data represent only a small proportion of child maltreatment victims since many incidents are never reported.[117] The CIS assesses child maltreatment by examining investigations in nation-wide representative samples of child protection agencies. There have been three reports to date, the latest of which was in 2008.[118] This report shows a rate of child protection investigations that is five times higher than those reported to the police: 39.16 investigations per 1000. This is most likely due to the inclusion of neglect and exposure to intimate partner violence. Neither of these categories of maltreatment is included in the *Criminal Code*, but they are the categories most frequently investigated by child protection agencies. The CIS findings, like the police data, identified infants as the most vulnerable to maltreatment, in this instance, neglect. What was particularly concerning in their data was that a third of substantiated maltreatment investigations were of children who previously had been referred for maltreatment.

There have been few methodologically sound community-based studies of child maltreatment. One province-wide study and one national survey are exceptions. They illustrate the extent of self-reported childhood maltreatment. The Ontario Child Health Study is a province-wide longitudinal study that started with children aged four to sixteen years in 1983.[119] When the children became young adults, aged twenty-one to thirty-five years, they were asked to rate the frequency with which they had experienced specific incidents of abuse in their childhoods. Their answers indicated that one-third had been physically abused, with one-fifth experiencing severe physical abuse, 15 percent sexual abuse, and 8 percent both physical and sexual abuse. Similar rates of child maltreatment were obtained in a large national sample. Tracie Afifi and her colleagues examined national data from the 2012 Canadian Community Health Survey and determined the prevalence of child maltreatment to be 32 percent of the population.[120] Again, physical abuse was the most common type experienced. It is interesting that among those with a history of maltreatment, only 7.6 percent had experienced any contact with a child protection or child welfare agency. Such community data lend strong support to the suggestions that both police and child protection investigations of reported child maltreatment vastly underestimate the scope of the problem. This is troubling given the well-documented, profound, and long-lasting effects of child maltreatment.

As well as the obvious immediate risk of harm, child maltreatment consistently is associated with adverse developmental outcomes across the lifespan. The extent of the relation between maltreatment and subsequent mental and physical health problems varies with its chronicity and severity. The longer the child is subjected to maltreatment and the more severe the maltreatment, the worse the outcomes.[121] In addition to health problems, from infancy to adolescence children who are maltreated are susceptible to poor impulse control, difficulties with emotion regulation, low self-worth, behaviour disorders, criminal offending, social withdrawal, and poor social relationships.[122] The difficulties continue.

Through adolescence and adulthood, maltreatment is associated with a range of physical and mental health difficulties. For example, the findings of the 2012 Canadian Community Health Survey showed childhood maltreatment increases the likelihood of subsequent obesity and a range of physician-diagnosed physical conditions including migraine headaches, bowel disease, and chronic bronchitis.[123] In addition, the Health Survey showed a strong relation between childhood maltreatment and substance abuse, suicidal ideation, and suicide attempts.[124] Similar findings are seen in research from the United States. In a rare prospective longitudinal study, Todd Herrenkohl and his colleagues compared a group of children with officially recorded histories of maltreatment with those without. The study started in 1976 when the children were eighteen months to six years old, with the last measure taken when they were adults (average age thirty-six).[125] Compared to their non-maltreated peers, those with a history of maltreatment showed significantly higher levels of depression, anxiety, alcohol problems, and risk of substance use, as well as poorer physical health. In another national study, conducted in the United States, it was found that childhood maltreatment predicted a number of disorders in adulthood, including depression, generalized anxiety disorder, and substance abuse.[126]

Perhaps most compelling are the findings of an extensive review and analysis of research from North America, Australia, New Zealand, and Western Europe.[127] With a focus on the effects of physical abuse, emotional abuse, and neglect, the analysis revealed a consistent pattern of adverse mental and physical health outcomes. Those with a history of maltreatment were at increased risk of depression and anxiety disorders, eating disorders, suicidal behaviour, risky alcohol use, risky sexual behaviour, sexually transmitted infections, obesity, arthritis, ulcers, and migraine headaches. Why this long list of adverse outcomes? Maltreatment is a powerful social toxin.

A growing body of research from neuroscience explains why maltreatment early in a child's development affects mental and physical functioning. As Sara Jaffee and Cindy Christian explain, when a child experiences maltreatment during infancy and early childhood, the immune system (which protects us from diseases), the neuroendocrine system (which has a critical role in the hormones that regulate functions such as stress responses, blood pressure, metabolism, and reproduction), and the central nervous system (the brain and spinal cord) are all profoundly affected.[128] These systems develop rapidly through the first few years of life—the time when maltreatment is most likely—and are highly responsive to environmental experiences. Maltreatment dysregulates these systems and in so doing, places the child at elevated risk of lifelong chronic physical and mental health problems.

Our responses to the problem of child maltreatment are incommensurate with its scope and adverse developmental outcomes. Given that the profile of the parent most at risk for abusive behaviour has been well documented, it is unconscionable that Canadian authorities do not take preventive actions to protect children from maltreatment. The CIS data underscore the importance of providing supports and training to parents who are young, are single, have few social supports, and are struggling with poverty, substance abuse, partner violence, and mental health issues.[129] This does not happen. Rather, child welfare authorities wait until the maltreatment is severe, respond with excess caution, and fail to take into account the rights of the child. The child protection system has been so flawed that an inquest into the maltreatment death of Ontario child Katelynn Sampson in 2016 came up with 173 recommendations that focus on what should be obvious—putting the child's interests first.[130]

Katelynn was at high risk for maltreatment. She was born into poverty, a broken family, and a crack-addicted mother, Bernice Sampson. When she was a toddler, police found her wandering the streets alone at 6:30 one morning. She was removed from her home but only for three days. Continuing to struggle with her addiction, Bernice later "gave" Katelynn to her friend Donna Irving. Donna had a criminal record as well as a history of addiction. Children's services previously had removed two of her birth children. Nonetheless a family court judge sanctioned the agreement between the two women, legally entrusting Katelynn to a caregiver with a history of and current dysfunction. We can only assume that the judge did not read the case details. No one bothered to consult Katelynn. Since Donna is half-Anishinabe, once Katelynn moved in with Donna, her case was referred to First

Nations Child and Family Services. Katelynn was not Indigenous but that did not seem to be of concern to anyone. What ensued were a number of calls to child protection agencies about the suspected abuse of Katelynn; it seems they did not reach the First Nations Child and Family Services supposedly supervising her placement. In the *Toronto Star*, columnist Catherine Porter reported that Katelynn's school principal called the Children's Aid Society to report burns on her face and arms; the staff said the file and information were forwarded to First Nations Child and Family Services. They told the inquest jury that they never received it.[131] No one spoke with Katelynn. And so it continued until she was found dead with extensive and severe injuries at age seven.

The lack of attention to the best interests of the child exemplified in Katelynn's case is not at all unusual. The Convention requires that alternative placements for children who are abused and neglected be of high quality, and that caregivers be well trained and competent to meet the developmental and recovery needs of the child.[132] This rarely happens. In fact, most children who are maltreated are either left with their family or are removed very briefly and then returned.[133]

Children who are reunified with their family of origin are at high risk of experiencing a recurrence of maltreatment. In Ontario, recorded rates of recurrence vary from 33 to 51 percent.[134] In Québec, Sonia Helie and her colleagues found that one-third of children were at risk of further maltreatment, and that each failed reunification increased the risk of recurrence.[135] The authors concluded that caseworkers pay insufficient attention to the family situation to which the child is returned, and underestimate the risk to the child. In contrast to all the evidence, there continues to be a belief in the endless resilience of young children to cope with multiple moves and significant instability. It is a belief without merit.[136] There also appears to be an unfounded belief in the effectiveness of services and parenting education programs to effect changes in maltreating parents' behaviour. Although there is compelling evidence that early supports and education can prevent maltreatment among high-risk parents, there is much less documented success at reducing maltreatment recidivism among parents.[137] For example, nurse visitation programs have been shown to be effective in preventing abuse and neglect in high-risk groups of parents. However, they, like other interventions, do little to reduce the risk of further maltreatment. A high risk of recurrence remains regardless of post-maltreatment interventions.[138] It seems the pattern of parenting is difficult to modify.

The probability that a child will be placed in alternative care increases with the number of times the child is investigated for maltreatment.[139] As a result, intervention is late. Children are shunted back and forth between temporary placements and their family of origin until their healthy development is seriously compromised. Frequent placement changes are associated with emotional and behavioural difficulties.[140] It is very difficult for children to establish their much-needed relationships with caregivers, peers, teachers, and their community when they are moved around. And for very young children the development of secure attachment is profoundly disrupted. Astonishingly, children in the first year of life—a critical developmental period requiring extensive nurturance and stability—have been found to experience four or more placements with changes occurring as quickly as within thirty-eight days of their initial removal.[141] Presumably these multiple moves resulted from failed reunification and the recurrence of maltreatment. Children are placed into alternative care arrangements only as a measure of last resort. As Richard Gelles so eloquently notes in *The Book of David*, "foster care [is] an expensive ambulance at the bottom of the cliff."[142]

Reluctance to place children in foster care is not without merit. There are difficulties with the foster care system. Tom Waldock, a specialist in child welfare and children's rights, points to the many shortcomings in foster care.[143] Among them are the following three key difficulties for children in need of out-of-home care.

First and perhaps most obvious is the shortage of appropriate placement options. As Waldock explains, placements should meet the needs of maltreated children as specified in the Convention. In contrast, a lack of available home situations means many children are separated from their siblings and many are inappropriately placed in group homes, residential care, and even hotel rooms. In response to some tragic deaths, the news media have highlighted the use of hotels to house apprehended children.[144] Among them were teenagers Tina Fontaine, who was found dead after going missing from her Best Western placement in Winnipeg, Manitoba, and Alex Gervais, who fell to his death from his hotel window in Abbotsford, British Columbia. In each case, the practice of hotel placements has come under scrutiny and governments have pledged to stop them. But they continue.

Second, our current approach of dependence on volunteer foster parents is neither consistent with the rights of the child nor commensurate with the need. Not surprisingly, it has become increasingly difficult to recruit and retain foster parents.[145] By the time children are placed in care, their needs are extensive. Not only have they experienced abuse or neglect, but many have experienced disrupted relationships, multiple placements, and maltreatment recurrences. Yet no mandatory training is provided for foster parents, there is little recognition of the complexities of their task, excessive administrative duties are expected from them, and they are provided inadequate supports and insufficient remuneration.

That the current system is failing is not questioned. Unfortunately, the response has not been to change and improve the system; authorities have instead responded by making increasing use of kinship care—the third key difficulty.[146] Kinship care is the term used to describe a placement in which the child lives with a relative other than a parent. It is assumed to be beneficial because typically the child has an existing relationship with the caregiver and so the move should be less disruptive.[147] In addition, with kinship placements, siblings may be accepted and care tends to be more stable. However, research to date indicates that for many children, kinship care is not at all in their best interests.

Kin caretakers have less education than other foster care providers, are more likely to live in poverty and have high rates of food insecurity, and are more likely to be lone parents who are older and have mental and physical health challenges.[148] A more critical problem is seen in the reality of intergenerational transmission of both risk factors for maltreatment and parenting style.[149] Despite this, the tolerance for risk in kinship placements is high and standards for placement are significantly reduced.[150] Many caseworkers have expressed their concern about the lowered standards for kinship placements, noting that children are often placed with a caregiver who exhibits many of the same challenges seen in the parent from whom the child was apprehended.[151] Several caseworkers also report discovering that both criminal and child welfare involvement records exist for kinship homes that were approved for alternative child care. Exacerbating these difficulties is that kinship caregivers receive fewer resources and less support than non-family foster parents, despite obviously being needier. More than a decade after the high-profile death of Jeffrey Baldwin from gross abuse and neglect by his grandparents, little has changed. Kimberly Brisebois and her colleagues report that almost half of the caseworkers they talked with had removed a child from kinship care because of protection issues.[152]

The scope of child maltreatment in Canada, its developmental outcomes, and the inadequacy of responses underscore the importance of adopting a proactive approach. A two-pronged approach with a focus on early prevention and early permanency planning would be in the best interests of the child. First, early supports and parenting education for high-risk families are established means of preventing much maltreatment, as noted earlier. Second, when a child is apprehended due to maltreatment, the focus should be on a permanent solution when the family situation is at high risk for recurrence. Early adoption should be a priority consideration. Where permanent arrangements, especially early ones, have been made for children who must be removed, positive outcomes are more likely.

Reviews of the early literature on the outcomes of adoption show that, overall, children who are adopted are developmentally indistinguishable from their non-adopted peers.[153] Exceptions are those children whose adverse early circumstances have caused damage too severe to permit positive development under any circumstances. The strongest evidence remains that of a prospective study in which the development of all children born in Britain during one week in 1958 was followed. A subgroup born into high-risk circumstances were placed for adoption, mostly within three months of birth. This allowed the researchers a rare opportunity to compare the development of those adopted with the socio-demographically equivalent group of children raised by their birth mothers. The findings showed that the early disadvantage of those in the high-risk circumstances remained and accumulated through childhood with notable academic and behavioural problems. The development of the children who were adopted, in comparison, was much more positive with success in education and adulthood.[154] More recently, in an extensive and methodologically sound study of recurrence of maltreatment among children in Québec, those adopted prior to age three were the least likely to re-report or have any further substantiated investigations of abuse.[155] Such data should not be ignored. Using the compelling and consistent evidence to reform policies and practices would be a much-needed step toward providing for children's rights to protection.

# CHAPTER 7

❧

# The Rights of Participation

How well has Canada performed in implementing children's rights of participation? This category of rights is a new and demanding one. However, as with the other categories of rights, Canada is obligated under the Convention to ensure that children enjoy the substance of their right to participate in decision-making. The intention of assuring children a voice is to enable them to be subjects rather than objects, and to be valued citizens in their community. We now review the state of children's participation in families, schools, and legal proceedings. Finding deficiencies in each area, we explain why participation is so important to meeting children's needs and so integral to the best interests of the child.

## Participation in Families

Child participation is one of the primary principles of the Convention. According to article 12, Canada and other states parties have the obligation to assure children who are capable of forming their own views "the right to express those views freely in all matters affecting the child, the views of the child being given due weight in accordance with the age and maturity of the child." Within families, this means that parents (and guardians) are responsible for ensuring that the child has a voice in decision-making. It does not mean that a child's view must be decisive. Participation does not mean self-determination.[1] It means allowing children meaningful input and genuinely listening to what they have to say, giving their views "due weight" in accordance with their age and maturity. Participation does not mean a voice in all matters. But it does mean a voice in "all matters affecting the child."[2]

As part of participation, the child also has the right to freedom of expression under article 13; the right to freedom of thought, conscience, and religion under article 14; and the right to freedom of association and peaceful assembly under article 15. As with similar rights granted to adults under many national constitutions, these rights are subject to reasonable limits. According to the Convention, children's rights may be limited by pressing interests such as public order, public safety, and the rights and freedoms of others. However, although governments may put limits on the voices of children, they also have the obligation to ensure that the child's participation rights are put into effect. Within families, parents have the responsibility to allow for and facilitate children's participation. This certainly does not rule out guidance. Under articles 5 and 14, parents have an obligation to provide appropriate direction and guidance to children as they exercise their rights. Such guidance is not open-ended. It must be "in a manner consistent with the evolving capacities of the child." In other words, while parents have the responsibility to provide direction, they also have the obligation to allow the child more autonomy as the child matures.[3]

Historically, in Canada as elsewhere, there was little regard for children's participation rights in families and society. It was a culture with a widespread belief that "children should be seen and not heard." However, with the global expansion of human rights consciousness after the Second World War, this changed significantly.[4] That Canada agreed to include children's participation rights in the Convention was a reflection of this change. But despite the change in culture, and despite the increased willingness of parents to hear children's voices, there has been little government support for children's participation rights in families. A controlling and strict authoritarian parent, for example, may silence or squelch a child's voice with impunity. Canadian governments could enact legislation that would make it a legal obligation for parents and guardians to allow for participation and consult with children in matters that affect them. This has been done in countries like Norway and Sweden.[5] According to Norway's *Children's Act*, for instance, parents have the legal responsibility to consult with and hear the views of children before making decisions on personal matters affecting children. Norway's Act also requires parents to allow children more autonomy to make their own decisions as they get older, in keeping with the Convention.

Canada has no such law. The *Charter* applies to governments, not to private associations such as families. Provincial human rights legislation does apply to private associations, but not to families and children's freedom of expression.[6] Child protection legislation in the provinces and the territories is more promising. It offers the possibility of supporting child participation by protecting children from emotional abuse, which could be interpreted to include suppressing children's voices and expression within families. However, it is not clear that authorities would consider the denial of voice and expression a form of emotional abuse.[7] There would have to be a pattern of denial—not simply an incident—and the showing of harm or substantial risk of harm to the child by the denial. And compared to most other forms of maltreatment, emotional abuse is harder to substantiate. So child protection legislation does not clearly or easily provide a legal basis for supporting children's participation rights within families.

Another possible means of supporting participation is through comprehensive parenting education. This has been the means urged by the UN Committee on the Rights of the Child to support parenting styles that are respectful of children's voices.[8] When properly implemented, such programs help parents gain an understanding of the Convention and the child's right to a voice, appreciate the importance of building mutual respect through listening to children, realize their responsibility to inform children of their rights including the right to participate, and appreciate the need to understand, respect, and promote children's evolving capacities. Parenting education programs also would help parents understand the benefits for children and families of parenting styles that are supportive of participation.[9]

Unfortunately, successive federal and provincial governments have failed to listen to the Committee. Although parenting education programs have grown in Canada in recent decades, they remain few in number and limited largely to specific purposes, such as responding to cases of child maltreatment, providing education on parenting after divorce, providing parenting skills to at-risk parents, or educating mothers about healthy pregnancies and infant health.[10] Some of the programs have been evaluated favourably for outcomes such as increasing the confidence of parents[11] and decreasing parental conflict after divorce.[12] But overall, parenting education programs have been of short duration and superficial in content. They have received little formal evaluation and funding from governments, have reached relatively few parents, and have made little or no reference to the Convention and to children's participation rights.[13]

That Canadian governments have failed to develop strong programs of parenting education with a children's rights focus again is reflective of a political culture with a prominent belief in individual responsibility. Although beliefs in social responsibility and children's rights are growing, they remain dominated by the view that parents are solely responsible for raising their children, not the state. According to this view, children's voices may be important, and public education programs for parents may be justified to address particular problems. But ultimately it is the individual responsibility of parents to meet the needs of their children. Parents know best.

## The Need for Democratic Parenting

Parenting style describes the strategies parents use to socialize children. Diana Baumrind described three basic styles of parenting in 1967: authoritative, authoritarian, and permissive.[14] The styles she described continue to be used to explain a wide variety of child and adolescent behaviours. The permissive category has since been divided into permissive-indulgent and permissive-indifferent. The styles vary in their combination of demanding behaviours (expectations for behaviour) and responsive parental behaviours. The authoritative (or democratic) category is the only style of parenting consistent with the Convention principles of participation and best interests.

The demanding behaviours of the democratic parent are setting and enforcing age-appropriate limits, expecting age-appropriate maturity, and monitoring and supervising the child. In terms of responsiveness, democratic parents are affectionate and supportive, they recognize the child's achievements, and they are involved in their children's social and academic development. Democratic parents do not simply allow their children's views to be heard; they encourage their children to express opinions on matters affecting them, and they encourage their children to explore options in decision-making. Socialization is focused on proactive teaching, modelling, and reward. Reasoning and explanation are used in response to unwanted behaviours, and when parents' actions are contrary to the child's expressed wishes.

The authoritarian and permissive categories describe ineffective parenting styles and are inconsistent with the Convention. Neither permissive nor authoritarian parents allow meaningful participation. Permissive parents, either indulgent or indifferent, have few demands or expectations for behaviour. There is little opportunity for children to express their views because they are free to do as they please. Authoritarian parents have excessive and inflexible demands for obedience and behavioural standards. Children's talents, interests, strengths, and weaknesses are not accommodated. Children are not respected as autonomous bearers of rights, and they are denied expression of opinion. There is no explanation for rules other than those that reflect parental authority, for example, "because I said so." Attempts at participation in decision-making by the child are seen as nothing more than signs of disrespect and are likely to be punished.

Democratic parenting, because it includes participation, increases the child's self-esteem, decision-making skills, and sense of being a full member of the family and community. Age-appropriate demands and responsiveness would not have such beneficial effects if the child were not allowed to participate. For example, parental involvement in the child's academic development (one characteristic of democratic parenting) has a strong facilitative effect on academic achievement because democratic parents ask for the child's opinions, listen to the child, and encourage and engage in discussion with the child. The child will not be told, "You are going to take French immersion classes." Instead, there will be discussion of the advantages and disadvantages of French immersion. The child's views will be sought and listened to, and the final decision will take them into account. If the child's views are not paramount in the final decision, the parent will explain his or her reasoning. A lot of learning about how to make a decision happens throughout the process. In turn, we see more socially and academically competent children. The findings from research are very compelling.

In Baumrind's 1967 study, the focus was on the social competence of preschool children—in essence how well children get along with other children and with adults. Preschoolers who showed the highest levels of social competence had democratic parents. Since that study, across time, culture, socioeconomic status, and gender of the child, positive developmental outcomes have been found among children raised by democratic parents, whereas children raised by permissive or authoritarian parents tend to exhibit poor developmental outcomes and a wide range of behaviour disorders.[15]

The research consistently shows that children of democratic parents, compared with those of authoritarian, indulgent, or neglectful parents, have high levels of self-esteem, self-reliance, self-control, social maturity, and academic competence, and fewer behaviour problems.[16] These optimum social, academic, and behavioural outcomes have been summarized well by Nadia Sorkhabi. Democratic parenting, she explains, "has been found to provide children with the experiential basis for optimally balancing agency (characterized by self-assertion, self-reliance, and prudential self-interest) with communion (characterized by prosocial engagement, cooperation, and moral concern for others' interests)."[17]

The findings of positive relations between democratic parenting and developmental outcomes in childhood were so consistent that researchers turned their attention to adolescence. Adolescence is a developmental stage when increasing independence and burgeoning identity require good decision-making, and when risk-taking behaviours become more common and have more serious consequences. Would democratic parenting show advantages in adolescence as it did in earlier childhood? The answer, overwhelmingly, is yes.

The early research finds that adolescents who have democratic parents, compared with those who have authoritarian or permissive ones, show higher self-esteem, more prosocial peer-group selection, and higher academic aspirations. Their social behaviours indicate lower levels of risk-taking: They report less sexual activity; less high-risk sexual behaviour; lower rates of tobacco, alcohol, and illicit drug use; low levels of interpersonal conflict or violence; and good conflict-resolution abilities.[18]

Subsequent research with adolescents has demonstrated that democratic parenting also promotes a sense of self as a moral person, civic participation, and support for democratic and rights-respecting ideals.[19] It does so through its three characteristic components. One is the warmth and responsiveness of the parent. Adolescents raised by such parents have a good relationship with their parents, and so are likely to internalize parental controls, develop prosocial behaviours and empathy, and have the motivation for positive interactions. Second is the participation and increasing autonomy provided by democratic parents. Through listening to the child's voice, and involving the child in decision-making discussions, the parents are modelling good decision-making. The child learns to take into account others' views, to think critically, and, as they grow, to make responsible and informed decisions. Third is the demanding aspect of democratic parenting. By having appropriate limits and demands for maturity, the child comes to understand the importance of principles of behaviour and the consequences of their violation. Together, the developmental outcomes associated with the three components are reflected in an adolescent who displays social trust—a belief that people generally are fair and trustworthy—and a belief in the self as a moral person.[20] In turn, these beliefs motivate prosocial behaviours and community involvement.[21] Such beliefs, behaviours, and involvement are critical not only to democratic governance, but also to the establishment and maintenance of a rights-respecting culture consistent with the Convention.

## Participation in Schools

Implementing children's participation rights is required in schools as well as families. According to the UN Committee on the Rights of the Child, "Respect for the right of the child to be heard within education is fundamental to the realization of the right to education."[22] Put another way, providing for a child's right to participation in education is an integral part of providing for a child's right to education. It is therefore essential that children have the opportunity to be heard and to express themselves in the school community. In order to do this, four basic things are necessary.

First, structures and procedures need to be in place to facilitate child participation. These include class councils, student councils, student representation on advisory boards and school committees, surveys of student views on issues, and procedures that allow for the right to be heard on matters such as discipline, suspension, and expulsions. Many of these structures have been implemented in schools across Canada. But there has been significant variation and inconsistency in the degree to which they have been put into place. Child participation thrives in some schools and school districts but not in others.[23] Reasons for this include the lack of incorporation of the Convention and participation rights into provincial and territorial education legislation, variation in legislation requiring participation, and the delegation of authority in many jurisdictions to individual school boards and schools.[24] Without a clear legislative requirement for participation, and with delegation of authority, many schools and boards have been left with the discretionary power to require or not require structures facilitating children's voices. Many have chosen not to do so, or to do so in a limited way. As Kathy Bickmore of the Ontario Institute for Studies in Education has noted, "Adults, including educators, are not necessarily disposed toward sharing power with young people."[25] As a result, the child's right to be heard has not always been provided. As a glaring example, in Ontario's system for hearing appeals of decisions to suspend or expel a student, a child under age eighteen has no standing in the procedure.[26] The only persons allowed to appeal are parents or guardians.

A second requirement for participation is that children have the opportunity to exercise their rights to freedom of expression, thought, and religion as extensively as possible, subject to reasonable limits. Here also, Canadian schools have a mixed record. On the positive side, significant progress has been made in assuring freedom of religion and conscience. Virtually all provinces, territories, and school districts, mindful of the *Charter*, human rights laws, and constitutional protection of religious freedom, have taken steps to ensure respect for religious diversity in schools.[27] The principle of respect for religious freedom has been given explicit expression in most education legislation. Reference has been made in legislation, regulations, and policies that school boards are to ensure educational practices such that no religious dogma or creed is taught; that allowance is made for students wearing certain symbols, clothing, head coverings, and hairstyles dictated by religious affiliation; and that allowance be made for religious holidays. Education authorities at times have attempted to restrict ceremonial daggers and veils.[28] But in *Multani v. Commission scolaire Marguerite-Bourgeoys*, [2006] 1 S.C.R. 256, the Supreme Court of Canada ruled that such restrictions violate the section 2(b) religious freedoms of students under the *Charter*.[29]

However, in providing children their more general right to freedom of expression, there have been problems. Historically, departments of education, school boards, and schools were overly restrictive in regulating what children could say, read, or learn about, and how they could express themselves.[30] Education authorities used their broad discretionary power in an almost dictatorial way to approve learning materials, censor material in student newspapers and other communications, and impose codes of student speech and dress. When students challenged the restrictions in court on the basis of freedom of expression, judges commonly sided with the authorities. Since the signing of the Convention, school policies and practices have become much less restrictive. Obvious examples are the general relaxation of rules on student clothing and speech and a move—though incomplete—to respect the expressive rights of students who identify as LGBTQ2.[31] But in decisions on the scope of children's expression and on restrictions on it, children commonly have not been given a voice, contrary to article 12 of the Convention.[32] Consistency with the Convention requires that school officials ensure that children have input into decisions on the appropriate balance between their expressive rights and competing considerations. Their views need not be decisive. But they do have the right to be heard and to have their views taken into account.

A third requirement for participation is that children be aware of their rights. Participation rights in schools are more likely to be realized if children (as well as adults) know that they have the right to be heard. That children become aware of their rights of participation—as well as of provision and protection—is a requirement of the Convention.[33] Under article 29, education is to be directed at the development of respect for human rights and fundamental freedoms, including those of children. And under article 42, the principles and provisions of the Convention are to be made known to children as well as to adults. Schools are an obvious place to provide knowledge, understanding, and respect for basic rights. However, apart from a few classrooms, schools, and districts, there has been little systematic effort and little interest among educators in implementing children's rights education in Canadian schools.[34] As a result, the rights of the child have been "Canada's best-kept secret."[35] It is not that children do not learn about rights. The problem, as Pat Pitsula has put it, is that they most likely learn about their rights from Hollywood.[36] But there is more to know than the right to remain silent. Thus it is important and in keeping with the Convention that schools provide children with full knowledge and understanding of the rights of the child. This is why the UN Committee on the Rights of the Child urged Canada in 1995 and again in 2012 to incorporate children's rights education into the curricula, teaching materials, and teacher education.[37]

## The Need for Democratic Schooling

There is no question that the role of the teacher has changed. Today's teacher, in the absence of specialized training, is also expected to fill the roles of parent, friend, counsellor, confessor, psychologist, and IT specialist. At the same time, cutbacks in government funding have resulted in larger classes, fewer resources, loss of programs, and loss of support personnel. But children's developmental needs have not changed. Few schools meet children's participation needs or participation rights. For the most part, the way schools are organized and administered, the greater the need for participation, the less the opportunity will be afforded. Whereas many kindergartens allow for self-direction and participation in classroom decision-making, with increasing age come more expectations for obedience and rote learning. This, of course, is inconsistent with article 12, which states that children's views should be given *increased* weight as they mature.

Opportunities for participation are especially important in early adolescence. During this period, development is characterized by increased desire for independence and self-determination, increased opportunity for peer interaction, and greater capacity to engage in more abstract and hypothetical thinking.[38] Adolescents therefore need a school environment that is intellectually challenging, and in which they feel safe questioning ideas and exploring issues with peers as well as teachers. They also need to have their ideas listened to, respected, and appreciated. This does not often happen. At a developmental stage where a sense of autonomy and efficacy is needed for well-being, children are being subjected to authoritarian styles of management that make them feel powerless.[39] There are few opportunities for peer interaction or for peer decision-making. Yet it is through peer discussion and problem solving that children learn how to make sound decisions, how to deal with dissenting opinions, and how to consider multiple perspectives on controversial issues—in short, how to be a good citizen in a democratic society.[40]

Studies of children's meaningful participation in their education identify its benefits. Democratic teaching, like democratic parenting, promotes a sense of personal efficacy, social responsibility, self-esteem, critical thinking, and good decision-making. Teachers who are supportive, who recognize children's accomplishments, who have clear expectations for behaviour, and who encourage children's participation in the classroom and in the school have a positive impact on prosocial behaviour, school engagement, and academic achievement.[41] There are also benefits beyond the school. Democratic teaching is associated with community involvement and civic participation.[42]

Despite such evidence, allowing children to participate in their schooling has not been easy for teachers and it remains uncommon.[43] Teachers cite pragmatic concerns such as time and organizational needs, and the need to deliver the full mandated curriculum.[44] More likely reasons are teachers' lack of trust in children's capacity for meaningful participation and lack of appropriate teacher training.[45] Teachers lack training in the Convention and the pedagogy it requires; they are not taught the importance of children's voices or agency in their own learning.[46] As a result, teachers are poorly prepared to teach in any but traditional methods. As Laura Lundy describes, too often children's participation in schools is limited to student councils.[47] But councils rarely provide for meaningful participation. Often student councils are controlled by teachers who set the agenda and limit the issues to be discussed. And typically their membership is restricted to students unlikely to challenge teachers or administrators. Issues of real concern to students are often disallowed—their relationships with teachers, for example, or the school's disciplinary practices. It is often difficult for students to express their thoughts on matters that are important to them without fear of reprisal. They are afraid of being shouted at and having their expression seen as an attempt to undermine adult authority rather than their fundamental human right.[48] Rarely is open expression or discussion of alternative viewpoints allowed in student councils, school newspapers, class discussions, or elsewhere in school.[49]

One notable exception is a rights-based school initiative assessed first in Nova Scotia and then more fully implemented in Hampshire County, England.[50] The initiative requires not only teaching children about their rights, but also respecting them through classroom and school practices—including participation. When the initiative was implemented in Hampshire, it was at the school and district level. The widespread and holistic adoption of the Rights, Respect and Responsibility (RRR) initiative, as it became known, allowed for extensive assessment of the effects of student participation within a rights framework. Participation was implemented as follows.

Teaching in the RRR classroom is democratic, with the teacher primarily playing the role of guide or facilitator. Children participate in their own learning through self-directed and cooperative group learning, critical thinking, social issues discussion, role-play, and project-based learning. To establish standards of behaviour, at the beginning of each year, students and teachers collaboratively develop and display a classroom charter of rights and corresponding responsibilities. These often have included such statements as "We have the right to be heard and the responsibility to listen to and respect other people's ideas."[51] At the level of the school, children are democratically elected by their peers to represent the student body on issues of budgetary allocations, spending, hiring, disciplinary practices, and school renovation plans. Student councils and school newspapers are run with rights as the overarching framework for issues, and teachers play supportive rather than directive roles. And importantly, participation is not tokenistic. Even in hiring decisions, the children's views are taken seriously. One noteworthy example is seen in the hiring of a "dinner lady." In many schools in England, community adults—usually women—are hired to prepare and serve a hot lunch. A four-year-old committee member added her interview questions: "Are you a good cook? Do you like children? Do you shout?"[52]

It may be that this type of fully democratic schooling is made possible by the rights context in which the school functions. Because children are learning about their rights and the rights of other children, they are able to use rights as a standard and framework for problem solving, discussion, critical thinking, and the evaluation of ideas. The shared value of children's rights among all members of the school also facilitates participation. In discipline practices, for example, staff and students can collaborate to determine expectations and infractions from a rights perspective. They can jointly consider what rights must be respected so that every child can learn and play without fear of bullying. And standards for behaviour can be developed from these considerations.

Evaluation of the RRR schools over a decade demonstrated the many benefits of democratic teaching and schools.[53] The opportunities provided for participation in the RRR schools were found to enhance children's engagement in school and confidence in learning. This was reflected in their commitment to learning, achievement, academic aspirations, enjoyment of school, self-esteem, and optimism for the future. Over time, the children participated more in the classroom and in school committees and activities. And as their participation increased, the children became increasingly respectful of their peers and their teachers. Children were reported by their teachers to be more and more cooperative, inclusive, and sensitive to the needs of children with learning difficulties. Incidents of bullying and other inappropriate behaviours concomitantly decreased. Classroom and school climate became significantly more positive. And as we would predict from the existing literature, participation at school elicited involvement in prosocial activities in the community. In sum, the RRR schools demonstrate how democratic schooling is consistent with the Convention and very much in the best interests of the child.

## Participation in Legal Proceedings

The Convention is quite specific about the child's right to be heard in legal proceedings. Article 12(2) states that the child shall be provided "the opportunity to be heard in any judicial and administrative proceedings affecting the child." This may be done either directly or indirectly through "a representative or an appropriate body." It is important to note that the term *proceedings* refers not only to formal judicial proceedings such as in a court. According to the UN Committee on the Rights of the Child, it refers also to informal administrative proceedings such as in mediation after separation or divorce and in decisions about child protection.[54] Children have the right to express their views, or not express them, in *any* proceeding and in *all* matters affecting the child. Children having a voice, says the Committee, is an integral part of their best interests.[55]

Since the 1990s, Canada has made some progress in implementing children's participation rights in proceedings. Youth justice is a leading example. Under the federal *Youth Criminal Justice Act*, enacted in 2003, youth in conflict with the law (ages twelve to seventeen inclusive) have been assured the right to be heard in legal proceedings and to have legal representation, consistent with article 12 as well as with articles specifically on youth justice (articles 37 and 40).[56] In addition, in procedures related to extrajudicial sanctions and community programs such as restorative justice, youth have been given the right to consent (or withhold consent) to their involvement in programs and the right to consult a lawyer before making a decision. Another example is child testimony. Through a number of reforms in Canada's criminal justice system, children have been better able to give testimony in court, their competency and reliability as witnesses has been more recognized, and child-friendly means have been employed—screens, videotapes, closed-circuit television, and assistance of support persons—to facilitate children's testimony.[57] A further example is civil law proceedings under Québec's *Civil Code* (1991), which took effect in 1994. In all proceedings affecting children, the *Code* requires courts to "give the child an opportunity to be heard if his [*sic*] age and power of discernment permit it."[58] In child custody and access cases, for example, it is the practice of judges to make every effort to seek out and hear what children have to say.[59] It is not a matter of discretion as it is in many other provinces. Québec law requires that this be done, in keeping with the Convention.

However, in other proceedings, Canada's implementation of children's participation rights has been inconsistent and problematic. In child protection legal proceedings, as stated in all provincial and territorial legislation, decisions are to be based on the best interests of the child.[60] And as part of determining best interests, the views of the child are to be considered, consistent with the Convention. But at what age and by what means children's views are taken into account varies with jurisdiction. In Manitoba, for instance, the child has the right to be heard only at age twelve. Children's views may be heard in different ways: through court-ordered assessments, children's lawyers, written statements by children, and, less frequently, children's testimony and judicial interviews. But these methods often involve restrictions and a great deal of discretion. For example, the legislation generally states that courts *may*—rather than *shall*—appoint lawyers or order assessments or grant judicial interviews. And in some provinces, the methods apply only to children of a certain age. For example, in Nova Scotia, children are entitled to a lawyer at age sixteen, which is remarkably late. Moreover, only in some jurisdictions (e.g., Ontario) are children's lawyers government funded. In other jurisdictions, although children may have a formal right to a lawyer, they are not always able to exercise this right because of a lack of resources and legal aid.[61] In summary, children's participation rights are hampered by uneven and sometimes limited application.

Outside of formal proceedings, problems also exist in the child protection process. This is well illustrated in the tragic child abuse death of Katelynn Sampson in Ontario, discussed in the previous chapter. In 2016, in response to her death and to the failure of children's services to consult with her about her well-being—which could have prevented her death—the jury at the inquest announced "Katelynn's Principle."[62] It declares, among other things, that children who come to the attention of child protection authorities should be given every opportunity to express their views—directly or through a representative—before decisions are made affecting them. This principle is to apply not only in formal hearings but also in the process as a whole. Child advocates have urged that, consistent with the Convention, the principle be applied across Canada.[63] That Katelynn's Principle had to be declared has shown a general failure in the child protection process to take seriously the participation rights of the child. In 2016 Ontario did introduce new child protection legislation that incorporated Katelynn's Principle.[64] But the failure to take such action elsewhere reflects a continuing lack of commitment to children's participation.

Lack of participation continues to be common among children taken into care. In all Canadian jurisdictions, once children are removed from the home, they are placed in care, in the form of foster homes, staffed group homes, or institutional care.[65] Beginning in Québec in 1977 and Ontario in 1984, these children were provided with a number of participation rights in law. These include the right to consult with a lawyer and with the office of the Child Advocate (or children's representative or ombudsperson), to participate in the development of plans of care, to initiate a review of a placement decision, and to express views in major decisions such as about medical treatment and education. If their rights are violated, children may initiate a complaint to the ministry responsible and to the office of the Child Advocate. However, as noted by Tom Waldock, there is variation across the country in the rights provided and in children's awareness of their rights.[66] Also, as pointed out by Waldock, there is a problem in the day-to-day practice of participation. Because children in care are at risk and often feel powerless, it is important that their care providers advocate for them and support their participation in decision-making. However, foster parents, who are the most common care providers, receive little training in effective communication and facilitation of participation. And workers in group homes and institutions, who could be important advocates for the children, often fail to fulfill this role because of high caseloads and bureaucratic paperwork. So it comes as no surprise that although children have the formal right to participate, they are not always able to practise it.

Participation is also problematic in adoption proceedings. As with child protection, adoption is largely a provincial and territorial responsibility. In all jurisdictions, decisions on adoptions are to be based on the best interests of the child.[67] But there is significant variation in the extent to which children's views are part of determining best interests. Older children have the right to consent to an adoption in all jurisdictions. In Ontario, it is at age seven, at which point legal advice and counselling are available.[68] But in other jurisdictions, it is at age twelve, and not necessarily with legal advice and counselling. In all jurisdictions, children under the age of consent are allowed to be involved in adoption hearings. But again, there is major variation.[69] In Ontario, children's participation rights are relatively well implemented. Young children—where their views can be reasonably ascertained—have the right to be heard in decisions not only about adoption placements but also about details such as continuing contact with birth parents and relatives. Other jurisdictions are more restrictive. In Yukon, the involvement of children in hearings means only that they have "the right to be present." In Prince Edward Island, the child may be heard but only when practicable. And in many other jurisdictions, if children are granted an opportunity to be heard in a decision, they are not provided with the right to consult with a lawyer and they are not assured input into important details of an adoption order, such as contact with birth parents.

Finally, in child custody and access proceedings, children's participation rights have not been fully put into practice.[70] One problem is that the right to be heard has not been made explicit in all law. In provincial and territorial family law, which governs matters of custody when parents are seeking separation, custody is to be determined on the basis of the best interests of the child. In doing this, judges are instructed to consider the child's views and preferences. But in the federal *Divorce Act*, which governs matters of custody when married parents are seeking divorce, there is no reference to the child's views. Judges under the Act are instructed to decide custody on the basis of the child's best interests. In practice, although they often interpret best interests to include considering the child's views, they are reluctant to do so directly through interviewing the child. And there is no legal requirement to seek the child's views or to seriously listen to the child. Discretion is practised widely.[71] The result is that some children have no voice. Even if children are given a voice in the courtroom, they are not assured a right to be heard during mediation and in informal meetings outside the courtroom, which often produce agreements on custody.[72] Parents, lawyers, and mediators may consult with the children affected. But there is no requirement that they do so and no way of knowing whether genuine consultation takes place.

A further problem is that the main methods used for hearing children's views allow for a gap between the principle and practice of participation.[73] First, in all jurisdictions, courts *can* order assessments by an independent third party to gather information on the family situation, including the views of the child, which then are brought into court through a report or testimony. But this is not always a requirement and assessments can be very costly for families, which means most families do not proceed. Second, courts *can* appoint private lawyers or government-funded lawyers (e.g., in Ontario) to represent children. But the appointment of lawyers is often discretionary, costs are high for private lawyers, and legal aid is not available in many jurisdictions. A problem also is that the role of lawyers varies by jurisdiction. In some jurisdictions, it is to represent the child's views. In others, it is to represent what the lawyer believes is the child's best interests. However, judges are under no obligation to hear children's lawyers, read their reports, or give them any weight. As a result, the child's voice is not always assured. Third, judges *can* gather the views of children through judicial interviews in private. But again, this is up to the discretion of judges and most judges are reluctant to interview children. With all these limits on the right to be heard, the evidence suggests that the views of children are taken into account in only a minority of judicial decisions about custody and access.[74]

In summary, since the signing of the Convention, certain progress has been made in advancing children's participation rights in legal and administrative proceedings affecting the child. However, contrary to the early hopes of child advocates, the progress to date has been underwhelming.

## *The Need to Hear Children in Proceedings*

The lack of progress in ensuring children's participation rights in proceedings is of particular concern. Since the legal reforms of the past decades, there has been a considerable increase not only in the numbers of children involved in proceedings, but also in research demonstrating that such participation is both possible and desirable. The research findings clearly show the following. First, practices continue to seriously compromise children's participation in proceedings. Second, from early childhood, children can provide valuable and accurate information when appropriately asked. Third, being heard in proceedings that affect them is very important to children. We now examine each area in turn.

First, despite the many legal reforms to expand participation, practices have not always changed and have tended to remain biased toward ignoring or discrediting children.[75] The use of testimonial aids is one example. In 2006, the *Criminal Code* was amended to allow the expanded use of screens, closed-circuit televisions, and videotaped statements. This was in response to evidence that their use makes children more comfortable and more likely to give accurate testimony.[76] However, researchers report that even in so-called child-friendly courts where children are recounting sexual abuse, the use of testimonial aids is strongly discouraged because of concerns that their use will jeopardize the child's credibility.[77] And the most commonly used aid in sexual abuse cases, videotaped testimony, is also the most likely to be discredited.[78] It can be very difficult for children to talk about their abuse in front of others and especially in front of their abuser. Without testimonial aids, participation is significantly compromised.

Judicial interviewing is another example of a faulty practice. As previously discussed, judges are reluctant to interview children. But even when they do, there is a lack of appropriate interviewing, which limits meaningful participation. Research shows many benefits of child participation in divorce or post-separation parenting arrangements.[79] Participation is empowering for the child because it makes the experience much less negative, and it is enlightening to the judge because the information the child provides can improve decision-making. Yet, with the exception of Québec, judges rarely meet with children in post-separation decision-making.[80] Some judges believe that protecting the child from what they see as a traumatic event is more important than respecting the child's right to participate. Others argue that judges lack the training needed to reliably assess what children are saying, or that children cannot be expected to provide useful information.[81] It is true that judges lack training in talking with children. And with inadequate training, children's participation is unlikely to be empowering to the child or enlightening to the decision-maker.

Not only do judges lack training, again with the exception of Québec, but so do forensic interviewers (most often police and social workers) who work with children.[82] Interviewing children is challenging and comprehensive training is essential. Outside the context of legal proceedings, when a child is asked a question, most often it is either a reprimand ("Did you forget to wash your hands again?"), a test of knowledge ("How do you say apple in French?"), or a simple request for information ("Do you want ice cream now or later?"). Rarely is a detailed answer sought. And rarely are children in the role of experts when answering adults' questions.[83] As a result, it is difficult for children to understand what is expected of them, and so they tend to provide incomplete descriptions of events. Children also are vulnerable to suggestibility. Ineffective or inappropriate styles of questioning can easily result in false statements.

With inadequate training and little knowledge of evidence-based techniques or sometimes even of legislative changes, interviewers continue to use inappropriate means of questioning and to engage in abolished practices such as competency testing.[84] Interviewers also report other challenges. For example, in cases of allegations of maltreatment, a parent may be present and sending cues to the child that limit or even prevent the child from talking. Sometimes interviews are held in the place where the abuse occurred, thus making the child very uncomfortable. And interviewers report experiencing particular challenges when talking with children with developmental delays or mental health issues. Significant training is essential to all those in the legal system who meet with children. In its absence, participation may be meaningless.

Second, researchers find that when children are asked appropriate questions in appropriate settings, they can provide detailed and accurate information. The two key questions addressed in the competency research are at what age are children able to reliably give testimony, and what are the best interview strategies for eliciting accurate accounts of events, including how deception can be identified.

It is rare in Canada for children younger than age five to give their views in any legal proceedings. However, there is evidence that by age three children can provide accurate testimony. Carole Peterson and her colleagues have conducted extensive studies of children's capacity to provide accurate testimony both when a stressful event occurs and over time.[85] Their work indicates that children even as young as age two can describe traumatic events that happened to them not only at the time but also five years later. Other researchers have found that children as young as age four who have lived in out-of-home care for some time are able to provide vivid and accurate details about their experiences at home prior to being taken into care.[86] In fact, young children's accounts have been of such value that researchers have recommended—consistent with Katelynn's Principle—that children's perspectives be an integral part of risk assessment. Overall, the data suggest that once children are verbal, their participation rights should be respected and their voices heard.

How best to hear those voices has been the subject of much research. The first and very important step is to make sure children know the roles of those involved, the meaning and purpose of the procedures, what is expected of them, and the fact that they have a right to be heard. Legal terminology and the roles and functions of professionals are not well understood by children, and they are not always comfortable asking for clarification. "I did not understand what a placement meant," one maltreated child told a researcher. "Then I asked my friend. He said it meant I had to go to another family."[87] Another child recounted that the social worker said, "We will think of a new family and then we will go and get acquainted with them and see what it would be like to live there.... It was not said that I would have to stay there until I was 18 years old."[88] Children's legal knowledge does increase with age.[89] But generally, without intervention, such knowledge remains inadequate to allow for informed participation. Ensuring understanding and providing opportunities for questions would obviously be helpful for facilitating children's participation. Inadequate understanding elicits misinformation and anxiety. And children who are anxious because they do not understand what is happening are less likely to talk and are more prone to suggestive questions by an interviewer.[90]

The means by which children's accounts are sought are of critical importance. Particularly in cases of alleged abuse, children may be interviewed a number of times prior to a court appearance. Multiple interviews are not necessarily damaging to the child's memory. However, if interviewers use leading or suggestive questions, false memories or misinformation can easily become incorporated into the child's recounting of events. The more frequent the inappropriate interviewing, the more contaminated the child's evidence.[91] Contaminated evidence is not the only problem. The types of questions asked can compromise the information the child gives, and in turn the child's credibility. For example, in one study of police and social worker interviews with maltreated children in Ontario, few subjective questions were asked.[92] This is critical because children who do not talk about their feelings are seen as less credible. But children do need to be asked to describe their feelings. Clearly, objective information—what happened—is important. But subjective information—the child's thoughts and feelings—is important in assessing credibility in cases of maltreatment and in deciding post-divorce parenting arrangements.[93] There is considerable evidence on best practices for interviewing children.[94] Nicholas Bala, a Canadian expert on legal processes involving children, has provided excellent and comprehensive child interview guidelines for family court judges that could be readily adapted to forensic contexts.[95]

In addition to knowing the best strategies for interviewing children, it is important for professionals to know how to detect deception. Children too easily can be manipulated into telling fabricated accounts of events. They may lie to please or protect a parent, or in response to parental threat, interviewer bias, or inappropriate questioning.[96] They are excellent at it, too. Children can recount fabricated events in highly credible ways. Generally, adults' rates of success in identifying the truth of a child's story are around chance levels.[97] Fortunately, there is software available that shows promise in identifying when children are fabricating reports. The first study to analyze children's narratives with the Linguistic Inquiry and Word Count (LIWC) software used four-to-seven-year-olds in a mock courtroom setting.[98] Children were coached by a parent to "testify" either about an event they had experienced or one they had not. Their narratives were transcribed and given to adults, who were asked to assess their truthfulness, and the same narratives were analyzed using the LIWC. The software program identified differences between the true and fabricated narratives that were missed by the adults. Overall, the success rate of the LIWC in detecting fabrication was over 72 percent. The adults correctly identified deception in only 45 percent of the narratives. Was this a fair comparison? It might be argued that relying on transcripts would make deception more difficult to detect than if the adults had observed the children's behaviours during their testimony. Might body language reveal deception more than linguistic variables? The unfortunate reality is that even preschoolers are able to regulate their non-verbal behaviours such that they appear honest; this ability increases with age, as does children's ability to maintain consistency in describing untrue reports.

Third, not only do children have a right to be heard, but cross-national research consistently shows it is of great importance to them. Children in a variety of countries and across ages have been asked about their participation in either post-separation parenting arrangements or child protection proceedings.[99] Overwhelmingly, children express a strong desire to have their thoughts and feelings heard. And overwhelmingly, children are clear that they want only to be consulted, not to make decisions. However, they do want control in the way their views are presented. Children want their opinions heard directly by the decision-maker in order to avoid possible misinterpretation by an intermediary. They want to be able to disclose their feelings in private without concerns about upsetting a parent or being subjected to retaliation. And importantly, they want to feel that whomever they are meeting with is taking their opinions seriously. An example is illustrative. There are jurisdictions in the United States where maltreated children routinely participate in hearings to determine if they will be placed in care and if parental rights will be terminated. Stephanie Block and her colleagues talked to seven-to-ten-year-olds after their hearings.[100] Two-thirds of the children felt that they did not get to tell the judge what they wanted, and over a third reported that they felt neither believed nor listened to. Surprisingly, over half did not even know the outcome of their case.

Such findings underscore the importance of having well-trained interviewers and of providing opportunities for children to meet directly with judges, unless they choose otherwise. In addition, it would be helpful to monitor children's participation experiences to ensure they feel heard. In child protection proceedings, when children do feel their views have been heard, believed, and seriously taken into account, they are more trusting of the decision-makers, see the decisions as fairer, and have a better understanding of their case and its outcomes.[101] In cases of separation and divorce, children who participate in decisions about parenting arrangements are less negative about the changes to their family and more likely to maintain positive relationships with both parents.[102] In short, children not only have a right to be heard but also want to be listened to, and they should be listened to. Participation is in children's best interests whether in the family, at school, or in legal proceedings. And as we have seen in the tragedy of Katelynn Sampson, listening to children can be life-saving.

# CHAPTER 8

ৎ

# Meeting the Challenge

When Canada ratified the UN Convention on the Rights of the Child in 1991, child advocates were optimistic. They hoped the Convention would inspire Canadian governments to advance the rights of children and improve children's lives. But their hopes have not been fully realized. The gap between the promise of the Convention and its implementation means that many children in Canada continue to be raised in socially toxic environments. The questions we address in this final chapter are these. Why has there been a failure in Canada to meet the challenge of children's rights? What is required to fully implement children's rights? And is this likely to happen?

## Failure to Meet the Challenge

Canada has made some progress in implementing the rights of children since signing the Convention. In the area of provision rights, child benefits have been steadily increasing, rates of infant mortality have been reduced, and Québec has developed the most progressive system of early childhood education and care in North America. In the area of protection rights, the Supreme Court of Canada has limited the availability of the section 43 defence, child pornography laws have been created to protect children from sexual exploitation, and child maltreatment has been defined more broadly to increase the protection of children from abuse and neglect in homes and institutions. Finally, in the area of participation rights, the child's right to be heard has widened in schools, in the youth justice system, and in family law proceedings (especially in Québec), and, to a greater degree than before, provision has been made for taking the child's views into account in decisions about child protection, adoption, and child custody.

But despite these positive steps, there has been an overall failure to meet the challenge of children's rights. International comparisons show that among the wealthier countries of the world, Canada has been a laggard in reducing the number of children living in poverty, in improving child health, and in expanding early childhood education and care programs.[1] Canada also has trailed behind in banning corporal punishment and in developing a more preventive and child-focused approach to child protection. Efforts by Canadian governments to assure children their participation rights have been uneven and inadequate. No greater evidence of the silencing of voice is the general failure to put Katelynn's Principle into effect, which directs child welfare officials to give children every opportunity to express their views.

If Canadian governments were serious about meeting the challenge of children's rights, they would have incorporated the Convention into federal, provincial, and territorial law, making the implementation of children's rights more focused and achievable. But they have failed to do so. Although the Supreme Court has used the Convention as an aid in interpreting statutes, only in a few pieces of legislation is the Convention even referenced. The UN Committee on the Rights of the Child has repeatedly expressed concern about this.[2] To address the problem, the Committee has urged Canadian governments at all levels to work together and develop a comprehensive legal framework that fully incorporates the provisions of the Convention. Some progress has been made. In Saskatchewan, for example, thanks to pressure by Saskatchewan's Child Advocate, the government in 2009 approved the Child and Youth First Principles based on the Convention, serving as a guiding framework for establishing new child-related legislation.[3] In Ontario, after pressure by the province's Child Advocate and other groups, the government in 2016 proposed new child welfare legislation affirming the rights of children under the Convention.[4] However, important though these steps have been, the full and direct incorporation of the Convention into law has yet to be accomplished federally or provincially.

Across the country children do not have the same right to be heard in legal proceedings, the same protection from abuse, or the same access to programs such as early childhood education. In addition, major social inequalities persist in Canada, particularly for Indigenous children, who continue to suffer disproportionately from poverty, health problems, suicide, maltreatment, and sexual exploitation.

Finally, if Canadian governments were serious about meeting the challenge of children's rights, they would have adopted a more proactive approach to improving the lives of children and securing their rights. In child welfare systems, the best interests of children are not served by merely reacting to cases of maltreatment and sending children into multiple, short-term foster care placements. Appropriate responses are important, but children's best interests require more. They require the early identification of risk and strong programs of prevention. Prevention needs action outside formal systems of child welfare to reduce child poverty rates, improve pre-natal and infant health outcomes, expand early childhood education and care programs, ban corporal punishment, and ensure children a voice in matters that affect them. If the broad range of children's rights were put into effect, children would be more likely to experience healthy development and to enjoy the substance of their rights under the Convention.

## Why the Failure?

What accounts for Canada's failure? Our analysis points to significant deficits in political commitment and public pressure to advance the rights of children.[5] With political party agreement and public support, Canada's ratification of the Convention in 1991 showed commitment to children's rights. And since that time, as we have acknowledged, progress has been made in a number of areas. But political commitment has not been deep and public pressure to implement the Convention has not been strong. If it were strong, Canadian governments would have worked hard to overcome the chief obstacles to implementation—federalism, enforcement of treaties, financial concerns—and they would have achieved much more success in the progressive realization of children's rights. The achievements in northern Europe show what can be done when governments are fully committed to implementing children's rights. Canada's mediocre record, compared to other countries, speaks volumes.

Why Canadian governments have failed to honour their commitment is not difficult to understand. Ratifying the Convention in 1991 was a relatively easy thing to do. Declaring intentions to help children and to support human rights is always politically popular. But the heavy lifting of overcoming the obstacles and giving priority to children's rights amidst all the competing demands on governments for attention and funding is neither easy nor popular.

One reason for the failed implementation is that governments have come and gone since 1991. Newly elected governments come in with different priorities. In its 2005 report, the Senate Standing Committee on Human Rights was surprised that few politicians or government officials had even the most basic knowledge or understanding of the Convention.[6] In accounting for this lack of awareness, the Committee noted the absence of a permanent governmental mechanism or structure to spread awareness and ensure officials are always aware of their international human rights obligations.

Another reason for Canada's failure is that Canada has an unfortunate tradition of not fully honouring its international human rights obligations. It has become standard practice to proudly ratify international conventions and then, once the party is over, not live up to their terms. In 2008, Amnesty International, in a review of Canada's compliance with human rights treaties, found that in most cases, Canada had failed to act on UN Committee recommendations, including those of the Committee on the Rights of the Child.[7] According to Amnesty, Canadian governments used federalism as an excuse for inaction, despite the 1969 Vienna Convention on the Law of Treaties, which disallows this.[8]

Amnesty pointed to another problem: government secrecy and lack of transparency.[9] When Canadian officials were asked by UN committees about how Canada plans to follow up with their recommendations, the officials replied that matters would be dealt with by the obscure Federal, Provincial, and Territorial Continuing Committee of Officials on Human Rights. As part of implementation, the Continuing Committee is to keep government officials informed of the comments and recommendations of UN committees. But a major problem, said Amnesty, is that the Continuing Committee conducts most of its work in secret, is unknown to most Canadians, allows little public or parliamentary input into its discussions, and never reports to the public. With this lack of awareness and accountability, Canadian governments can ignore or evade their human rights obligations.

Canadian governments would be more inclined to honour their children's rights commitments if they were under strong and sustained pressure to do so. One possible source of pressure is from the chief stakeholders— children. Although it is obviously in children's best interests that their rights under the Convention be fully implemented, the simple fact is that children have little political power. They do not vote and they do not organize into interest groups that could pressure governments. Few interest groups are even partially composed of children and youth. Without large organizations and power of their own, children have to depend on others to apply pressure on their behalf. And since children's rights education is also lacking, most people do not even know that pressure needs to be applied.

Pressure to implement children's rights has been applied repeatedly by a wide range of individual advocates, child advocacy organizations, and other concerned groups. Within the structures of government, all provinces and territories have official offices of child and youth advocacy (except for the Northwest Territories and Prince Edward Island).[10] Although funded by the legislature, these offices are independent from government and act to some degree as critical watchdogs and advocates for children. However, their main function is to respond to complaints, monitor the situation of children receiving government care or services, and address grievances and problems. They do important work within their jurisdictions. But they do not have the broader role of monitoring the rights of the child on a comprehensive basis and pressuring for implementation of the Convention.

A national association of advocacy offices, the Canadian Council of Child and Youth Advocates, was created in 2001 to act as a forum for the exchange of information and to promote the rights of the child more widely.[11] Again, this association does important work for children. But without resources and a significant public profile, and without a national Children's Commissioner to champion the rights of children in the federal jurisdiction, the Council has lacked the clout and capacity to advocate for Canadian children as a whole, and to apply strong pressure for implementing the Convention.

Outside of government, a variety of child advocacy organizations and interest groups have also applied pressure. These include child rights and child welfare organizations with a broad focus such as Save the Children Canada, UNICEF Canada, Children First Canada, the Canadian Coalition for the Rights of Children, and the National Alliance for Children and Youth. They also include groups that focus on specialized issues such as Campaign 2000 (child poverty), the Child Care Advocacy Association (early childhood education and care), and the Child Welfare League of Canada (child protection). And they include professional organizations such as the Canadian Bar Association, which advocates for implementing the Convention. All of these groups have done important work in promoting children's rights. However, there are also individuals and organizations that support corporal punishment, oppose the expansion of early childhood education, and promote parental rights and the family preservation approach to child welfare.[12]

Amidst these competing groups urging governments to act in different ways, children's rights advocates have had limited success. The children's rights deficit continues.

Child advocates, inside and outside government, could have more success if public opinion were more strongly on their side. But this has not been the case. So far, public opinion has failed to be a sufficiently powerful force to back child advocates, and to compel Canadian governments to act on behalf of children. The main reason for this is that most Canadians have little knowledge or awareness of children's rights.[13] Contrary to article 42 of the Convention, political and educational authorities in Canada have failed to spread awareness. Public opinion can be a significant force in influencing governments only if it is unified and strong.[14] But this is not the case.

There is even opposition to teaching children about their rights. In celebration of the tenth anniversary of the Convention, UNICEF Canada and Elections Canada organized a student vote in schools across the country.[15] Students were given the opportunity to discuss the Convention and vote on the rights they thought were most important. Three-quarters of a million students in almost 2000 schools participated. However, participation was blocked in some schools by conservative interest groups. Their reasons included that children already have too many rights and that promoting awareness of rights would weaken adult authority. As stated by one school trustee in British Columbia, the Convention "undermines the integrity of the family and involves children in a political undertaking. There is a gradual erosion of parental authority and this is one more step in that direction."[16] An irony of the voting was that the right thought most important to the children who participated in the exercise was the right to a family upbringing. Clearly, the concepts and principles of the Convention have not permeated Canadian political culture and public consciousness.

At the core of the Convention is the concept that children are independent bearers of rights. However, the older concept of children as the property of their parents persists. Although few Canadians support absolute parental rights, there is a lingering notion that parental authority over children should be upheld as much as possible. This is why Alberta, after much hesitation, belatedly approved the Convention in 1999 with the understanding that it would not "usurp or override the authority of parents."[17] The older concept of children as vulnerable not-yets also persists. This has certain benefits. It has influenced opinions in support of government measures such as reducing child poverty rates and improving child welfare systems. But underlying this concept is the belief that children are not yet ready for rights, but are in need of compassion and charity. It is an influential belief that is reflected in resistance to children's knowledge of rights and their participation in schools, legal proceedings, health decisions, and civic affairs.[18] Because these older concepts continue to inform public thinking, children's rights have failed to gain ascendancy in Canada's political culture.

Another concept of the Convention is social responsibility. The Convention affirms the principle that safeguarding and promoting the rights of children is a sovereign duty. Indeed, every UN member state apart from the United States has endorsed this principle by ratifying the Convention. Consistent with the Convention, the concept of social responsibility for children has been gaining strength in Canada, particularly in Québec. However, it remains weaker than in many other Western industrialized countries. According to Danish sociologist Gøsta Esping-Andersen, common-law countries (including Canada) compare unfavourably to European countries in the strength of social welfare policies and the willingness to use government as agencies of social responsibility.[19] In the Nordic nations, he says, the political cultures are social democratic and progressive. There are strong beliefs in social responsibility, social justice, and social welfare. In European countries such as Germany and France, there is less emphasis on direct government action and more on governments working with voluntary groups, religious institutions, and private organizations to achieve social welfare objectives. But in Canada and the United States, there are stronger beliefs in individual responsibility, economic freedom, and limited government. Social welfare policies are considered to be residual, applying only as a limited safety net rather than as a right. Unlike cultures in Europe, in Canada and the United States social welfare is not considered to be a right that is to be provided for on a regular and comprehensive basis.

This persistent belief in individual responsibility has underpinned the view held by many Canadians that parents—not governments—are individually responsible for the economic welfare of their children, the discipline of their children, and decisions about vaccinations, health care, and sexual health education for their children.[20] Without a strong belief in children's rights and social responsibility, and without powerful public pressure on governments to honour their commitment to children, it is not surprising that Canada lags behind other countries in implementing the rights of the child.

## Meeting the Challenge

As Nelson Mandela said, "Education is the most powerful weapon which you can use to change the world."[21] Over time, and with education about the Convention, there is every reason to believe that public attitudes toward children can be changed to produce a culture strongly committed to the rights of the child.

Canada should provide widespread, comprehensive education on the Convention and its benefits to children, families, and society. Currently, education about the rights of the child is limited to government pamphlets, National Child Day celebrations, and other isolated initiatives. Education about children's rights should be provided in K–12 schools, colleges and universities, and professional programs. In addition, education directed at expanding public consciousness and building a culture supportive of children's rights should be provided by a national Children's Commissioner working with child advocacy offices, human rights commissions, and educators.

*Children's Rights Education in K–12 Schools.* The UN Committee on the Rights of the Child has stressed that "[c]hildren do not lose their human rights by virtue of passing through the school gates."[22] The Committee has repeatedly urged Canada to create a national strategy for children's rights education in all primary and secondary schools.[23] Even very young children can learn the meaning of rights, the importance of respecting rights, and the link between having rights and having the responsibility to protect and promote the rights of others.[24] Children quickly realize that if they disrespect the rights of others, their own rights may be at risk.[25] When educated in a rights-respecting environment, children develop rights-supportive attitudes, as well as the skills, knowledge, and motivation needed to promote and protect the rights of others. These children will carry with them the value of children's rights into adulthood and parenthood. To date, departments of education and the Canadian Council of Ministers of Education (the collective provincial voice on educational matters) have ignored the Committee.

*Colleges, Universities, and Professional Schools.* Courses in children's rights at the university level would spread awareness of the Convention and of children as bearers of human rights because the vast majority of Canadian youth attend either college or university.[26] Many will become parents, and many will pursue careers that involve working with or for children—teachers, lawyers, nurses, doctors, social workers, therapists, public service workers, and policy-makers. But few will learn about the rights of the child as part of their training. Courses on children's rights are rarely a core requirement. Yet basic education on the Convention, and its benefits to children, has been found effective in changing the attitudes of undergraduate students.[27]

At the graduate level and in professional programs, children's rights education should be extended to include implementation strategies. In education, for example, one of the difficulties teachers have with implementing children's rights in the classroom is a lack of training in democratic teaching and the facilitation of participation.[28] Research shows that when teachers learn not just a content area but also the strategies for teaching it, the topic becomes more valued by them. They become more confident in their ability to teach the topic, and more likely to make efforts to do so.[29] This is important for all those who will work with or for children.

The major components of graduate and professional training in children's rights are threefold: learning the importance and benefits of proactive interventions, learning how to critically analyze and use evidence as a basis for program development, and learning how to use child impact assessments to guide programs and policies. The emphasis given to each component will, of course, vary with the target group of students.

First, given the importance of the prenatal environment to healthy child development, students need to be taught the importance of implementing preventive programs to reduce developmental vulnerability and build resilience. These programs should be provided early in the prenatal period and continue until the child is of kindergarten or preschool age. As the late child champion Clyde Hertzman concluded, Canada must focus on improving developmental paths in early childhood.[30] The unfortunately common quick-fix reactive approach may be well suited to politicians, but it is not in the best interests of children. Proactive interventions can significantly minimize the numbers of children who need later interventions for difficulties associated with abuse, neglect, sexual exploitation, harsh punishment, or exposure to prenatal toxins. And proactive interventions can help build resilience.

Second, those who will be funding, designing, or implementing programs for children and families should learn how to conduct and assess research studies and program evaluations. This education will help avoid the implementation of inappropriate programs that are not in the best interests of the child, and will facilitate optimum use of resources. Failure to identify biased reporting or inappropriate samples, for example, can result in expensive implementation of programs with no valid evidence.[31]

Third, all students who will be working with or for children need to be taught how to conduct child impact assessments, as urged by the UN Committee on the Rights of the Child. They are to be used for any proposed new programming, policy, or change of policy, laws, or budgets. In Sweden, for example, the routine use of child impact assessments helps ensure that actions are evidence-based and in the child's best interests.[32]

*Children's Rights Education for Parents.* Few parenting programs in Canada include discussion of the Convention, or of the democratic parenting strategies that are consistent with the child's rights. The Convention is not the threat to parents that some believe it to be. Rather, it is supportive of the family as the ideal rearing environment for children. The Convention identifies parents—both parents in two-parent families—to have the primary responsibility for guiding children in the exercise of their rights. To help parents with their child-rearing, the Convention identifies the responsibilities of governments to provide supports to children and families, as detailed throughout this book. Educating parents about the Convention and the benefits of rights to child development is important for promoting children's rights both within and outside the family. Knowledge of the relation among child rights, rights-consistent parenting strategies, and positive developmental outcomes improves parenting practices and, as a result, child behaviours. And learning the responsibilities of governments would encourage parents to pressure for and obtain the services and supports they need. Canada has relatively high rates of childhood difficulties and low rates of accessible help for parents.[33] Parents across the country have sought help, but few are able to access a parenting program of any type.[34] Would child-rights-based parenting programs really make a difference? We think so. Efforts to end corporal punishment demonstrate this.

Using corporal punishment as a discipline strategy is inconsistent with children's rights because of its potential for harm and its negative effects on development. In addition to its negative outcomes, it is ineffective in teaching desired behaviours. In fact, corporal punishment has a deleterious effect on parent–child relationships and makes parenting more difficult. Education about corporal punishment and non-violent discipline strategies has been demonstrated to change parental attitudes toward its use, and hence to significantly reduce its use. For example, in a study of support for section 43 of Canada's *Criminal Code*, researchers found that when they provided information about the links between corporal punishment and harmful child outcomes, support for section 43 dropped significantly.[35] And provision of information on the use of strategies such as redirection, praise, and removal of privileges allows parents to alter their discipline strategies to those consistent with positive outcomes and the Convention.[36]

Education is effective in changing attitudes and behaviours, but it would be even more effective if accompanied by supports for parents. All parents may need support at times. But supports are of particular importance to the healthy development of children whose parents live in challenging circumstances. Children are vulnerable to negative developmental outcomes when they are raised in high-risk conditions, especially in the first four years of life. Education without supports may not be effective where there is emotional, social, or material deprivation that results in a stressful parenting environment. Although a lack of knowledge of developmental milestones and positive child-rearing strategies can be overcome with education, parents living with domestic violence, separation from family support networks, addictions, and physical or mental health challenges need supports in the community. Appropriate education with early supports and with proactive interventions would eliminate much developmental vulnerability.[37]

The time to start is early in the pregnancy. Those who have extensively studied prenatal care in Canada emphasize that although smoking and drinking rates have decreased during pregnancy, they continue to be a significant concern.[38] Given the risks to birth outcomes and the long-term effects on children's health and daily functioning, there is an urgent need for prevention efforts. Simply informing someone that smoking or drinking in pregnancy is bad for the infant, without providing cessation strategies, may not elicit changed behaviour. But smoking cessation programs during pregnancy do result in fewer low-birth-weight and preterm births.[39] Addiction services, cessation programs, and family supports to reduce stress are essential.

*A National Children's Commissioner.* An important contribution to public education can be made by a national Children's Commissioner. Unlike countries such as Norway, Sweden, England, New Zealand, and Australia, Canada does not have a national Children's Commissioner (or ombudsperson or official advocate) to champion the rights of children.[40] Although child advocacy offices perform significant work at provincial and territorial levels, there is no independent national body to advocate for children in the federal jurisdiction—Indigenous children, refugees or immigrants, or children of divorce—and for children in areas of joint federal, provincial, territorial, and Indigenous responsibility. As suggested by the Senate Standing

Committee on Human Rights, a Children's Commissioner could perform important roles in monitoring Canada's implementation of the Convention, conducting systemic investigations of child rights issues, seeking input from children, and collaborating with child advocacy offices to improve the practice of children's rights across the country.[41] But it is of crucial importance, said the Senate Committee, that the Commissioner be given the role of raising public awareness and educating Canadians about the Convention and children's rights.

Internationally, with strong mandates and appropriate resources, national children's commissioners or ombudspersons have proven to be effective.[42] In Norway, for example, the Children's Ombudsman has had considerable success in raising the profile of children's rights, increasing public support, and pressuring for government action in reforming laws and policies, consistent with the Convention.[43] Similar success can be achieved by a Commissioner in Canada. Through press releases, annual and special reports, and collaboration with child advocates and with the Canadian Council of Child and Youth Advocates, a Commissioner could increase public understanding of the Convention, increase knowledge of issues, and build a culture that is supportive of children's rights.

A national Children's Commissioner could provide leadership in numerous ways. First, the office could partner with the Council of Child and Youth Advocates, human rights commissions, and educators to implement children's rights education in schools, teacher training, professional training, and parenting education programs. Second, a Commissioner could work for Canada's signing and ratification of the Optional Protocol to the Convention on the Rights of the Child on a communications procedure. Approving this protocol would allow children or their representatives to bring forward complaints about violations of their rights (if not resolved domestically) to the UN Committee on the Rights of the Child.[44] The value of this procedure is that it would bring media and public attention to problems and further help to publicize the Convention. By 2017, fifty-one states had signed the protocol and thirty-six had ratified it. Canada has yet to act. Third, over the longer term and with the successful building of public support, a Commissioner could work with the child advocacy community for the wider implementation of the Convention and for its incorporation into Canadian law. Achieving incorporation in itself would be of great importance not only in giving children legal protections, but also in educating the public and promoting cultural change in support of the rights of the child.

*Incorporation of the Convention.* Where the Convention has been incorporated into legislation, it has had an important educational and cultural impact. Laura Lundy and her colleagues found that a significant outcome of incorporation was the elevation of the status of children and children's rights.[45] Their study involved an analysis of implementation in twelve countries—Canada, Australia, New Zealand, South Africa, Norway, Sweden, Denmark, Iceland, Belgium, Germany, Ireland, and Spain. The fullest incorporation of the Convention into law was in Belgium (in the constitution and legislation), Norway (in key legislation), and Spain (in the constitution and legislation). In those countries, citizens were most aware of the Convention, and children were more likely to be perceived as bearers of rights rather than as parental property or not-yets.

This impact should not be surprising. Although law has the general function of regulating society and protecting the rights and interests of citizens, it also functions as an educational force and an agent of cultural change. When the Convention is incorporated into law and when judges and officials make reference to it in applying the law, the principle of children's rights becomes more embedded in the culture. Thus, for Canada, incorporating the Convention into law would help build a culture of respect for children's rights.

## Prospects for Change

Over the long term, there is reason to believe that significant progress can be made. Since the Second World War, Canada's political culture and public attitudes have embraced rights consciousness, as evident in the establishment of the *Canadian Charter of Rights and Freedoms* and various human rights laws and policies. Canadians have become more supportive of the principle that human rights are of paramount importance.[46] With this growing consciousness has been increasing support for the rights of children, as reflected in Canada's approval of the Convention and, to a degree at least, the widening practice of children's rights. It is certainly true that progress has been halting, imperfect, and disappointing. But it also is true that respect for children's rights is greater now than it was when Canada ratified the Convention more than a quarter of a century ago.

In this environment of growing rights consciousness, children's rights advocates have reason to be optimistic. The Internet barely existed in 1991. Now it provides powerful tools for disseminating and exchanging information and strategies to promote the rights of the child. Social networking sites, for example, provide an effective means of participatory learning.[47] The immediacy of electronic interaction and the opportunity to ask questions have been identified as important factors in promoting knowledge, thought, and discussion about human rights.[48] The opportunities afforded by technology, together with the more formal education measures discussed above, suggest the possibility of extensive consciousness raising and social transformation.

One key message to be disseminated is that Canada has committed itself to implementing the rights of the child. It needs to be clearly explained to Canadians that the concept of children having human rights is far from radical. We are confident that once the majority of Canadians understand the reasonableness of children's rights, and their consistency with Canadian values, they will support efforts at their fuller implementation. At the same time, it is important that Canadians be educated about the fact that many children in Canada are denied the substance of their rights. Information needs to be conveyed about the negative consequences for children that are associated with living in poverty, poor health care, fetal alcohol spectrum disorder, maltreatment, sexual exploitation, and lack of participation. Learning about children's rights is powerful. But it is even more powerful when combined with learning about children who are deprived of their rights.

As we have noted at various points in this book, "Enjoyment of the substance of a right is socially guaranteed ... only if all social institutions, as well as individual persons, avoid depriving people of the substance of the right and some provide, if necessary, aid to anyone who has nevertheless been deprived of the substance of the right."[49] As a society, we are still quite a long way from this ideal. Ratification of the Convention cannot, in and of itself, guarantee that everyone will abandon proprietary notions about children, or that all children will be able to enjoy the substance of their rights in every social and institutional context in which they find themselves, including within families. This remains one of the most important challenges of children's rights for Canada.

In this book, we have argued that social toxins such as poverty and violence are as harmful to children's independent welfare and developmental interests as environmental toxins, and that both must be eradicated if Canada is to fulfill its commitments under the Convention. We have also argued that if Canada wishes to ensure the substance of the rights described in the Convention are socially guaranteed, an attitudinal or cultural shift is required concerning the moral and legal status of children. This is why article 42 of the Convention mandates children's rights education for children *and* adults.[50]

Canadian governments have not honoured their official commitment to children's rights. Canadians need to know that our country has been a laggard in addressing problems including our high child poverty and infant mortality rates, our lack of high-quality early childhood education and care programs, our lack of prevention programs, our failure to ban corporal punishment, and our failure to establish a national Children's Commissioner. Social change and social development of this nature tend to be generational in scope and to require ongoing children's rights education for young people in general and aspiring professionals in particular. We hope this book will help meet the challenge of children's rights for Canadian academics, policy-makers, parents, teachers, social workers, and human service professionals—for everyone who cares about and for children.

# Notes

## CHAPTER 1

1. J. Uechi, "Kitsilano Resident Shocked to See School Children Playing in the Water after Toxic Spill," *Vancouver Observer,* April 14, 2015, http://www.vancouverobserver.com/news/kitsilano-resident-shocked-see -schoolchildren-playing-water-after-toxic-spill.
2. P. J. Landrigan and L. R. Goldman, "Children's Vulnerability to Toxic Chemicals: A Challenge and Opportunity to Strengthen Health and Environmental Policy," *Health Affairs* 30, no. 5 (2011): 842–50, doi:10.1377/ hlthaff.2011.0151.
3. P. Grandjean and P. J. Landrigan, "Neurobehavioural Effects of Developmental Toxicity," *The Lancet Neurology* 13, no. 3 (2014): 330–38.
4. M. Wente, "A Ban on Spanking: Who'd Be Hurt Most?" *Globe and Mail,* December 21, 2015, http://www.theglobeandmail.com/opinion/a-ban-on -spanking-whod-be-hurt-the-most/article27896251/.
5. J. Garbarino, *Raising Children in a Socially Toxic Environment* (San Francisco: Jossey-Bass, 1995).
6. K. Ard and M. Fairbrother, "Pollution Prophylaxis? Social Capital and Environmental Inequality," *Social Science Quarterly* 98, no. 2 (2017): 584–607, doi/10.1111/ssqu.12324.
7. J. Bulanda and T. B. Johnson, "A Trauma-Informed Model for Empowerment Programs Targeting Vulnerable Youth," *Child and Adolescent Social Work Journal* 33 (2016): 303–12. doi:10.1007/s10560-015-0427-z.
8. S. Gaetz, T. Gulliver, and T. Richter, *The State of Homelessness in Canada* (Toronto: Homeless Hub Press, 2014); S. Gaetz, B. O'Grady, K. Buccieri, J. Karabanow, and A. Allyson, eds., *Youth Homelessness in Canada: Implications for Policy and Practice* (Toronto: Canadian Homelessness Research Network Press, 2013).
9. United Nations Committee on the Rights of the Child, *General Comment No. 21 on Children in Street Situations,* June 21, 2017; see also Terre des Hommes, *Children in Street Situations,* 2010, http://www.ohchr.org/Documents/Issues/ Children/Study/TerreDesHommes.pdf; see also D. Stoecklin, "The General Comment on Children in Street Situations: Insights into the Institutionalisation of Children's Rights," *International Journal of Children's Rights* 25, nos. 3–4 (2017): 817–69, doi:10.1163/15718182-02503014.

10. M. J. MacKenzie, E. Nicklas, J. Waldfogel, and J. Brooks-Gunn, "Corporal Punishment and Child Behavioural and Cognitive Outcomes through 5 Years of Age: Evidence from a Contemporary Urban Birth Cohort Study," *Infant and Child Development* 21, no. 1 (2012): 3–33, doi:10.1002/iccl.758; H. Jung et al., "Gendered Pathways from Child Abuse to Adult Crime through Internalizing and Externalizing Behaviours in Childhood and Adolescence," *Journal of Interpersonal Violence* (2015), doi:10.1177/0886260515596146; A. Oshri et al., "Developmental Pathways to Adolescent Cannabis Abuse and Dependence: Child Maltreatment, Emerging Personality, and Internalizing Versus Externalizing Psychopathology," *Psychology of Addictive Behaviours* 25, no. 4 (2011): 634–44.

11. K. Covell and R. B. Howe, *Children, Families and Violence: Challenges for Children's Rights* (London: Jessica Kingsley, 2009); R. E. Norman et al., "The Long-Term Health Consequences of Child Physical Abuse, Emotional Abuse, and Neglect: A Systematic Review and Meta-Analysis," *PLoS Medicine* 9, no. 11 (2012): e1001349, doi:10.1371/journal.pmed.1001349.

12. R. B. Howe and K. Covell, *Education in the Best Interests of the Child: A Children's Rights Perspective on Closing the Achievement Gap* (Toronto: University of Toronto Press, 2013), 53–67.

13. W. T. Church II, J. W. Jaggers, and J. K. Taylor, "Neighborhood, Poverty, and Negative Behaviour: An Examination of Differential Association and Social Control Theory," *Children and Youth Services Review* 34, no. 5 (2012): 1035–41.

14. Howe and Covell, *Education in the Best Interests of the Child*, 59–67.

15. L. J. Berlin et al., "The Effectiveness of Early Intervention: Examining Risk Factors and Pathways to Enhanced Development," *Preventive Medicine* 27, no. 2 (1998): 238–45, doi:10.1006/pmed.1998.0282.

16. A. Khanna, *2017 Report Card on Child and Family Poverty in Canada: A Poverty-Free Canada Requires Federal Leadership* (Toronto: Campaign 2000 / Family Service Toronto, November 2017), https://campaign2000.ca/wp-content/uploads/2017/11/EnglishNationalC2000ReportNov212017.pdf.

17. Covell and Howe, *Children, Families and Violence*, 32–62.

18. S. C. Aitken, "Children's Geographies: Tracing the Evolution and Involution of a Concept," *Geographical Review* 108, no. 1 (2018): 3–23, doi:10.1111/gere.12289; M. J. Meaney, "Epigenetics and the Biological Definition of Gene x Environment Interactions," *Child Development* 81, no. 1 (2010): 41–79.

19. M. Boivin and C. Hertzman, eds., *Early Childhood Development: Adverse Experiences and Developmental Health* (Ottawa: Royal Society of Canada, 2012).

20. Covell and Howe, *Children, Families and Violence*, 33–37.

21. Boivin and Hertzman, *Early Childhood Development*.

22. J. F. Cryan and T. G. Dinan, "Unraveling the Longstanding Scars of Early Neurodevelopmental Stress," *Biological Psychiatry* 74, no. 11 (2013): 788–89, doi:10.1016/j.biopsych.2013.10.004; P. A. Kelly et al., "Cortical Thickness,

Surface Area, and Gyrification Abnormalities in Children Exposed to Maltreatment: Neural Markers of Vulnerability?" *Biological Psychiatry* 74 (2013): 845–52, doi:10.1016/j.biopsych.2013.06.020.

23. R. Gilbert et al., "Burden and Consequences of Child Maltreatment in High-Income Countries," *The Lancet* 3 (2009): 68–81, doi:10.1016/S0140 -6736(08)61706-7; Norman et al., "The Long-Term Health Consequences."

24. C. P. Carr et al., "The Role of Early Life Stress in Adult Psychiatric Disorders: A Systematic Review According to Childhood Trauma Subtypes," *Journal of Nervous and Mental Disorders* 201, no. 12 (2013): 1007–20, doi:10.1097/NMD.0000000000000049; Norman et al., "The Long-Term Health Consequences."

25. Norman et al., "The Long-Term Health Consequences."

26. K. Kelly and M. Totten, *When Children Kill: A Social-Psychological Study of Youth Homicide* (Toronto: University of Toronto Press, 2002).

27. G. Rice and T. Thomas, "James Bulger—A Matter of Public Interest?" *International Journal of Children's Rights* 21 (2013): 1–11, doi:10.1163/ 157181812X633842.

28. A. Gillan, "Did Bad Parenting Turn Thompson and Venables into Killers?" *Guardian,* November 1, 2000, http://www.theguardian.com/uk/2000/nov/01/ bulger.familyandrelationships.

29. D. P. Boots and K. M. Heide, "Parricides in the Media: A Content Analysis of Available Reports across Cultures," *International Journal of Offender Therapy and Comparative Criminology* 50, no. 4 (2006): 418–45, doi:10.1177/0306624X05285103.

30. D. P. Farrington and D. West, "The Cambridge Study in Delinquent Behaviour (United Kingdom)," in *Prospective Longitudinal Research: An Empirical Basis for the Primary Prevention of Psychosocial Disorder,* ed. S. Mednick, A. Beart, and B. P. Backmann (Oxford: Oxford University Press, 1981).

31. J. Fallon, *The Psychopath Inside* (New York: Penguin, 2013).

32. J. S. Mejdoubi et al., "The Effect of VoorZorg, the Dutch Nurse-Family Partnership, on Child Maltreatment and Development," *PLOS ONE* 10, no. 4 (2015): e0120182, doi:10.1371/journal.pone.0120182; S. M. Jack et al., "Adapting, Piloting and Evaluating Complex Public Health Interventions: Lessons Learned from the Nurse-Family Partnership in Canadian Public Health Settings," *Health Promotion and Chronic Disease Prevention in Canada* 35, no. 8/9 (2015), doi.org/10.24095/hpcdp.35.8/9.07.

33. W. S. Barnett and E. Frede, "The Promise of Preschool: Why We Need Early Education for All," *American Educator* 34, no. 1 (2010): 21–29.

34. J. Heckman, R. Pinto, and P. A. Savelyev, "Understanding the Mechanisms through Which an Influential Early Childhood Program Boosted Adult Outcomes" (working paper, Vanderbilt University Department of Economics, 2012), http://www.accessecon.com/pubs/VUECON/VUECON-12-00011.

pdf; S. Loeb, "Missing the Target: We Need to Focus on Informal Care Rather than Preschool," *Evidence Speaks Report* 1, no. 19 (Washington, DC: Brookings Institute, 2016): 1–5.

35. Berlin et al., "The Effectiveness of Early Intervention"; L. A. Karoly et al., *Investing in Our Children: What We Know and Don't Know about the Costs and Benefits of Early Childhood Interventions* (Santa Monica, CA: Rand, 1998).

36. Covell and Howe, *Children, Families and Violence*, 32–94.

37. U. Bronfenbrenner, *Making Human Beings Human: Bioecological Perspectives on Human Development* (London: Sage, 2005).

38. Howe and Covell, *Education in the Best Interests of the Child*, 50–80.

39. Covell and Howe, *Children, Families and Violence*, 95–128.

40. M. E. Malakoff, J. M. Underhill, and E. Zigler, "Influence of Inner-City Environment Head Start Experience on Effectance Motivation," *American Journal of Orthopsychiatry* 68, no. 4 (1998): 630–38, doi:10.1037/h0080371.

41. R. M. Ryan and E. L. Deci, *Self-Determination Theory: Basic Psychological Needs in Motivation, Development, and Wellness* (New York: Guilford Press, 2017).

42. K. Covell, *Seen, Heard and Believed: What Youth Say about Violence* (Toronto: UNICEF, 2006).

43. M. Freeman, *A Commentary on the United Nations Convention on the Rights of the Child: Article 3—The Best Interests of the Child* (Leiden: Martinus Nijhoff, 2007), 16.

44. G. Lansdown, "Children's Rights to Participation and Protection: A Critique," in *Participation and Empowerment in Child Protection,* ed. C. Cloke and M. Davies (London: Pitman, 1995), 19–37.

45. UNICEF Innocenti Research Centre, "Promoting the Rights of Children with Disabilities," *Innocente Digest no. 13* (Florence, Italy: UNICEF Innocente Research Centre, 2007).

46. T. Waldock, ed., *A Question of Commitment: The Status of Children in Canada* (Waterloo, ON: Wilfrid Laurier University Press, 2018); M. D. Ruck, M. Peterson-Badali, and M. Freeman, eds., *Handbook of Children's Rights: Global and Multidisciplinary Perspectives* (New York: Routledge, 2017); J. Becker, *Campaigning for Children: Strategies for Advancing Children's Rights* (Stanford, CA: Stanford University Press, 2017); A. B. Smith, ed., *Enhancing Children's Rights: Connecting Research, Policy and Practice* (New York: Palgrave Macmillan, 2015); W. Vandenhole, ed., *Routledge International Handbook of Children's Rights Studies* (New York: Routledge, 2015); G. H. Jacobsen, ed., *Rights of Children in the Nordic Welfare States* (Copenhagen: NSU Press, 2015); M. Kanyal, ed., *Children's Rights 0–8: Promoting Participation in Education and Care* (New York: Routledge, 2014); E. K. M. Tisdall, A. M. Gadda, and U. M. Butler, eds., *Children and Young People's Participation and Its Transformative Potential* (New York: Palgrave Macmillan, 2014); K. Hanson and O. Nieuwenhuys, eds., *Reconceptualizing Children's Rights in International Development: Living Rights,*

*Social Justice, Translations* (New York: Cambridge University Press, 2013);
C. Butler, ed., *Child Rights: The Movement, International Law, and Opposition*
(West Lafayette, IN: Purdue University Press, 2012); M. Liebel, ed., *Children's
Rights from Below: Cross-Cultural Perspectives* (New York: Palgrave Macmillan,
2012); C. Bernard and J. Shea, eds., *Giving Children a Voice: The Transforming
Role of the Family* (Newcastle upon Tyne, UK: Cambridge Scholars, 2009);
T. O'Neill and D. Zinga, eds., *Children's Rights: Multidisciplinary Approaches
to Participation and Protection* (Toronto: University of Toronto Press, 2008);
K. Covell and R. B. Howe, eds., *A Question of Commitment: Children's Rights
in Canada* (Waterloo, ON: Wilfrid Laurier University Press, 2007).

## CHAPTER 2

1. S. Svidal, "Government Endorses UN Convention on Children's Rights—Sort
   Of," *Alberta Teachers Association News* 33, no. 16 (1999).
2. R. Dworkin, *Taking Rights Seriously* (Cambridge, MA: Harvard University
   Press, 1977).
3. R. B. Howe, "Evolving Policy on Children's Rights in Canada," in *Readings in
   Child Development*, ed. K. Covell (Toronto: Nelson, 1991), 4–27.
4. R. Joyal, *Les enfants, la société et l'état au Québec, 1608–1989* (Montreal:
   Hurtubise, 1999); D. Marshall, *The Social Origins of the Welfare State: Quebec
   Families, Compulsory Education, and Family Allowances, 1940–1955* (Waterloo,
   ON: Wilfrid Laurier University Press, 2006); Commission des droits de la
   personne et droits de la jeunesse, *Les droits des enfants et des jeunes*, 2018,
   http://www.cdpdj.qc.ca/fr/droits-de-la-personne/vos-droits-au-quebec/Pages/
   enfants.aspx.
5. S. N. Hart, "From Property to Person Status: Historical Perspective
   on Children's Rights," *American Psychologist* 46, no. 1 (1991): 53–59;
   M. A. Mason, *From Father's Property to Children's Rights* (New York:
   Columbia University Press, 1994).
6. N. Bala, "Setting the Context: Child Welfare Law in Canada," in *Child
   Welfare: Connecting Research, Policy, and Practice,* ed. K. Kufeldt and
   B. McKenzie (Waterloo: Wilfrid Laurier University Press, 2011), 2.
7. A. Rowland, F. Gerry, and M. Stanton, "Physical Punishment of Children:
   Time to End the Defence of Reasonable Chastisement in the UK, USA and
   Australia," *International Journal of Children's Rights* 25, no. 1 (2017), 165–95,
   doi:10.1163/15718182-02501007.
8. S. Bell, *Young Offenders and Youth Justice: A Century after the Fact* (Toronto:
   Nelson, 2012), 9–16.
9. N. Sutherland, *Children in English-Canadian Society: Framing the Twentieth
   Century Consensus* (Waterloo: Wilfrid Laurier University Press, 2000).
10. Bala, "Setting the Context," 2–4.

11. Bell, *Young Offenders and Youth Justice*, 33–37.

12. R. J. Thomlison and C. E. Foote, "Children and the Law in Canada: The Shifting Balance of Children's, Parents' and State's Rights," *Journal of Comparative Family Studies* 18, no. 2 (1987): 231–45.

13. R. N. Bezeau and J. R. Hoskins, *The Fallen Feather* (Surrey, BC: Fallen Feather Productions, 2007), video recording; T. King, *The Inconvenient Indian: A Curious Account of Native People in North America* (Toronto: Anchor, 2012); Truth and Reconciliation Commission of Canada, *Final Report of the Truth and Reconciliation Commission of Canada, Vol. One: Summary—Honouring the Truth, Reconciling for the Future* (Toronto: Lorimer, 2015).

14. A. B. Smith, *Children's Rights: Towards Social Justice* (New York: Momentum, 2016); J. Wall, *Children's Rights: Today's Global Challenge* (Lanham, MD: Rowman & Littlefield, 2017).

15. Bell, *Young Offenders and Youth Justice*, 40–61.

16. Thomlison and Foote, "Children and the Law," 233–35; Bala, "Setting the Context," 11–12.

17. S. Detrick, *A Commentary on the United Nations Convention on the Rights of the Child* (The Hague: Martinus Nijhoff, 1999).

18. "UN Lauds Somalia as Country Ratifies Landmark Children's Rights Treaty," UN News Centre, January 15, 2015, http://www.un.org/apps/news/story .asp?NewsID=49845#.Wn2o3WaZOTc; "UN Lauds South Sudan as Country Ratifies Landmark Children's Rights Treaty," UN News Centre, May 4, 2015, http://www.un.org/apps/news/story.asp?NewsID=50759#.Wn2pY2aZOTc.

19. Canadian Council on Children and Youth, *Admittance Restricted: The Child as Citizen in Canada* (Ottawa: Canadian Council on Children and Youth, 1978), 153–60.

20. B. MacLaurin and N. Bala, "Children in Care," in *Canadian Child Welfare Law*, ed. N. Bala et al. (Toronto: Thompson, 2004), 116–19.

21. M. Guggenheim, *What's Wrong with Children's Rights* (Cambridge, MA: Harvard University Press, 2005); P. Alderson, "Common Criticisms of Children's Rights and 25 Years of the IJCR," *International Journal of Children's Rights* 25, no. 2 (2017): 307–19, doi:10.1163/15718182-02502001.

22. M. Hill and K. Tisdale, *Children and Society* (London: Addison-Wesley Longman, 1997), 26–28; L. Purdy, *In Their Best Interest? The Case against Equal Rights for Children* (Ithaca, NY: Cornell University Press, 1992).

23. For example, R. Farson, *Birthrights* (Harmondsworth, UK: Penguin, 1978).

24. For example, M. Freeman, *The Rights and Wrongs of Children* (London: Frances Pinter, 1983), 45–48.

25. N. Cantwell, "The Origins, Development and Significance of the United Nations Convention on the Rights of the Child," in *The United Nations Convention on the Rights of the Child,* ed. S. Detrick (Dordrecht: Martinus Nijhoff, 1992), 26.

26. T. Hammarberg, "The UN Convention on the Rights of the Child—and How to Make It Work," *Human Rights Quarterly* 12, no. 1 (1990): 97–105.

27. J. Eekelaar, "The Role of the Best Interests Principle in Decisions Affecting Children and Decisions about Children," *International Journal of Children's Rights* 23 (2015): 3–26, doi:10.1163/15718182-02301003; L.-G. Sund and M. Vackermo, "The Interest Theory, Children's Rights and Social Authorities," *International Journal of Children's Rights* 23 (2015): 752–68, doi:10.1163/15718182-02304002; S. C. Grover, *Children Defending Their Human Rights under the CRC Communication Procedure: On Strengthening the Convention on the Rights of the Child Complaint Mechanism* (Berlin: Springer, 2015), doi:10.1007/978-3-662-44443-6_3.

28. K. Marshall, *Children's Rights in the Balance: The Participation-Protection Debate* (Edinburgh: Stationery Office, 1997), 8–11.

29. Ibid., 13–16.

30. G. Melton, "The Child's Rights to a Family Environment," *American Psychologist* 51, no. 12 (December 1996): 1234–38.

31. E. Peters and C. M. Kamp Dush, *Marriage and Family Perspectives and Complexities* (New York: Columbia University Press, 2009).

32. P. Veerman, "The Ageing of the UN Convention on the Rights of the Child," in *The Future of Children's Rights,* ed. M. Freeman (Leiden: Brill Nijhoff, 2014), 16–49.

33. R. Hodgkin and P. Newell, *Implementation Handbook for the Convention on the Rights of the Child* (New York: UNICEF, 2007), 49–50.

34. Senate of Canada, Standing Committee on Human Rights, *Children: Silenced Citizens* (Ottawa: Senate Standing Committee on Human Rights, 2007), 8–10 and 40–43.

35. L. Lundy, U. Kilkelly, and B. Byrne, "Incorporation of the United Nations Convention on the Rights of the Child in Law: A Comparative Review," *International Journal of Children's Rights* 21 (2013): 442–63, doi:10.1163/15718182-55680028.

36. T. M. Collins, "The Significance of Different Approaches to Human Rights Monitoring: A Case Study of Child Rights," *International Journal of Human Rights* 12, no. 2 (2008): 159–87, doi:10.1080/13642980801899626; Hodgkin and Newell, *Implementation Handbook*, 637–56.

37. R. B. Howe and K. Covell, *Empowering Children: Children's Rights as a Pathway to Citizenship* (Toronto: University of Toronto Press, 2007), 29–35; R. Mitchell, "Postmodern Reflections on the UNCRC: Towards Utilizing Article 42 as an International Compliance Indicator," *International Journal of Children's Rights*, 13 (2005): 315–31.

38. Howe and Covell, *Empowering Children*, 37–40.

39. Canadian Coalition for the Rights of Children, *The UN Convention on the Rights of the Child: The Canadian NGO Response* (Ottawa: CCRC, 1994).

40. UN Committee on the Rights of the Child, *UN Committee on the Rights of the Child: Concluding Observations: Canada*, June 20, 1995, CRC/C/15/Add.37, http://www.refworld.org/docid/3ae6af5a14.html.

41. L. A. White, "Understanding Canada's Lack of Progress in Implementing the UN Convention on the Rights of the Child," *International Journal of Children's Rights* 22 (2014): 164–88, doi:10.1163/15718182-02201002.

42. R. B. Howe, "Introduction," in *A Question of Commitment: Children's Rights in Canada*, ed. R. B. Howe and K. Covell (Waterloo: Wilfrid Laurier University Press, 2007), 4–5.

43. Senate Standing Committee, *Children: Silenced Citizens*, 12–13; Howe, "Introduction," 11–12.

44. Howe, "Introduction," 12; L. Monsebraaten, "Ontario Introduces 'Historic' Changes to Child-Protection Laws," *Toronto Star,* December 8, 2016, https://www.thestar.com/news/gta/2016/12/08/ontario-introduces-historic-changes-to-child-protection-laws.html.

45. See *Baker v. Canada (Minister of Citizenship and Immigration),* [1999] 2 S.C.R. 817, which we discuss in detail in Chapter 4.

46. J. Brunnee and S. Toope, "A Hesitant Embrace: Baker and the Application of International Law by Canadian Courts," in *Canadian Yearbook of International Law 40,* ed. D. M. McRae (Vancouver: UBC Press, 2002), 3–60.

47. Senate Standing Committee, *Children: Silenced Citizens*, 48–49; Howe, "Introduction," 6–7.

48. Senate Standing Committee, *Children: Silenced Citizens*, 14–16.

49. S. Toope, "The Convention on the Rights of the Child: Implications for Canada," in *Children's Rights: A Comparative Perspective,* ed. M. Freeman (Aldershot, UK: Dartmouth, 1996), 51–52.

50. E. Y. Cho, "Child Benefit Portfolios Across OECD Countries," *Social Indicators Research* 132, no. 3 (2017): 1099–1115, doi:10.1007/s11205-016-1334-1.

51. J. Himes, *Implementing the United Nations Convention on the Rights of the Child* (Florence: UNICEF International Child Development Centre, 1992).

52. T. M. Collins and L. Pearson, "The Role and Impact of Civil Society upon Child Rights in Canada," *The Philanthropist* 23, no. 4 (2011): 451–61.

53. Senate Standing Committee, *Children: Silenced Citizens*, 193–98; Howe, "Introduction," 8; Howe and Covell, *Empowering Children*, 35–42.

54. C. Goodwin-De Faria and V. Marinos, "Youth Understanding and Assertion of Legal Rights: Examining the Roles of Age and Power," *International Journal of Children's Rights* 20 (2012): 343–64, doi:10.1163/157181812X652607.

55. M. Clarke, "The Rights and Wrongs of Canada's Policies for Children," in *Human Rights in Canada: Into the 1990s and Beyond*, ed. R. Cholewinski (Ottawa: Human Rights Research and Education Centre, 1990), 198–200.

56. M. Friendly, "Child Care and the Rights of Young Children," in *On the Right Side: Canada and the Convention on the Rights of the Child,* ed. Canadian Council on Children and Youth (Ottawa: CCCY, 1990), 34–37.

57. Canadian Coalition, *The UN Convention*, 7–8.
58. A. Genereux, "Corporal Punishment: Is it Violence Against Children?" in *On the Right Side*, 29–33.
59. N. Bala, "Pornography and Prostitution: Does Canada Comply with the Convention?" in *On the Right Side*, 22–26.
60. Canadian Coalition, *The UN Convention*, 8–9.
61. Canadian Coalition for the Rights of Children, *The United Nations Convention on the Rights of the Child: The Views of Canadian Youth* (Ottawa: CCRC, 1990).

## CHAPTER 3

1. For more detailed accounts of rights (or claims) as correlates of duties, see W. N. Hohfeld, "Some Fundamental Legal Conceptions as Applied in Judicial Reasoning," *Yale Law Journal* 23 (1914): 16–59; M. Cowden, *Children's Rights: From Philosophy to Public Policy* (Basingstoke, UK: Palgrave Macmillan, 2016), 27–33; J. G. Dwyer, *The Relationship Rights of Children* (Cambridge: Cambridge University Press, 2006), 291–307; L. Ferguson, "Not Merely Rights for Children but Children's Rights: The Theory Gap and the Assumption of the Importance of Children's Rights," *International Journal of Children's Rights* 27 (2013): 177–208, doi:10.1163/15718182-55680015; and J. C. Blokhuis, "Student Rights and the Special Characteristics of the School Environment in American Jurisprudence," *Journal of Philosophy of Education* 49, no. 1 (2015): 65–85, doi:10.1111/1467-9752.12096.
2. I. Kant, *The Metaphysics of Morals,* trans. M. Gregor (1797; repr. Cambridge: Cambridge University Press, 1996), 64–65.
3. J. S. Mill, *On Liberty,* 1859, reprinted as "Education and the Limits of State Authority," in *Philosophy of Education: An Anthology,* ed. R. Curren (Oxford: Blackwell, 2006), 157.
4. J. S. Mill, *On Liberty*, 158.
5. J. S. Mill, "Utilitarianism," in *Great Books of the Western World,* ed. R. M. Hutchins, vol. 43 (Chicago: Encyclopaedia Britannica, 1952), 470–71.
6. H. Steiner, *An Essay on Rights* (Oxford: Blackwell, 1994), 93.
7. J. A. Ballentine, *Ballentine's Law Dictionary: With Pronunciations*, 3rd ed., ed. W. S. Anderson (San Francisco: Bancroft-Whitney, 1969).
8. S. Grover, *The Child's Right to Legal Standing* (Toronto: LexisNexis, 2008).
9. J. Feinberg, "The Nature and Value of Rights," *Journal of Value Inquiry* 4 (1970): 251.
10. J. C. Blokhuis, "Whose Custody Is It, Anyway? Homeschooling from a *Parens Patriae* Perspective," *Theory and Research in Education* 8, no. 2 (2010): 212.
11. D. Lovinsky and J. Gagne, *Legal Representation of Children in Canada* (Ottawa: Department of Justice, 2016).
12. *Code civil du Québec*, S.Q. 1991, c. 64a, 159.

13. CBC News, "Quebec Dad Sued by Daughter after Grounding Loses His Appeal," April 7, 2009, http://www.cbc.ca/news/canada/montreal/quebec-dad-sued-by-daughter-after-grounding-loses-his-appeal-1.803756.

14. Blokhuis, "Student Rights," 79.

15. H. Shue, *Basic Rights* (Princeton, NJ: Princeton University Press, 1980), 75 (emphasis added).

16. *Smoke-Free Ontario Act*, S.O. 1994, c. 10.

17. K. Covell, R. B. Howe, and A. McGillivray, "Implementing Children's Education Rights in Schools," in *Handbook of Children's Rights: Global and Multidisciplinary Perspectives,* ed. M. D. Ruck, M. Peterson-Badali, and M. Freeman (New York: Routledge, 2017), 306.

18. Curateur public du Québec, "L'émancipation du mineur," 2017, http://www.curateur.gouv.qc.ca/cura/fr/mineur/tutelle-biens/droits/emancipation/index.html.

19. *Family Law Act*, R.S.O. 1990, c. F.3.

20. *Education Act*, R.S.O. 1990, c. E.2.

21. *Education Act*, R.S.O. 1990, c. E.2, as amended 2006, c. 28, s. 5(1).

22. *Highway Traffic Act*, R.S.O. 1990, c. H.8.

23. *Smoke-Free Ontario Act*, S.O. 1994, c. 10; see also Ministry of Labour, "In the Workplace: FAQs," 2016, https://www.labour.gov.on.ca/english/hs/faqs/workplace.php.

24. Blokhuis, "Student Rights," 69.

25. National Defence and the Canadian Armed Forces, "FAQs," 2017, http://www.forces.ca/en/page/faq-220.

26. *Tackling Violent Crime Act*, S.C. 2008, c. 6.

27. *Health Care Consent Act*, 1996, S.O. 1996, c. 2 (Schedule A); see . J. C. Blokhuis and Amy Smoke, "The Extraordinary Cases of J. J. and Makayla Sault," in *The Status of Children in Canada: A Children's Rights Perspective,* ed. T. Waldock (Waterloo, ON: Wilfrid Laurier University Press, 2018).

28. Blokhuis, "Whose Custody," 200.

29. Blokhuis, "Student Rights," 70.

30. Cowden (*Children's Rights*, 77) distinguishes between latent capacity, capacity, competence, and "ableness."

31. *Children's Law Reform Act*, R.S.O. 1990, c. 12, s. 20(2).

32. M. Liebel, "From Evolving Capacities to Evolving Capabilities: Contextualizing Children's Rights," in D. Stoecklin and J.-M. Bonvin (eds.), *Children's Rights and the Capability Approach, Children's Wellbeing: Indicators and Research* 8 (2014), 67–84, doi:10.1007/978-94-017-9091-84; N. Peleg, "Reconceptualising the Child's Right to Development: Children and the Capability Approach," *International Journal of Children's Rights* 21 (2013): 523–42, doi:10.1163/15718182-02103003.

33. Blokhuis, "Student Rights," 74.

34. F. C. Ensign, *Compulsory School Attendance and Child Labor* (Iowa City: Athens Press, 1921); L. Kotin and W. F. Aikman, *Legal Foundations of Compulsory School Attendance* (Port Washington, NY: Kennikat Press, 1980); M. Imber et al., *Education Law,* 5th ed. (New York: Routledge, 2014); Blokhuis, "Student Rights," 74.

35. R. Curren and J. C. Blokhuis, "The *Prima Facie* Case against Homeschooling," *Public Affairs Quarterly* 25, no. 1 (2011): 1–19; P. Kitcher, "Public Knowledge and Its Discontents," *Theory and Research in Education* 9, no. 2 (2011): 103–124; Blokhuis, "Student Rights," 74.

36. K. Hammer, "Father Sues Ontario School Board for Not Accommodating His Religious Beliefs," *Globe and Mail* (Toronto), September 10, 2012, http://www.theglobeandmail.com/news/toronto/father-sues-ontario-school-board-for-not-accommodating-his-religious-beliefs/article4533186/.

37. R. Curren, "Developmental Liberalism," *Educational Theory* 56, no. 4 (2006), 456–57.

38. I. Kant, *Grounding for the Metaphysics of Morals*, 3rd ed. trans. J. W. Ellington (1785; repr. Indianapolis, IN: Hackett, 1993), 36.

39. J. Griffin, "Do Children Have Rights?" in *The Moral and Political Status of Children*, ed. D. Archard and C. M. Macleod (New York: Oxford University Press, 2002), 20.

40. Curren and Blokhuis, "The *Prima Facie* Case," 9.

41. L.-G. Sund and M. Vackermo, "The Interest Theory, Children's Rights and Social Authorities," *International Journal of Children's Rights* 23 (2015): 752–68, doi:10.1163/15718182-02304002; L-G. Sund, "The Rights of the Child as Legally Protected Interests," *International Journal of Children's Rights* 14 (2006): 327–37, doi:10.1163/1571811806779050159; S. Brennan, "Children's Choices or Children's Interests: Which Do Their Rights Protect?" in *The Moral and Political Status of Children*, ed. D. Archard and C. M. Macleod (New York: Oxford University Press, 2002), 53–69.

42. D. Archard, *Children: Rights and Childhood*, 3rd ed. (New York: Routledge, 2015), 58.

43. K. Covell, R. B. Howe, and A. McGillivray, "Children's Education Rights in Schools," in *Handbook of Children's Rights: Global and Multidisciplinary Perspectives*, ed. M.D. Ruck, M. Peterson-Badali, and M. Freeman (New York: Routledge, 2017), 306.

44. Curren, "Developmental Liberalism," 457; citing J. Locke, *A Letter Concerning Toleration* (1689; repr. New York: Prometheus Books, 1990) and J. Locke, *Second Treatise of Government* (1690; repr. Indianapolis, IN: Hackett, 1980).

45. J. Wall, *Children's Rights: Today's Global Challenge* (Lanham, MD: Rowman & Littlefield, 2017), 11.

46. K. Strike, *Liberty and Learning* (New York: St. Martin's Press, 1982), 132.

47. Griffin, "Do Children Have Rights?" 20.

48. I. Robeyns, "The Capability Approach," *Stanford Encyclopedia of Philosophy,* 2016, https://plato.stanford.edu/entries/capability-approach/; M. Nussbaum, *Creating Capabilities* (Cambridge, MA: Belknap Press, 2011); A. Sen, *Development as Freedom* (New York: Oxford University Press, 1999); M. Biggieri, J. Ballet, and F. Comim (eds.), *Children and the Capability Approach* (Basingstoke, UK: Palgrave Macmillan, 2011); N. Peleg, "Reconceptualising the Child's Right to Development: Children and the Capability Approach," *International Journal of Children's Rights* 21 (2013): 523–42, doi:10.1163/15718182-02103003.

49. R. M. Ryan, R. Curren, and E. L. Deci, "What Humans Need: Flourishing in Aristotelian Philosophy and Self-Determination Theory," in *The Best Within Us: Positive Psychology Perspectives on Eudaimonia,* ed. A. S. Waterman (Washington, DC: American Psychological Association, 2013), 57–75.

50. Mill, *On Liberty*, 9.

51. Strike, *Liberty and Learning*, 127.

52. D. Archard and C. M. Macleod, "Introduction," in *The Moral and Political Status of Children*, ed. D. Archard and C. M. Macleod (Oxford: Oxford University Press, 2002), 2.

53. J. Feinberg, "The Child's Right to an Open Future," in Curren, *Philosophy of Education,* 113.

54. Strike, *Liberty and Learning*, 128.

55. R. S. Peters, "Education as Initiation," in Curren, *Philosophy of Education,* 57.

56. R. B. Howe, "Introduction," in *Children's Rights in Canada: A Question of Commitment*, ed. R. B. Howe and K. Covell (Waterloo, ON: Wilfrid Laurier University Press, 2007), 5.

## CHAPTER 4

1. We have not discussed the following six Supreme Court decisions in which the Convention was invoked because it was inapplicable in the circumstances: *M.M. v. United States of Americ*a, [2015] S.C.J. no. 62; *Kazemi Estate v. Islamic Republic of Iran*, [2014] S.C.J. no. 62; *R. v. C.D.* and *R. v. C.D.K.*, [2005] S.C.J. no. 79; *Trinity Western University v. British Columbia College of Teachers*, [2001] S.C.J. no. 32; *United States of America v. Burns*, [2001] S.C.J. no. 8; and *V.W. v. D.S.*, [1996] S.C.J. no. 53.

2. *Youth Criminal Justice Act,* S.C. 2002, c. 1.

3. United Nations, Universal Declaration of Human Rights, 1948, http://www.un.org/en/universal-declaration-human-rights/.

4. League of Nations, Geneva Declaration on the Rights of the Child, 1924, http://www.un-documents.net/gdrc1924.htm.

5. Office of the UN High Commissioner for Human Rights, "Fact Sheet no. 2," June 1996, http://www.ohchr.org/_layouts/15/WopiFrame.aspx?sourcedoc

=/Documents/Publications/FactSheet2Rev.1en.pdf&action=default
&DefaultItemOpen=1.

6. W. N. Hohfeld, "Some Fundamental Legal Conceptions as Applied in Judicial Reasoning," *Yale Law Journal* 23 (1914): 16–59. For a detailed account of rights (or Hohfeldian claims) as correlates of duties, see M. Cowden, *Children's Rights: From Philosophy to Public Policy* (Basingstoke, UK: Palgrave Macmillan, 2016), 27–33.

7. J. C. Blokhuis, "Student Rights and the Special Characteristics of the School Environment in American Jurisprudence," *Journal of Philosophy of Education* 49, no. 1 (2015): 76, doi:10.1111/1467-9752.12096.

8. L. Lundy, U. Kilkelly, and B. Bryne, "Incorporation of the United Nations Convention on the Rights of the Child in Law: A Comparative Review," *International Journal of Children's Rights* 21 (2013): 442–63, doi:10.1163/15718182-55680028.

9. H. L. A. Hart, *The Concept of Law*, 3rd ed. (New York: Oxford University Press, 2012), 84.

10. E. M. Hafner-Burton, "Sticks and Stones: Naming and Shaming the Human Rights Enforcement Problem," *International Organization* 62 (2008): 689–716, doi:10.1017/S0020818308080247.

11. Michael Ignatieff, ed., *American Exceptionalism and Human Rights* (Princeton, NJ: Princeton University Press, 2005).

12. J. C. Blokhuis, "Whose Custody Is It, Anyway? Homeschooling from a *Parens Patriae* Perspective," *Theory and Research in Education* 8, no. 2 (2010): 214.

13. J. Feinberg, "The Nature and Value of Rights," *Journal of Value Inquiry* 4 (1970): 251.

14. S. Clarke, "Children's Rights: Canada" (Washington, DC: Library of Congress), http://www.loc.gov/law/help/child-rights/canada.php.

15. J.-F. Noël, "The Convention on the Rights of the Child" (Ottawa: Department of Justice, 2015), http://www.justice.gc.ca/eng/rp-pr/fl-lf/divorce/crc-crde/conv2a.html.

16. L. A. White, "Understanding Canada's Lack of Progress in Implementing the UN Convention on the Rights of the Child," *International Journal of Children's Rights* 22 (2014): 164–88, doi:10.1163/15718182-02201002.

17. N. Bala, "Child Welfare Law in Canada: An Introduction," in *Canadian Child Welfare Law*, ed. N. Bala et al. (Toronto: Thompson, 2004), 4–5.

18. T. R. van Geel, *Understanding Supreme Court Opinions* (New York: Longman, 2009), 11.

19. M. Morin, "La compétence *parens patriae* et le droit privé québécois: Un emprunt inutile, un affront à l'histoire," *Revue du barreau* 50, no. 5 (1990): 827–923.

20. R. Sullivan, *Driedger on the Construction of Statutes*, 3rd ed. (Toronto: Butterworths, 1994), 330; R. Sullivan, *Statutory Interpretation* (Toronto: Irwin

Law, 2007); see also S. Beaulac and P.-A. Côté, "Driedger's 'Modern Principle' at the Supreme Court of Canada: Interpretation, Justification, Legitimization," *Revue Juridique Thémis* (2007), https://papers.ssrn.com/sol3/papers2.cfm ?abstract_id=987199.

21. *Immigration and Refugee Protection Act*, S.C. 2001, c. 27, s. 25(1).

22. Customs and Immigration Canada, "Humanitarian and Compassionate Assessment: Best Interests of a Child," March 2, 2016, http://www.cic.gc.ca/ english/resources/tools/perm/hc/processing/child.asp.

23. R.S.C., 1985, c. C-4.

24. UN Committee on the Rights of the Child, *Consideration of Reports Submitted by State Parties under Article 44 of the Convention*, 2003, 34th Session, CRC/C/15/ Add. 215, paras. 32–33; cited by Justice Louise Arbour at para. 188.

25. *Youth Criminal Justice Act*, S.C. 2002, c. 1.

26. J. V. Roberts and N. Bala, "Understanding Sentencing under the Youth Criminal Justice Act," *Alberta Law Review* 41 (September 2003): 396; cited by Justice Louise Charron at para. 19.

27. J. Eekelaar, "The Interests of the Child and the Child's Wishes: The Role of Dynamic Self-Determination," *International Journal of Law and the Family* 8 (1994): 42–61, doi:10.1093/lawfam/8.1.42.

## CHAPTER 5

1. M. Freeman, "Article 3: The Best Interests of the Child," in *A Commentary on the United Nations Convention on the Rights of the Child,* ed. A. Allen et al. (Leiden: Martinus Nijhoff, 2007), 1–79; T. Hammarberg, "The Principle of the Best Interests of the Child: What It Means and What It Demands from Adults" (lecture, Warsaw, May 30, 2008), Council of Europe, https://wcd .coe.int/wcd/ViewDoc.jsp?id=1304019; R. B. Howe and K. Covell, *Education in the Best Interests of the Child: A Children's Rights Perspective on Closing the Achievement Gap* (Toronto: University of Toronto Press, 2013), 20–28.

2. K. Battle, "Child Poverty: The Evolution and Impact of Child Benefits," in *A Question of Commitment: Children's Rights in Canada*, ed. R.B. Howe and K. Covell (Waterloo, ON: Wilfrid Laurier University Press, 2007), 21.

3. M. Black, *Children First* (New York: Oxford University Press, 1996).

4. Government of Canada, *Brighter Futures: Canada's Action Plan for Children* (Ottawa: Ministry of Supply and Services, 1992).

5. M. Daly, "Parenting Support as a Policy Field: An Analytic Framework," *Social Policy & Society* 14, no. 4 (2015): 597–608, doi:10.1017/ S1474746415000226.

6. Battle, "Child Poverty," 21–44; K. Battle, *Child Benefits in Canada: Politics versus Policy* (Ottawa: Caledon Institute of Social Policy, 2015), http:// www.caledoninst.org/Publications/PDF/1074ENG.pdf.

7.  K. Battle, *Child Benefits and the 2015 Federal Budget* (Ottawa: Caledon Institute of Social Policy, 2015), http://www.caledoninst.org/Publications/PDF/1064ENG.pdf.

8.  UNICEF Innocenti Research Centre, "Measuring Child Poverty: New League Tables of Child Poverty in the World's Rich Countries," *Innocenti Report Card 10* (Florence, Italy: UNICEF Innocenti Research Centre, 2012).

9.  P. Albanese, *Children in Canada Today* (Toronto: Oxford University Press, 2016), 183–86.

10. Campaign 2000, *2017 Report Card on Child and Family Poverty in Canada* (Toronto: Campaign 2000, 2017).

11. Ibid.

12. Food Banks Canada, *HungerCount 2016* (Toronto: Food Banks Canada, 2016), https://www.foodbankscanada.ca/hungercount2016.

13. UNICEF Office of Research, "Fairness for Children: A League Table of Inequality in Child Well-Being in Rich Countries," *Innocenti Report Card 13* (Florence: UNICEF Office of Research—Innocenti, 2016), 4–5, https://www.unicef-irc.org/publications/pdf/RC13_eng.pdf.

14. Albanese, *Children in Canada Today*, 190–97.

15. S. Heyman, K. Penrose, and A. Earle, "Meeting Children's Needs: How Does the United States Measure Up?" *Merrill-Palmer Quarterly* 52, no. 2 (2006): 189–215; R. B. Howe and K. Covell, *Children, Families and Violence* (London: Jessica Kingsley, 2009): 165–67; G. Olsen, *The Politics of the Welfare State* (Toronto: Oxford University Press, 2002).

16. OECD, *Public Spending on Family Benefits* (October 2013). OECD Family Database, http://www.oecd.org/els/family/PF1_1_Public_spending_on_family_benefits.pdf.

17. U. Bronfenbrenner, *Making Human Beings Human: Bioecological Perspectives on Human Development* (London: Sage, 2005); W. E. Cross, Jr., "Ecological Factors in Human Development," *Child Development* 88, no. 3 (2017): 767–69, doi:10.1111/cdev.12784; J. R. H. Tudge et al., "Still Misused After All These Years? A Reevaluation of the Uses of Bronfenbrenner's Bioecological Theory of Human Development," *Journal of Family Theory & Review* 8, no. 4 (2016): 427–45, doi:10.1111/jftr.12165.

18. Albanese, *Children in Canada Today*, 195–97; M. Eichler, *Family Shifts: Families, Policies and Gender Equality* (Toronto: Oxford University Press, 1997), 123–64; Howe and Covell, *Children, Families and Violence*, 196–208; M. Sandbæk, "European Policies to Promote Children's Rights and Combat Child Poverty," *International Journal of Environmental Research and Public Health* 14 (2017): 837–51, doi:10.3390/ijerph14080837.

19. Eichler, *Family Shifts*, 88–109; Howe and Covell, *Children, Families and Violence*, 208–214.

20. H. Yoshikawa, J. L. Aber, and W. R. Beardsley, "The Effects of Poverty on the Mental, Emotional, and Behavioural Health of Children and Youth," *American Psychological Association* 67, no. 4 (2012): 272–84, doi:10.1037/a0028015.

21. C. Blair et al., "Cumulative Effects of Early Poverty on Cortisol in Young Children: Moderation by Autonomic Nervous System Activity," *Psychneuroendroncrinology* 38, no. 11 (2013): 2666–75.

22. T. M. Marteau and P. A. Hall, "Breadlines, Brains and Behaviour," *British Medical Journal* 347 (November 12, 2013): 86750, doi:10,1136/bmj.f6750.

23. Marteau and Hall, "Breadlines, Brains and Behaviour"; C. C. Raver, C. Blair, and M. Willoughby, "Poverty as a Predictor of Executive Function: New Perspectives on Models of Differential Susceptibility," *Developmental Psychology* 49, no. 2 (2013): 292–304.

24. D. A. Hackman et al., "Mapping the Trajectory of Socioeconomic Disparity in Working Memory: Parental and Neighborhood Factors," *Child Development* 85, no. 4 (2014): 1433–45, doi:10.1111/cdev.12242.

25. D. A. Hackman et al., "Socioeconomic Status and Executive Function: Developmental Trajectories and Mediation," *Developmental Science* 18, no. 5 (2015): 686–702, doi:10.1111/desc.12246.

26. Marteau and Hall, "Breadlines, Brains and Behaviour."

27. A. McEwen and J. M. Stewart, "The Relationship between Income and Children's Outcomes: A Synthesis of Canadian Evidence," *Canadian Public Policy* (2014): 99–109, doi:10.3138/cppCRDCN.

28. G. W. Evans and P. Kim, "Childhood Poverty, Chronic Stress, Self-Regulation, and Coping," *Child Development Perspectives* 7, no. 1 (2013): 43–48.

29. E. T. B. Mathis and K. L. Bierman, "Dimensions of Parenting Associated with Child Prekindergarten Emotion Control in Low-Income Families," *Social Development* 24, no. 3 (2015): 601–20, doi:10.111/sode.12112.

30. W. T. Church II, J. W. Jaggers, and J. K. Taylor, "Neighborhood Poverty and Negative Behaviour: An Examination of Differential Association and Social Control Theory," *Children and Youth Services Review* 34, no. 5 (2012): 1035–41.

31. J. A. Kalil, "Childhood Poverty and Parental Stress: Important Determinants of Health," *UBC Medical Journal* 6, no. 1 (2015): 41–43; McEwen and Stewart, "The Relationship between Income and Children's Outcomes."

32. Evans and Kim, "Childhood Poverty, Chronic Stress, Self-Regulation, and Coping."

33. B. Fallon et al., "Opportunities for Prevention and Intervention with Young Children: Lessons from the Canadian Incidence Study of Reported Child Abuse and Neglect," *Child and Adolescent Psychiatry* 7, no. 4 (2013), http://capmh.biomedcentral.com/articles/10.1186/1753-2000-7-4.

34. H. MacMillan et al., "Child Physical and Sexual Abuse in a Community

Sample of Young Adults: Results from the Ontario Child Health Study," *Child Abuse & Neglect* 37, no. 1 (2013): 14–21, doi:10.1016/j.chiabu.2012.06.005.

35. Kalil, "Childhood Poverty and Parental Stress."

36. D. T. Browne and J. M. Jenkins, "Health across Early Childhood and Socioeconomic Status: Examining the Moderating Effects of Differential Parenting," *Social Science and Medicine* 74, no. 10 (2012): 1622–29, doi:10.1016/j.socscimed.2012.01.017.

37. Evans and Kim, "Childhood Poverty, Chronic Stress, Self-Regulation, and Coping"; L. Kakinami et al., "Poverty's Latent Effect on Adiposity during Childhood: Evidence from a Quebec Cohort," *Journal of Epidemiology and Community Health* 68, no. 3 (2014): 239–45, doi:10.1136/jech-2012-201881.

38. P. Sidebotham et al., "Understanding Why Children Die in High-Income Countries," *The Lancet* 384, no. 9946 (2014): 915–27, doi:10.1016/S0140-6736(14)60581-X.

39. Evans and Kim, "Childhood Poverty, Chronic Stress, Self-Regulation, and Coping."

40. Sidebotham et al., "Understanding Why Children Die."

41. F. Reiss, "Socioeconomic Inequalities and Mental Health Problems in Children and Adolescents: A Systematic Review," *Social Science and Medicine* 90 (August 2013): 24–31.

42. N. Slopen et al., "Poverty, Food Insecurity and the Behaviour for Childhood Internalizing and Externalizing Disorders," *Journal of the American Academy of Child and Adolescent Psychiatry* 49, no. 5 (2010): 444–52.

43. C. A. Holtz, R. A. Fox, and J. R. Meurer, "Incidence of Behaviour Problems in Toddlers and Preschool Children from Families Living in Poverty," *Journal of Psychology* 149, no. 2 (2015): 161–74.

44. C. Waddell et al., *Child and Youth Mental Disorders: Prevalence and Evidence-Based Interventions* (Vancouver: Children's Health Policy Centre, Simon Fraser University, 2014), http://childhealthpolicy.ca/wp-content/uploads/2014/06/14-06-17-Waddell-Report-2014.06.16.pdf.

45. I. Schoon et al., "Family Hardship, Family Instability and Children's Cognitive Development," *Journal of Epidemiology and Community Health* 66, no. 8 (2012): 716–22, doi:10.1136/jech.2010.121228.

46. A. Dickerson and G. K. Popli, "Persistent Poverty and Children's Cognitive Development: Evidence from the U.K. Millennium Cohort Study," *Journal of the Royal Statistical Society* 179, no. 2 (2016): 535–58; N. S. Sorhagen, "Early Teacher Expectations Disproportionately Affect Poor Children's High School Performance," *Journal of Educational Psychology* 105, no. 2 (2013): 465–77.

47. J. A. Baker et al., "Evidence for Population-Based Perspectives on Children's Behavioural Adjustment and Needs for Service Delivery in Schools," *School Psychology Review* 35, no. 1 (2006): 31–46.

48. Browne and Jenkins, "Health across Early Childhood and Socioeconomic Status"; Evans and Kim, "Childhood Poverty, Chronic Stress, Self-Regulation, and Coping."

49. Baker et al., "Evidence for Population-Based Perspectives"; Mathis and Bierman, "Dimensions of Parenting."

50. K. Benzies et al., "Two-Generation Preschool Program: Immediate and 7-Year-Old Outcomes for Low-Income Children and Their Parents," *Child & Family Social Work* 19, no. 2 (2014): 203–14, doi:10.1111/j.1365-2206.2012.00894.x; T. Koponen et al., "Cognitive Predictors of Single-Digit and Procedural Calculation Skills and Their Covariation with Reading Skill," *Journal of Experimental Child Psychology* 97, no. 3 (2007): 220–41, doi:10.1016/j.jecp.2007.03.001; B. M. Phillips and J. Lonigan, "Variations in the Home Literacy Environment of Preschool Children: A Cluster Analytic Approach," *Scientific Studies of Reading* 13, no. 2 (2009): 146–74.

51. Howe and Covell, *Education in the Best Interests of the Child*; Phillips and Lonigan, "Variations in the Home Literacy Environment of Preschool Children."

52. Howe and Covell, *Education in the Best Interests of the Child.*

53. Dickerson and Popli, "Persistent Poverty"; Mathis and Bierman, "Dimensions of Parenting."

54. Mathis and Bierman, "Dimensions of Parenting."

55. Howe and Covell, *Education in the Best Interests of the Child.*

56. K. Kokko et al., "Trajectories of Prosocial Behaviour and Physical Aggression in Middle Childhood: Links to Adolescent School Dropout and Physical Violence," *Journal of Research on Adolescence* 16, no. 3 (2006): 403–28, doi:10.1111/j.1532-7795.2006.00500.x.

57. Benzies et al., "Two-Generation Preschool Program"; G. J. Duncan, M. Kathleen, and A. Kalil, "Early Childhood Poverty and Adult Attainment, Behaviour and Health," *Child Development* 81, no. 1 (2010): 306–25, doi:10.1111/j.1467-8624.2009.01396.x.

58. R. Hodgkin and P. Newell, *Implementation Handbook for the Convention on the Rights of the Child* (New York: UNICEF, 2007), 344.

59. C. van Daalen-Smith, "A Right to Health," in Howe and Covell, *A Question of Commitment,* 83.

60. Statistics Canada, "Infant Mortality Rates, by Province and Territory," February 23, 2018, http://www.statcan.gc.ca/tables-tableaux/sum-som/l01/cst01/health21a-eng.htm.

61. Public Health Agency of Canada, *Sudden Infant Death Syndrome (SIDS) in Canada*, http://publications.gc.ca/collections/collection_2015/aspc-phac/HP35-51-2014-eng.pdf.

62. A. P. Thakrar, A. D. Forrest, M. G. Maltenfort, and C. B. Forrest, "Child Mortality in the US and 19 OECD Comparator Nations: A 50-Year Time-Trend Analysis," *Health Affairs* 37, no. 1 (2018), doi:10.1377/hlthaff.2017.0767.

63. Statistics Canada, "Low Birth Weight Babies," December 10, 2012, http://
    www5.statcan.gc.ca/cansim/a26?lang=eng&id=1020701.

64. Public Health Agency of Canada, *Measuring Up: Results from the National
    Immunization Coverage Survey, 2002,* March 1, 2004, http://www.phac-aspc
    .gc.ca/publicat/ccdr-rmtc/04vol30/dr3005a-eng.php; Government of Canada,
    *Vaccine Coverage in Canada: Highlights of the 2013 Childhood National
    Immunization Coverage Survey,* October 13, 2016, http://healthycanadians
    .gc.ca/publications/healthy-living-vie-saine/immunization-coverage-children
    -2013-couverture-vaccinale-enfants/index-eng.php.

65. Statistics Canada, "Suicide and Suicide Rate, by Sex and by Age Group,"
    February 23, 2018, http://www.statcan.gc.ca/tables-tableaux/sum-som/
    l01/cst01/hlth66d-eng.htm; Statistics Canada, *Suicide Rates: An Overview,*
    June 16, 2017, http://www.statcan.gc.ca/pub/82-624-x/2012001/article/
    chart/11696-02-chart6-eng.htm.

66. J. Finlay and L. Akbar, "Caught between Two Worlds: The Voices of Youth
    from Four First Nations in Northern Ontario," *Canadian Journal of Children's
    Rights* 3, no. 1 (2016): 68–99.

67. Statistics Canada, *Study: Prevalence of Obesity among Children and Adolescents
    in Canada and the United States, 1976 to 2013,* August 26, 2015, http://
    www.statcan.gc.ca/daily-quotidien/150826/dq150826a-eng.htm.

68. Canadian Institute for Health Information, *Trends in Income-Related Health
    Inequalities in Canada, Revised July 2016* (Ottawa: CIHI, 2016), https://
    secure.cihi.ca/free_products/trends_in_income_related_inequalities_in_
    canada_2015_en.pdf; D. Raphael, "Social Determinants of Children's Health
    in Canada: Analysis and Implications," *International Journal of Child, Youth
    and Family Studies* 5, no. 2 (2014): 220–39.

69. Albanese, *Children in Canada Today,* 168–69; Bennett, M., "Aboriginal
    Children's Rights," in Howe and Covell, *A Question of Commitment,* 275–78;
    van Daalen-Smith, "A Right to Health," in Howe and Covell, *A Question of
    Commitment,* 77–79.

70. UNICEF Office of Research, "Fairness for Children," 8–9.

71. UNICEF Office of Research, "Child Well-Being in Rich Countries: A
    Comparative Overview," *Innocenti Report Card 11* (Florence: UNICEF Office
    of Research, 2013), 11–15.

72. Sidebotham et al., "Understanding Why Children Die."

73. OECD, "Health Spending," 2014, https://data.oecd.org/healthres/health
    -spending.htm#indicator-chart.

74. *R. v. Drummond,* [1997] O.J. no. 6390. The decision was made in 1996 and
    reported in 1997.

75. J. H. G. Williams and L. Ross, "Consequences of Prenatal Toxin Exposure for
    Mental Health in Children and Adolescents: A Systematic Review," *European
    Child & Adolescent Psychiatry* 16, no. 4 (2007): 243–53, doi:10.1007/
    s00787-006-0596-6.

76. G. Muckle et al., "Alcohol, Smoking and Drug Use among Inuit Women of Childbearing Age during Pregnancy and the Risk to Children," *Alcoholism: Clinical and Experimental Research* 35, no. 6: 1081–91, doi:10.1111/j.1530-0277.2011.01441.x.; G. Thomas et al., "The Effectiveness of Alcohol Warning Labels in the Prevention of Fetal Alcohol Spectrum Disorder: A Brief Review," *International Journal of Alcohol and Drug Research* 3, no. 1 (2014): 91–103, doi:10.7895/ijadr.v3i1.126.

77. Williams and Ross, "Consequences of Prenatal Toxin Exposure."

78. S. Popova et al., "Comorbidity of Fetal Alcohol Spectrum Disorder: A Systematic Review and Meta-Analysis," *The Lancet* 387, no. 10022 (2016), doi:10.1016/S0140-6736(15)01345-8.

79. D. J. Bonthius, Jr., et al., "Importance of Genetics in Fetal Alcohol Effects: Null Mutation of the nNOS Gene Worsens Alcohol-Induced Cerebellar Neuronal Losses and Behavioural Deficits," *NeuroToxicology* 46 (January 2015): 60–72, doi:10.1016/j.neuro.2014.11.009.

80. Popova et al., "Comorbidity of Fetal Alcohol Spectrum Disorder."

81. Popova et al., "Cost Attributable to Fetal Alcohol Spectrum Disorder in the Canadian Correctional System," *International Journal of Law and Psychiatry* 41 (July 2015): 76–81, doi:10.1016/j.ijlp.2015.03.010.

82. Muckle et al., "Alcohol, Smoking and Drug Use among Inuit Women."

83. N. N. Brown et al., "Prenatal Alcohol Exposure: An Assessment Strategy for the Legal Context," *International Journal of Law and Psychiatry* 42–43 (2015): 144–48, doi:10.1016/j.ijlp.2015.08.019.

84. Popova et al., "Cost Attributable to Fetal Alcohol Spectrum Disorder."

85. Thomas et al., "The Effectiveness of Alcohol Warning Labels."

86. Popova et al., "Comorbidity of Fetal Alcohol Spectrum Disorder."

87. Muckle et al., "Alcohol, Smoking and Drug Use among Inuit Women."

88. Brown et al., "Prenatal Alcohol Exposure."

89. Statistics Canada, "Percentage Who Reported Drinking 5 or More Drinks on One Occasion at Least 12 Times in the Last Year, by Age Group and Sex, Household Population Aged 12 or Older, Canada, 2008," September 28, 2016, http://www.statcan.gc.ca/pub/82-229-x/2009001/deter/desc/hdx-desc2.2-eng.htm.

90. E. Oulman et al., "Prevalence and Predictors of Unintended Pregnancy among Women: An Analysis of the Canadian Maternity Experiences Survey," *BMC Pregnancy and Childbirth* 15 (October 2015): 260, doi:10.1186/s12884-015-0663-4.

91. Statistics Canada, "Percentage Who Reported Drinking 5 or More Drinks."

92. Oulman et al., "Prevalence and Predictors of Unintended Pregnancy among Women."

93. M. Al-hamandi, "The Case for Stringent Alcohol Warning Labels: Lessons from the Tobacco Control Experience," *Journal of Public Health Policy* 35, no. 1 (2014): 65–74.

94. A. Joannou, "Yukon's Alcohol Label Study Back on but without a Cancer Warning," *Yukon News*, February 16, 2018, https://www.yukon-news.com/news/yukons-alcohol-label-study-back-on-but-without-a-cancer-warning/.

95. Ontario Agency for Health Protection and Promotion (Public Health Ontario), J. LeMar, E. Berenbaum, and G. Thomas, *Focus on: Standard Alcohol Labels* (Toronto: Queen's Printer for Ontario, 2015), http://www.publichealthontario.ca/en/eRepository/FocusOn-Standard_Alcohol_Labels_2015.pdf.

96. M. Rabson, "Warning Label Such a Simple Thing," *Winnipeg Free Press*, June 18, 2011, http://www.winnipegfreepress.com/special/fasd/prevention-and-solutions/warning-label-such-a-simple-thing-124123739.html.

97. Ibid.

98. Al-hamandi, "The Case for Stringent Alcohol Warning Labels"; Thomas et al., "The Effectiveness of Alcohol Warning Labels."

99. Al-hamandi, "The Case for Stringent Alcohol Warning Labels."

100. C. Fitzpatrick, T. A. Barnett, and L. S. Pagani, "Parental Bad Habits Breed Bad Behaviours in Youth: Exposure to Gestational Smoke and Child Impulsivity," *International Journal of Psychophysiology* 93, no. 1 (2014): 17–21, doi:10.1016/j.ijpsycho.2012.11.006.

101. J. C. Duby and D. L. Langkamp, "Another Reason to Avoid Second-Hand Smoke," *Journal of Pediatrics* 167, no. 2 (2015): 224–25, doi:10.1016/j.jpeds.2015.04.049; E. Simons et al., "Maternal Second-Hand Smoke Exposure in Pregnancy Is Associated with Childhood Asthma Development," *Journal of Allergy and Clinical Immunology: In Practice* 2, no. 2 (2014): 201–7, doi:10.1016/j.jaip.2013.11.014.

102. Fitzpatrick, Barnett, and Pagani, "Parental Bad Habits Breed Bad Behaviours in Youth"; Muckle et al., "Alcohol, Smoking and Drug Use among Inuit Women."

103. A. C. Erickson and L. T. Arbour, "Heavy Smoking during Pregnancy as a Marker for Other Risk Factors of Adverse Birth Outcomes: A Population-Based Study in British Columbia, Canada," *BMC Public Health* 12, no. 102 (2012), doi:10.1186/1471-2458-12-102.

104. S. Lange et al., "Alcohol Use, Smoking and Their Co-occurrence during Pregnancy among Canadian Women, 2003 to 2011/12," *Addictive Behaviours* 50 (November 2015): 102–9, doi:10.1016/j.addbeh.2015.06.018.

105. Muckle et al., "Alcohol, Smoking and Drug Use among Inuit Women."

106. Lange et al., "Alcohol Use, Smoking and Their Co-occurrence during Pregnancy."

107. Erickson and Arbour, "Heavy Smoking during Pregnancy as a Marker."

108. Fitzpatrick, Barnett, and Pagani, "Parental Bad Habits Breed Bad Behaviours in Youth."

109. Public Health Agency of Canada, *Perinatal Health Indicators for Canada 2013: A Report from the Canadian Perinatal Surveillance System* (Ottawa: Public Health Agency of Canada, 2013), http://publications.gc.ca/collections/collection_2015/aspc-phac/HP7-1-2013-2-eng.pdf.

110. N. L. Gilbert, C. R. M. Nelson, and L. Greaves, "Smoking Cessation during Pregnancy and Relapse after Childbirth in Canada," *Journal of Obstetrics and Gynaecology Canada: JOGC/Journal D'obstetrique et Gynecologie Du Canada: JOGC* 37, no. 1 (2015): 32–39.

111. M. Friendly, B. Grady, L. Macdonald, and B. Forer, *Early Childhood Education and Care in Canada* (Toronto: Childcare Resource and Research Unit, 2015, revised 2016), http://childcarecanada.org/sites/default/files/ECEC-2014-full -document-revised-10-03-16.pdf.

112. M. Friendly, "Early Learning and Child Care: Is Canada on Track?" in Howe and Covell, *A Question of Commitment*, 47.

113. Howe and Covell, *Education in the Best Interests of the Child*, 88–89.

114. E. R. Bell et al., "Peer Play as a Context for Identifying Profiles of Children and Examining Rates of Growth in Academic Readiness for Children Enrolled in Head Start," *Journal of Educational Psychology* 108, no. 5 (2016): 740–59, doi:10.1037/edu0000084.

115. M. Sinha, *Child Care in Canada* (Ottawa: Statistics Canada, 2012), http:// www.statcan.gc.ca/pub/89-652-x/89-652-x2014005-eng.htm.

116. Child Care Advocacy Association of Canada, *From Patchwork to Framework: A Child Care Strategy for Canada* (Ottawa: Child Care Advocacy Association of Canada, 2004).

117. Ibid., 10–12.

118. Albanese, *Children in Canada Today*, 126–28; C. Ferns and M. Friendly, *The State of Early Childhood Education and Care in Canada 2012,* http:// www.movingchildcareforward.ca, 6–9; Sinha, *Child Care in Canada*.

119. For example, Friendly, "Early Learning and Child Care."

120. C. G. Landolt, *The Child Care Debate* (Ottawa: Real Women of Canada, 2009), http://www.realwomenofcanada.ca/wp-content/uploads/2016/01/ Brief-127-The-Child-Care-Debate-COLF-Mar.-25-09.pdf.

121. Albanese, *Children in Canada Today*, 130–32; Friendly, "Early Learning and Child Care," 52–64.

122. Albanese, *Children in Canada Today*, 130–31; Friendly, "Early Learning and Child Care," 55–56.

123. Ferns and Friendly, *The State of Early Childhood Education*.

124. Economist Intelligence Unit, *Starting Well: Benchmarking Early Education Across the World*, 2012, http://graphics.eiu.com/upload/eb/Lienstartingwell .pdf.

125. OECD, *Public Spending on Child Care and Early Education*, OECD Family Database, 2008, https://www.oecd.org/edu/school/44975840.pdf.

126. UN Committee on the Rights of the Child, *UN Committee on the Rights of the Child: Concluding Observations: Canada*, October 5, 2012, CRC/C/ CAN/CO/3-4, http://www2.ohchr.org/english/bodies/crc/docs/co/CRC -C-CAN-CO-3-4_en.pdf.

127. See L. White, "Understanding Canada's Lack of Progress in Implementing the UN Convention on the Rights of the Child," *International Journal of Children's Rights* 22, no. 1 (2014): 164–88, doi:10.1163/15718182-02201002.
128. Albanese, *Children in Canada Today*, 131–32.
129. J. Belsky, "Infant Day-Care: A Cause for Concern?" *Zero to Three* 6, no. 4 (1986): 1–7.
130. M. Baker, J. Gruber, and K. Mulligan, "Universal Child Care, Maternal Labor Supply, and Family Well-Being," *Journal of Political Economy* 116, no. 4 (2008): 709–45, doi:10.1086/591908.
131. M. J. Kottelenberg and S. F. Lehrer, "New Evidence on the Impacts of Access and Attending Universal Child-Care in Canada," *Canadian Public Policy* 39, no. 2 (2016): 263–85.
132. M. Wente, "Universal Daycare Debate Deserves More Than a Brawl," *Globe and Mail* (Toronto), September 26, 2015, http://www.theglobeandmail.com/opinion/is-universal-daycare-a-smart-idea-lets-have-a-debate-guided-by-facts/article26548245/.
133. T. Kheiriddin, "Several Studies Have Now Shown the Dangers of Daycare," *National Post* (Toronto), September 23, 2015, http://news.nationalpost.com/full-comment/tasha-kheiriddin-several-studies-have-now-shown-the-dangers-of-daycare.
134. "If You Could Do It Over, Would You Want to Start School at Age Two?" *Maclean's*, December 6, 2011, http://www.macleans.ca/general/if-you-could-do-it-over-would-you-want-to-start-school-at-age-two/.
135. A. Miller, "Potential Dangers of Unlicensed Daycares," *Canadian Medical Association Journal CMAJ* 185, no. 18 (2013): 1566, doi:10.1503/cmaj.109-4643.
136. CBC News, "Daycare Deaths and Injuries in Canada," May 27, 2015, http://www.cbc.ca/news/canada/daycare-deaths-and-injuries-in-canada-1.3089068; Ontario Coalition for Better Child Care, "Unlicensed Child Care Incidents across Canada," February 27, 2014, http://www.childcareontario.org/unlicensed_child_care_incidents.
137. M. Geoffroy et al., "Daycare Attendance, Stress, and Mental Health," *Canadian Journal of Psychiatry. Revue canadienne de psychiatrie* 51, no. 9 (2006): 607–15; T. W. Morrissey, "Multiple Child-Care Arrangements and Young Children's Behavioural Outcomes," *Child Development* 80, no. 1 (2009): 59–76.
138. Morrissey, "Multiple Child-Care Arrangements."
139. C. Haeck, P. Lefebvre, and P. Merrigan, "Canadian Evidence on Ten Years of Universal Preschool Policies: The Good and the Bad," *Labour Economics* 36 (October 2015): 137–57, doi:10.1016/j.labeco.2015.05.002.
140. J. Quan, J. F. Bureau, and K. Yurowski, "The Association between Time Spent in Daycare and Preschool Attachment to Fathers and Mothers: An Exploration of Disorganization," *International Journal of Arts and Sciences* 6, no. 2 (2013): 415–22.

141. A. C. Huston, K. C. Bobbitt, and A. Bentley, "Time Spent in Child Care: How and Why Does It Affect Social Development?" *Developmental Psychology* 51, no. 5 (2015): 621–34.

142. D. L. Vandell et al., "Do Effects of Early Child Care Extend to Age 15 Years? Results from the NICHD Study of Early Child Care and Youth Development," *Child Development* 81, no. 3 (2010): 737–56, doi:10.1111/j.1467-8624.2010.01431.x.

143. Baker, Gruber, and Mulligan, "Universal Child Care, Maternal Labor Supply, and Family Well-Being."

144. Huston, Bobbitt, and Bentley, "Time Spent in Child Care."

145. Ibid.

146. Geoffroy et al., "Daycare Attendance, Stress, and Mental Health."

147. Haeck, Lefebvre, and Merrigan, "Canadian Evidence on Ten Years of Universal Preschool Policies."

148. Ibid.

149. Huston, Bobbitt, and Bentley, "Time Spent in Child Care."

150. Geoffroy et al., "Daycare Attendance, Stress, and Mental Health."

151. E. Gartsbein et al., "Lack of Oral Care Policies in Toronto Daycares," *American Association of Public Health Dentistry* 69, no. 3 (2009): 190–96, doi:10.1111/j.1752-7325.2009.00123.x; P. Tucker et al., "Physical Activity at Daycare: Childcare Providers' Perspectives for Improvements," *Journal of Early Childhood Research* 9, no. 3 (2011): 207–19, doi:10.1177/1476718X10389144.

152. M. Lang, "Health Implications of Children in Child Care Centres Part B: Injuries and Infections," *Paediatrics & Child Health* 14, no. 1 (2009): 40–43, reaffirmed February 1, 2016, http://www.cps.ca/en/documents/position/child-care-centres-injuries-infections.

153. Huston, Bobbitt, and Bentley, "Time Spent in Child Care."

154. E. Dearing, K. McCartney, and B. A. Taylor, "Does Higher Quality Early Child Care Promote Low-Income Children's Math and Reading Achievement in Middle Childhood?" *Child Development* 80, no. 5 (2009): 1329–49.

155. Ibid.

156. L. Lemay, N. Bigras, and C. Bouchard, "Educational Daycare from Infancy and Externalizing and Internalizing Behaviours in Early Childhood: Differential Effect by Children's Vulnerability," *Procedia—Social and Behavioural Sciences* 55 (October 5, 2012): 115–27, doi:10.1016/j.sbspro.2012.09.485; Vandell et al., "Do Effects of Early Child Care Extend to Age 15 Years?"

157. Huston, Bobbitt, and Bentley, "Time Spent in Child Care."

158. Lemay, Bigras, and Bouchard, "Educational Daycare from Infancy and Externalizing and Internalizing Behaviours in Early Childhood."

159. Haeck, Lefebvre, and Merrigan, "Canadian Evidence on Ten Years of Universal Preschool Policies."

160. Dearing, McCartney, and Taylor, "Does Higher Quality Early Child Care Promote Low-Income Children's Math"; Vandell et al., "Do Effects of Early Child Care Extend to Age 15 Years?"

## CHAPTER 6

1. R. Hodgkin and P. Newell, *Implementation Handbook for the Convention on the Rights of the Child* (New York: UNICEF, 2007), 260–64.
2. K. Covell and R. B. Howe, *Children, Families and Violence* (London: Jessica Kingsley, 2009), 63–64; J. E. Durrant, "Corporal Punishment: A Violation of the Rights of the Child," in *A Question of Commitment: Children's Rights in Canada*, ed. R. B. Howe and K. Covell (Waterloo, ON: Wilfrid Laurier University Press, 2007), 100.
3. P. Albanese, *Children in Canada Today* (Toronto: Oxford University Press, 2016), 224–28; B. J. Saunders, "Ending the Physical Punishment of Children by Parents in the English-Speaking World: The Impact of Language, Tradition and Law," *International Journal of Children's Rights* 21 (2013): 278–304, doi:10.1163/15718182-02102001; M. Freeman and B. J. Saunders, "Can We Conquer Child Abuse If We Don't Outlaw Physical Chastisement of Children?" *International Journal of Children's Rights* 22 (2014): 681–709, doi:10.1163/15718182-02204002; J. E. Durrant and A. Stewart-Tufescu, "What Is Discipline in the Age of Children's Rights?" *International Journal of Children's Rights* 25, no. 2 (2017): 359–79, doi:10.1163/15718182-02502007; A. S. Brown, G. W. Holden, and R. Ashraf, "Spank, Slap, or Hit? How Labels Alter Perceptions of Child Discipline," *Psychology of Violence* 8, no. 1 (2018): 1–9, doi:10.1037/vio0000080.
4. Truth and Reconciliation Commission of Canada, *Final Report of the Truth and Reconciliation Commission of Canada, Vol. One: Summary—Honouring the Truth, Reconciling for the Future* (Toronto: Lorimer, 2015); R. N. Bezeau and J. R. Hoskins, *The Fallen Feather* (Surrey, BC: Fallen Feather Productions, 2007), video recording.
5. Global Initiative to End All Corporal Punishment of Children, *Corporal Punishment of Children in Canada*, 2016, http://www.endcorporalpunishment .org/assets/pdfs/states-reports/Canada.pdf.
6. Durrant, "Corporal Punishment," 102–7; Repeal 43 Committee, "Constitutional Challenge," 2016, http://www.repeal43.org/constitutional-challenge/; S. Turner, *Something to Cry About: An Argument Against Corporal Punishment of Children in Canada* (Waterloo, ON: Wilfrid Laurier University Press, 2002).
7. *Canadian Foundation for Children, Youth and the Law v. Canada (Attorney General)*, [2004] 1 S.C.R. 76.
8. Truth and Reconciliation Commission of Canada, *Final Report*.

9. Ibid., 144.

10. J. Smith, "Liberal Government Commits to Repealing So-Called 'Spanking Law,'" *Toronto Star*, December 21, 2015, https://www.thestar.com/news/canada/2015/12/21/liberal-government-commits-to-repealing-spanking-law.html.

11. Global Initiative to End All Corporal Punishment of Children, "States Which Have Prohibited All Corporal Punishment," 2017, http://www.endcorporalpunishment.org/progress/prohibiting-states/.

12. J. Durrant, "Legal Reform and Attitudes toward Physical Punishment in Sweden," *International Journal of Children's Rights* 11, no. 2 (2003): 147–73.

13. J. Durrant and R. Ensom, "Physical Punishment of Children: Lessons from 20 Years of Research," *Canadian Medical Association Journal* 184, no. 12 (2012): 1373–77, doi:10.1503/cmaj.101314.

14. E. T. Gershoff, "More Harm Than Good: A Summary of Scientific Research on the Intended and Unintended Effects of Corporal Punishment on Children," *Law and Contemporary Problems* 73, no. 31 (2010): 31–56.

15. Covell and Howe, *Children, Families and Violence*.

16. Covell and Howe, *Children, Families and Violence*; E. T. Gershoff et al., "Parent Discipline Practices in an International Sample: Associations with Child Behaviours and Moderation by Perceived Normativeness," *Child Development* 81, no. 2 (2010): 487–502, doi:10.1111/j.1467-8624.2009.01409.x.

17. Covell and Howe, *Children, Families and Violence*; Gershoff, "More Harm Than Good"; O. Gómez-Ortiz, E. M. Romera, and R. Ortega-Ruiz, "Parenting Styles and Bullying: The Mediating Role of Parental Psychological Aggression and Physical Punishment," *Child Abuse & Neglect* 51 (January 2016): 32–143, doi:10.1016/j.chiabu.2015.10.025.

18. Gershoff et al., "Parent Discipline Practices."

19. C. A. Taylor, J. A. Manganello, S. J. Lee, and J. C.Rice, "Mother's Spanking of 3-Year-Old Children and Subsequent Risk of Children's Aggressive Behavior," *Pediatrics* 125 (2010), doi:10.1542/peds 2009-2678.

20. L. Radford, N. Lombard, F. Meinck, E. Katz, and S. T. Mahati, "Researching Violence with Children: Experiences and Lessons from the UK and South Africa," *Families, Relationships and Societies* 6, no. 2 (2017): 239–56, doi:10.1332/204674317X14861128190401.

21. Durrant and Ensom, "Physical Punishment of Children."

22. Gershoff, "More Harm Than Good."

23. Ibid.

24. T. L. Taillieu and D. A. Brownridge, "Aggressive Parental Discipline Experienced in Childhood and Internalizing Problems in Early Adulthood," *Journal of Family Violence* 28, no. 5 (2013): 445–58, doi:10.1007/s10896-013-9513-1.

25. A. Tomoda et al., "Reduced Prefrontal Cortical Gray Matter Volume in Young Adults Exposed to Harsh Physical Punishment," *NeuroImage* 47, no. 2 (2009): T66–T71, doi:10.1016/j.neuroimage.2009.03.005.

26. Durrant and Ensom, "Physical Punishment of Children"; P. B. Fitzgerald et al., "A Meta-Analytic Study of Changes in Brain Activation in Depression," *Human Brain Mapping* 29, no. 6 (2008): 683–95, doi:10.1002/hbm.20426.

27. E. T. Gershoff, "Should Parents' Physical Punishment of Children Be Considered a Source of Toxic Stress That Affects Brain Development?" *Family Relations* 65, no. 1 (2016): 151–62, doi:10.1111/fare.12177.

28. L. M. Padilla-Walker, A. M. Fraser, and J. M. Harper, "Walking the Walk: The Moderating Role of Proactive Parenting on Adolescents' Value Congruent Behaviours," *Journal of Adolescence* 35, no. 5 (2012): 1141–52.

29. H. Chang et al., "Proactive Parenting and Children's Effortful Control: Mediating Role of Language and Indirect Intervention Effects," *Social Development* 24, no. 1 (2015): 206–23, doi:10.1111/sode.12069; Padilla-Walker, Fraser, and Harper, "Walking the Walk"; V. Rickert, A. L. Gilbert, and M. C. Aalsma, "Proactive Parents Are Assets to the Health and Wellbeing of Teens," *Journal of Pediatrics* 164, no. 6 (2014): 1390–95.

30. Chang et al., "Proactive Parenting and Children's Effortful Control."

31. F. Gardner et al., "Randomized Prevention Trial for Early Conduct Problems: Effects of Proactive Parenting and Links to Toddler Disruptive Behaviour," *Journal of Family Psychology* 21, no. 3 (2007): 398–406, doi:10.1037/0893-3200.21.3.398.

32. L. M. Padilla-Walker, K. J. Christensen, and R. D. Day, "Proactive Parenting Practices during Early Adolescence: A Cluster Approach," *Journal of Adolescence* 34, no. 2 (2011): 203–14; Padilla-Walker, Fraser, and Harper, "Walking the Walk."

33. Chang et al., "Proactive Parenting and Children's Effortful Control."

34. Rickert, Gilbert, and Aalsma, "Proactive Parents Are Assets."

35. Ibid.

36. Padilla-Walker, Christensen, and Day, "Proactive Parenting Practices"; Rickert, Gilbert, and Aalsma, "Proactive Parents Are Assets."

37. Padilla-Walker, Fraser, and Harper, "Walking the Walk."

38. L. Wray-Lake and C. A. Flanagan, "Parenting Practices and the Development of Adolescents' Social Trust," *Journal of Adolescence* 35, no. 3 (2012): 549–60, doi:10.1016/j.adolescence.2011.09.006.

39. Hodgkin and Newell, *Implementation Handbook*, 513.

40. A. McGillivray, "Child Sexual Abuse and Exploitation: What Progress Has Canada Made?" in Howe and Covell, *A Question of Commitment*, 127–51.

41. S. Grover, "Oppression of Children Intellectualized as Free Expression under the Canadian Charter: A Reanalysis of the *Sharpe* Possession of Pornography Case," *International Journal of Children's Rights* 11, no. 4 (2004): 311–31, doi:10.1163/157181804322985150; McGillivray, "Child Sexual Abuse," 138–39.

42. *R. v. Sharpe*, [2001] 1 S.C.R. 45.

43. Y. Akdeniz, *Internet Child Pornography Laws* (Aldershot, UK: Ashgate, 2008), 150–61; L. Casavant and J. Robertson, *The Evolution of Pornography Law in Canada* (Ottawa: Parliament of Canada, 2007), http://www.lop.parl.gc.ca/content/lop/researchpublications/843-e.htm#billc20.

44. Government of Canada, Justice Laws Website, *Tougher Penalties for Child Predators Act*, 2015, http://laws-lois.justice.gc.ca/eng/AnnualStatutes/2015_23/page-1.html.

45. Akdeniz, *Internet Child Pornography Laws*, 150–51; Casavant and Robertson, *The Evolution of Pornography Law*.

46. McGillivray, "Child Sexual Abuse," 139–40.

47. K. Bunzeluk, *Child Sexual Abuse Images: Analysis of Websites by Cybertip.ca* (Winnipeg, MB: Canadian Centre for Child Protection, 2009), https://cybertip.ca/pdfs/CTIP_ChildSexualAbuse_Report_en.pdf. See esp. pp. 11 and 44.

48. McGillivray, "Child Sexual Abuse," 136–37.

49. Ibid., 137–38.

50. ECPAT Canada, Beyond Borders, "Fact Sheet: Child Sex Tourism—Law," 2012, http://www.beyondborders.org/en/publications/fact-sheets/.

51. N. Barrett and M. Shaw, *Laws to Combat Sex Trafficking*, Canadian Women's Foundation, 2013, http://www.mamawi.com/wp-content/uploads/2016/02/National-Task-Force-Research-Report-Laws-to-Combat-Sex-Trafficking.pdf; Government of Alberta, *Protection of Sexually Exploited Children and Youth*, 2004, revised 2010, http://web.archive.org/web/20160409211120/http://www.humanservices.alberta.ca/documents/PSEC-manual.pdf.

52. S. Bittle, "Still Punishing to 'Protect,'" in *Selling Sex: Experience, Advocacy, and Research on Sex Work in Canada*, ed. E. van der Meulen, E. Durisin, and M. Love (Vancouver: UBC Press, 2013), 279–96.

53. L. McKay-Panos, *Using the Coercive Power of the State to Deal with Child Prostitution and Drug Abuse*, Alberta Law Foundation, 2009, 2–4, http://ablawg.ca/wp-content/uploads/2009/10/blog_lmp_protection_feb2009.pdf.

54. Ibid., 3–4.

55. Bittle, "Still Punishing," 292.

56. Barrett and Shaw, *Laws to Combat*, 46–47; Bittle, "Still Punishing," 292–94; McKay-Panos, *Using the Coercive Power of the State*, 1–2.

57. Y. Homma, D. Nicholson, and E. M. Saewyc, "A Profile of High School Students in Rural Canada Who Exchange Sex for Substances," *Canadian Journal of Human Sexuality* 21, no. 1 (2012): 29–40; H. Whittle et al., "A Review of Young People's Vulnerabilities to Online Grooming," *Aggression and Violent Behaviour* 18, no. 1 (2013): 135–46, doi:10.1016/j.avb.2012.11.008.

58. M. Hay, "Commercial Sexual Exploitation of Children and Youth," *BC Medical Journal* 46, no. 3 (2004): 119–22; S. Kidd and R. M. C. Liborio, "Sex Trade Involvement in Sao Paulo, Brazil, and Toronto, Canada: Narratives of Social Exclusion and Fragmented Identities," *Youth and Society* 43, no. 3 (2011): 982–1009; E. Quayle and E. Newman, "An Exploratory Study of Public Reports to Investigate Patterns and Themes of Requests for Sexual Images of Minors Online," *Crime Science* 5, no. 2 (2016), doi:10.1186/s40163-016-0050-0; Whittle et al., "A Review of Young People's Vulnerabilities."

59. Hay, "Commercial Sexual Exploitation of Children and Youth"; Homma, Nicholson, and Saewyc, "A Profile of High School Students"; J. M. Stoltz et al., "Associations between Childhood Maltreatment and Sex Work in a Cohort of Drug-Using Youth," *Social Science and Medicine* 65, no. 6 (2007): 1214–21, doi:10.1016/j.socscimed.2007.05.005.

60. Stoltz et al., "Associations between Childhood Maltreatment and Sex Work."

61. Hay, "Commercial Sexual Exploitation of Children and Youth"; Homma, Nicholson, and Saewyc, "A Profile of High School Students"; Whittle et al., "A Review of Young People's Vulnerabilities."

62. E. M. Saewyc et al., "Competing Discourses about Youth Sexual Exploitation in Canadian News Media," *Canadian Journal of Human Sexuality* 22, no. 2 (2013): 95–105, doi:10.3138/cjhs.2013.2041; Whittle et al., "A Review of Young People's Vulnerabilities."

63. Hay, "Commercial Sexual Exploitation of Children and Youth"; Saewyc et al., "Competing Discourses about Youth Sexual Exploitation."

64. Hay, "Commercial Sexual Exploitation of Children and Youth."

65. G. Shaw, "Amanda's Story: In Her Mother's Words," *Vancouver Sun*, October 12, 2012, http://vancouversun.com/news/staff-blogs/amandas-story-in-her-mothers-words.

66. Quayle and Newman, "An Exploratory Study."

67. M. L. Williams and K. Hudson, "Public Perceptions of Internet, Familial and Localized Sexual Grooming: Predicting Perceived Prevalence and Safety," *Journal of Sexual Aggression* 19, no. 2 (2013): 218–35.

68. R. Williams, I. A. Elliott, and A. R. Beech, "Identifying Sexual Grooming Themes Used by Internet Sex Offenders," *Deviant Behaviour* 34, no. 2 (2013): 135–52, doi:10.1080/01639625.2012.707550.

69. H. Whittle et al., "A Review of Online Grooming: Characteristics and Concerns," *Aggression and Violent Behaviour* 18, no. 1 (2013): 62–70, doi:10.1016/j.avb.2012.09.003.

70. Canadian Centre for Child Protection, "Preliminary Findings Provide New Insight into the Crime of Online Luring," October 19, 2012, https://protectchildren.ca/app/en/media_release_online_luring.

71. A. Todd, "My Story: Struggling, Bullying, Suicide, Self Harm," YouTube, 2012, https://www.youtube.com/watch?v=vOHXGNx-E7E.

72. Government of Canada, "Every Image, Every Child Backgrounder: Fast Facts and Statistics," Office of the Federal Ombudsman for Victims of Crime, 2013, http://www.victimsfirst.gc.ca/media/news-nouv/bg-di/20090507b.html.

73. J. Martin, "'It's Just an Image, Right?' Practitioners' Understanding of Child Sexual Abuse Images Online and Effects on Victims," *Child & Youth Services* 35, no. 2 (2014): 96–115, doi:10.1080/0145935X.2014.924334.

74. J. Martin, "Conceptualizing the Harms Done to Children Made the Subjects of Sexual Abuse Images Online," *Child & Youth Services* 36, no. 4 (2015): 267–87, doi:10.1080/0145935X.2015.1092832.

75. Martin, "It's Just an Image, Right?"
76. Canadian Resource Centre for Victims of Crime, "Brief to the Standing Committee on Access to Information, Privacy and Ethics re: PIPEDA review," 2007, p. 7, https://crcvc.ca/docs/PIPEDA.BRIEF.pdf.
77. J. Martin, "Conceptualizing the Harms."
78. Homma, Nicholson, and Saewyc, "A Profile of High School Students."
79. Homma, Nicholson, and Saewyc, "A Profile of High School Students"; F. Lavoie et al., "Buying and Selling Sex in Québec Adolescents: A Study of Risk and Protective Factors," *Archives of Sexual Behaviour* 39, no. 5 (2010): 1147–60, doi:10.1007/s10508-010-9605-4.
80. Kidd and Liborio, "Sex Trade Involvement in Sao Paulo."
81. Yonge Street Mission, "Changing Patterns for Street-Involved Youth," December 2009, http://www.publicinterest.ca/images/YSM_Report_-_Changing_Patterns_for_Street_Involved_Youth.PDF.
82. Hay, "Commercial Sexual Exploitation of Children and Youth."
83. B. D. L. Marshall et al., "Survival Sex Work and Increased HIV Risk among Sexual Minority Street-Involved Youth," *Journal of Acquired Immune Deficiency Syndromes* 53, no. 5 (2010): 661–64, doi:10.1097/QAI.0b013e3181c300d7.
84. Kidd and Liborio, "Sex Trade Involvement in Sao Paulo."
85. Ibid.
86. Yonge Street Mission, "Changing Patterns for Street-Involved Youth."
87. Hay, "Commercial Sexual Exploitation of Children and Youth."
88. Hodgkin and Newell, *Implementation Handbook*, 249.
89. UN Committee on the Rights of the Child, *General Comment 13*, 2011, http://www2.ohchr.org/english/bodies/crc/docs/CRC.C.GC.13_en.pdf; S. Hart, Y. Lee, and M. Wernham, "A New Age for Child Protection—General Comment 13: Why It Is Important, How It Was Constructed, and What It Intends," *Child Abuse & Neglect* 35, no. 12 (2011): 970–78, doi:10.1016/j.chiabu.2011.09.007.
90. S. Hallett and N. Bala, "Criminal Prosecutions for Abuse and Neglect," in *Canadian Child Welfare Law*, ed. N. Bala et al. (Toronto: Thompson, 2004), 311–31.
91. Bala, "Child Welfare Law in Canada," 1–25.
92. McGillivray, "Child Sexual Abuse," 141–44.
93. Bala, "Child Welfare Law in Canada," 18–19; M. Bernstein and K. Reitmeier, "The Child Protection Hearing," in Bala et al., *Canadian Child Welfare Law*, 71–73.
94. K. Swift, "Canadian Child Welfare: Child Protection and the Status Quo," in *Child Protection Systems: International Trends and Orientations*, ed. N. Gilbert, N. Parton, and M. Skivenes (New York: Oxford University Press, 2011), 42.
95. R. Vogl and N. Bala, "Initial Involvement," in Bala et al., *Canadian Child Welfare Law*, 41–43.

96. National Collaborating Centre for Aboriginal Health, *Child Welfare Services in Canada: Aboriginal and Mainstream*, 2009–2010, https://www.ccnsa-nccah.ca/docs/health/FS-ChildWelfareServices-EN.pdf.

97. Bala, "Child Welfare Law in Canada," 16–22; R. B. Howe, "Implementing Children's Rights in a Federal State: The Case of Canada's Child Protection System," *International Journal of Children's Rights* 9, no. 4 (2001), 361–82, doi:10.1163/15718180120495026; Swift, "Canadian Child Welfare," 39–43.

98. National Collaborating Centre for Aboriginal Health, *Child Welfare Services in Canada*.

99. C. Blackstock, "The Canadian Human Rights Tribunal on First Nations Child Welfare: Why if Canada Wins, Equality and Justice Lose," *Children and Youth Services Review* 33, no. 1 (2011): 187–94.

100. *First Nations Child and Family Caring Society of Canada et al. v. Attorney General of Canada (for the Minister of Indian and Northern Affairs Canada)*, [2013] F.C.J. no. 249.

101. B. MacLaurin and N. Bala, "Children in Care," in Bala et al., *Canadian Child Welfare Law*, 116–19.

102. Bala, "Child Welfare Law in Canada," 7–9; Swift, "Canadian Child Welfare," 52–53.

103. For example, N. McMurtry and M. Brownell, "Canada's Current Child Welfare System Fails Children," *Huffington Post*, October 20, 2015, http://www.huffingtonpost.ca/neeta-das-mcmurtry/child-welfare-canada_b_8304708.html.

104. Statistics Canada, "Family-Related Homicides, 2000 to 2009," 2015, http://www.statcan.gc.ca/pub/85-224-x/2010000/part-partie4-eng.htm.

105. Swift, "Canadian Child Welfare," 53.

106. Saskatchewan Advocate for Children and Youth, *2015 Annual Report* (Saskatoon: Saskatchewan Advocate for Children and Youth, 2016), 21–22.

107. K. Kufeldt, "Foster Care: An Essential Part of the Continuum of Care," in *Child Welfare*, ed. K. Kufeldt and B. McKenzie (Waterloo, ON: Wilfrid Laurier University Press, 2011), 157–59; MacLaurin and Bala, "Children in Care," 116–17; C. Waddell, H. Macmillan, and A. M. Pietrantonio, "How Important Is Permanency Planning for Children?" *Journal of Developmental and Behavioural Pediatrics: JDBP* 25, no. 4 (2004), 285–92.

108. Waddell, Macmillan, and Pietrantonio, "How Important Is Permanency Planning."

109. T. Esposito et al., "Family Reunification for Placed Children in Quebec, Canada: A Longitudinal Study," *Children and Youth Services Review* 44 (2014): 278–87, doi:10.1016/j.childyouth.2014.06.024; K. Kufeldt and B. McKenzie, "The Policy, Practice, and Research Connection," in Kufeldt and McKenzie, *Child Welfare*, 575–76.

110. K. Kufeldt and B. McKenzie, "Critical Issues in Current Practice," in Kufeldt and McKenzie, *Child Welfare*, 558–63.

111. K. Swift and M. Callahan, "Problems and Potential of Canadian Child Welfare," in *Toward Positive Systems of Child and Family Welfare,* ed. N. Freymond and G. Cameron (Toronto: University of Toronto Press, 2006), 118–147.

112. N. Gilbert, N. Parton, and M. Skivenes, "Changing Patterns of Response and Emerging Orientations," in *Child Protection Systems: International Trends and Orientations,* ed. N. Gilbert, N. Parton, and M. Skivenes (New York: Oxford University Press, 2011), 243–57.

113. For a detailed analysis of the Convention in relation to child welfare, see T. Waldock, "Theorising Children's Rights and Child Welfare Paradigms," *International Journal of Children's Rights* 24, no. 2 (2016): 1–26, doi 10.1163/15718182-02401007.

114. Swift, "Canadian Child Welfare," 36; Waldock, "Theorising Children's Rights," 17.

115. T. O. Afifi, "Child Maltreatment in Canada: An Understudied Public Health Problem," *Canadian Journal of Public Health/Revue canadienne de santé publique* 102, no. 6 (2011): 459–61.

116. T. Superle, "Section 3: Family Violence against Children and Youth," *Family Violence in Canada: A Statistical Profile*, Statistics Canada, 2013, http://www .statcan.gc.ca/pub/85-002-x/2014001/article/14114/section03-eng.htm.

117. H. L. MacMillan et al., "Child Physical and Sexual Abuse in a Community Sample of Young Adults: Results from the Ontario Child Health Study," *Child Abuse & Neglect* 37, no. 1 (2013): 14–21, doi:10.1016/j.chiabu.2012.06.005.

118. Public Health Agency of Canada, *Canadian Incidence Study of Reported Child Abuse and Neglect—2008* (Ottawa: Public Health Agency of Canada, 2010), http://www.phac-aspc.gc.ca/cm-vee/csca-ecve/2008/index-eng.php.

119. MacMillan et al., "Child Physical and Sexual Abuse."

120. T. O. Afifi et al., "Child Abuse and Mental Disorders in Canada," *CMAJ: Canadian Medical Association Journal/Journal de l'Association médicale canadienne* 186, no. 9 (2014): E324–32, doi:10.1503/cmaj.131792.

121. R. E. Norman et al., "The Long-Term Health Consequences of Child Physical Abuse, Emotional Abuse and Neglect: A Systematic Review and Meta-Analysis," *PLOS Medicine* 9, no. 11 (2012), e1001349.doi10.1371/journal.pmed.100349; L. Sugaya et al., "Child Physical Abuse and Adult Mental Health: A National Study," *Journal of Traumatic Stress* 25, no. 4 (2012): 384–92, doi:10.1002/ jts.21719.

122. Covell and Howe, *Children, Families and Violence*; A. Gonzalez et al., "Subtypes of Exposure to Intimate Partner Violence within a Canadian Child Welfare Sample: Associated Risks and Child Maladjustment," *Child Abuse & Neglect* 38, no. 12 (2014): 1934–44, doi:10.1016/j.chiabu.2014.10.007.

123. T. O. Afifi et al., "Child Abuse and Physical Health in Adulthood," Statistics Canada, March 16, 2016, http://www.statcan.gc.ca/pub/82-003-x/2016003/ article/14339-eng.htm.

124. Afifi et al., "Child Abuse and Mental Disorders in Canada."
125. T. Herrenkohl et al., "Developmental Impacts of Child Abuse and Neglect Related to Adult Mental Health, Substance Use and Physical Health," *Journal of Family Violence* 28, no. 2 (2013): 191–99. doi:10.1007/s10896-012-9474-9.
126. Sugaya et al., "Child Physical Abuse and Adult Mental Health."
127. Norman et al., "The Long-Term Health Consequences."
128. S. R. Jaffee and C. W. Christian, "The Biological Embedding of Child Abuse and Neglect: Implications for Policy and Practice," *Social Policy Report* 27, no. 4 (2013), http://www.srcd.org/sites/default/files/documents/spr_28_1.pdf.
129. B. Fallon et al., "Opportunities for Prevention and Intervention with Young Children: Lessons from the Canadian Incidence Study of Reported Child Abuse and Neglect," *Child and Adolescent Psychiatry and Mental Health* 7, no. 4 (2013), doi:10.1186/1753-2000-7-4; Gonzalez et al., "Subtypes of Exposure to Intimate Partner Violence."
130. *Sampson* (Re), 2016 CanLII 60525 (O.N. O.C.C.O.), http://canlii.ca/t/gtpvm.
131. C. Porter, "Katelynn Sampson Inquest Recommendations Focus on Putting Child First," *Toronto Star*, April 29, 2016, https://www.thestar.com/news/gta/2016/04/29/katelynn-sampson-inquest-recommendations-focus-on-information-sharing.html.
132. T. Waldock, "Enhancing the Quality of Care in Child Welfare: Our Obligations under the UN Convention on the Rights of the Child," *Relational Child and Youth Care Practice* 24, no. 3 (2011): 50–61; Waldock, "Theorising Children's Rights."
133. Esposito et al., "Family Reunification for Placed Children in Quebec"; M. Letarte, S. Normandeau, and J. Allard, "Effectiveness of a Parent Training Program 'Incredible Years' in a Child Protection Service," *Child Abuse & Neglect* 34, no. 4 (2010): 253–61, doi:10.1016/j.chiabu.2009.06.003.
134. H. MacMillan et al., "Effectiveness of Home Visitation by Public-Health Nurses in Prevention of the Recurrence of Child Physical Abuse and Neglect: A Randomised Controlled Trial," *Lancet* 365, no. 9473 (2005): 1786–93, doi:10.1016/S0140-6736(05)66388-X.
135. S. Helie, M. Poirier, and D. Turcotte, "Risk of Maltreatment Recurrence after Exiting Substitute Care: Impact of Placement Characteristics," *Child and Youth Services Review* 46 (November 2014): 257–64, doi:10.1016/j.childyouth.2014.09.002.
136. M. Courtney, R. J. Flynn, and J. Beaupré, "Overview of Out of Home Care in the USA and Canada," *Psychosocial Intervention* 22, no. 3 (2013): 163–73.
137. Jaffee and Christian, "The Biological Embedding of Child Abuse and Neglect."
138. MacMillan et al., "Effectiveness of Home Visitation by Public-Health Nurses."
139. T. Esposito et al., "Placement of Children in Out-of-Home Care in Quebec, Canada: When and for Whom Initial Out-of-Home Placement Is Most Likely to Occur," *Children and Youth Services Review* 35, no. 12 (2013): 2031–39, doi:10.1016/j.childyouth.2013.10.010.

140. K. Brisebois, P. D. Kernsmith, and A. I. Carcone, "The Relationship between Caseworker Attitudes about Kinship Care and Removal Decisions," *Journal of Family Social Work* 16, no. 5 (2013): 403–17, doi:10.1080/10522158.2013 .832459.

141. T. Esposito et al., "The Stability of Child Protection Placements in Québec, Canada," *Children and Youth Services Review* 42 (2014): 10–19, doi:10.1016/ j.childyouth.2014.03.015.

142. R. J. Gelles, *The Book of David: How Preserving Families Can Cost Children Their Lives* (New York: Basic Books, 1996), 131.

143. Waldock, "Enhancing the Quality of Care in Child Welfare"; T. Waldock, "The Rights of Children in Care: Consistency with the Convention?" in Howe and Covell, *A Question of Commitment*, 287–319.

144. K. B. Baum, "Manitoba Foster Children Still Being Left in 'Last Resort' Hotels," *Globe and Mail*, March 23, 2015, https://www.theglobeandmail.com/ news/national/Manitoba-foster-children-still-being-left-in-last-resort-hotels/ article23576306/; G. Leo, "13 Foster Kids Housed in Regina Hotel Sign of 'Looming Crisis': Advocate," CBC News, June 5, 2015, http://www.cbc.ca/ news/Canada/Saskatchewan/13-foster-kids-housed-in-regina-hotel-sign-of -looming-crisis-advocate-1.3102651; W. Stueck, "Hotel Stays for B.C. Foster Kids Reflect Overloaded System: Advocates," *Globe and Mail*, January 14, 2016, https://www.theglobeandmail.com/news/british-columbia/hotel-stays-for-bc -foster-kids-reflect-overloaded-system-advocates/article28208208/.

145. Waldock, "Enhancing the Quality of Care in Child Welfare."

146. Waldock, "Enhancing the Quality of Care in Child Welfare"; Waldock, "The Rights of Children in Care."

147. G. Perry, M. Daly, and J. Kotler, "Placement Stability in Kinship and Non-Kin Foster Care: A Canadian Study," *Children and Youth Services Review* 34, no. 2 (2012): 460–65.

148. Ibid.

149. Waldock, "Enhancing the Quality of Care in Child Welfare."

150. Waldock, "The Rights of Children in Care."

151. K. Brisebois, "Caseworker Attitudes of Kinship Care in Ontario," *Qualitative Social Work* 12, no. 3 (2013): 289–306.

152. Brisebois, Kernsmith, and Carcone, "The Relationship between Caseworker Attitudes about Kinship Care."

153. J. J. Haugaard, "Is Adoption a Risk Factor for the Development of Adjustment Problems?" *Clinical Psychology Review* 18, no. 1 (1998): 47–69.

154. B. Maughan, S. Collishaw, and A. Pickles, "School Achievement and Adult Qualifications among Adoptees: A Longitudinal Study," *Journal of Child Psychology and Psychiatry* 39, no. 5 (1998): 669–85.

155. Helie, Poirier, and Turcotte, "Risk of Maltreatment Recurrence."

## CHAPTER 7

1. R. Hodgkin and P. Newell, *Implementation Handbook for the Convention on the Rights of the Child* (New York: UNICEF, 2007), 1–4. See also R. Hart, "Stepping Back from the 'Ladder,'" in *Participation and Learning,* ed. A. Reid et al. (Dordrecht: Springer, 2008), 19–31.
2. M. Flekkoy and N. Kaufman, *The Participation Rights of the Child* (London: Jessica Kingsley, 1997), 33–34, 60–61, 90–98.
3. UN Committee on the Rights of the Child, *General Comment 12,* July 1, 2009, 8–9, http://www2.ohchr.org/english/bodies/crc/docs/AdvanceVersions/CRC-C-GC-12.pdf.
4. D. Stasiulis, "The Active Child Citizen: Lessons from Canadian Policy and the Children's Movement," *Citizenship Studies* 6, no. 4 (2002): 507–38.
5. K. Marshall, *Children's Rights in the Balance: The Participation-Protection Debate* (Edinburgh: Stationery Office, 1997), 34–35.
6. Human rights legislation in Saskatchewan, Québec, and Yukon are exceptions. In these jurisdictions, the legislation protects freedom of expression but not children's participation or freedom of expression in the family.
7. On the complications of detecting and substantiating cases of emotional maltreatment, see C. Chamberland et al., "Emotional Maltreatment in Canada," *Child Abuse & Neglect* 35, no. 10 (2011): 841–54, doi:10.1016/j.chiabu.2011.03.010.
8. UN Committee, *General Comment 12,* 18–19.
9. K. Campbell and L. Rose-Krasnor, "The Participation Rights of the Child: Canada's Track Record," in *A Question of Commitment: Children's Rights in Canada,* ed. R. B. Howe and K. Covell (Waterloo, ON: Wilfrid Laurier University Press), 215–16.
10. B. Bacon and B. McKenzie, "Parent Education after Separation/Divorce: Impact of the Level of Parental Conflict on Outcomes," *Family Court Review* 42, no. 1 (2004): 85–98; C. Matusicky and C. Russell, "Best Practices for Parents: What Is Happening in Canada?" *Paediatrics and Child Health* 14, no. 10 (2009): 664–65.
11. B. Skrypnek and J. Charchun, *An Evaluation of the Nobody's Perfect Parenting Program* (Ottawa: Canadian Association of Family Resource Programs, 2009).
12. Bacon and McKenzie, "Parent Education after Separation."
13. Campbell and Rose-Krasnor, "The Participation Rights of the Child," 216; Matusicky and Russell, "Best Practices for Parents," 664–65.
14. D. Baumrind, "Child Care Practices Anteceding Three Patterns of Preschool Behaviour," *Genetic Psychology Monographs* 75, no. 1 (1967): 43–88; D. Baumrind, "Current Patterns of Parental Authority," *Developmental Psychology Monographs* 4, no. 1 (1971): 1–103.

15. P. Braza et al., "Negative Maternal and Paternal Parenting Styles as Predictors of Children's Behavioural Problems: Moderating Effects of the Child's Sex," *Journal of Child and Family Studies* 24, no. 4 (2015): 847–56, doi:10.1007/s10826-013-9893-0.

16. Braza et al., "Negative Maternal and Paternal Parenting Styles"; S. A. Hardy et al., "Moral Identity and Psychological Distance: The Case of Adolescent Parental Socialization," *Journal of Adolescence* 33, no. 1 (2010): 111–23, doi:10.1016/j.adolescence.2009.04.008; M. Liu and F. Guo, "Parenting Practices and Their Relevance to Child Behaviours in Canada and China," *Scandinavian Journal of Psychology* 51, no. 2 (2010): 109–14, doi:10.1111/j.1467-9450.2009.00795.x.

17. N. Sorkhabi, "Applicability of Baumrind's Typology to Collective Cultures: Analysis of Cultural Explanations of Parent Socialization Effects," *International Journal of Behavioural Development* 29, no. 6 (2005): 552.

18. C. Jackson, L. Kenriksen, and V. Foshee, "The Authoritative Parenting Index: Predicting Health and Risk Behaviours among Children and Adolescents," *Health, Education and Behaviour* 25, no. 3 (1998): 319–37; M. F. Moghaddam, A. Validad, T. Rakhshani, and M. Assareh, "Child Self-Esteem and Different Parenting Styles of Mothers: A Cross-Sectional Study," *Archives of Psychiatry and Psychotherapy* 19, no. 1 (2017): 37–42. doi:10.12740/APP/68160; H. Masud, M. S. Ahmad, F. A. Jan, and A. Jamil, "Relationship between Parenting Styles and Academic Performance of Adolescents: Mediating Role of Self-Efficacy," *Asia Pacific Education Review* 17, no. 1 (2016): 121–31, doi:10.1007/s12564-015-9413-6; M. G. Minaie et al., "Parenting Style and Behavior as Longitudinal Predictors of Adolescent Alcohol Use," *Journal of Studies on Alcohol and Drugs* 76, no. 5 (2015): 671–79, doi:10.15288/jsad.2015.76.671; L. Kakinami, T. A. Barnett, L. Séguin, and G. Paradis, "Parenting Style and Obesity Risk in Children," *Preventive Medicine* (2015): 18–22, doi:10.1016/j.ypmed.2015.03.005.

19. Hardy et al., "Moral Identity and Psychological Distance"; M. Miklikowska and H. Hurme, "Democracy Begins at Home: Democratic Parenting and Adolescents' Support for Democratic Values," *European Journal of Developmental Psychology* 8, no. 5 (2011): 541–57; M. W. Pratt et al., "Earth Mothers (and Fathers): Examining Generativity and Environmental Concerns in Adolescents and Their Parents," *Journal of Moral Education* 42, no. 1 (2013): 12–27, doi:10.1080/03057240.2012.714751; L. Wray-Lake and C. A. Flanagan, "Parenting Practices and the Development of Adolescents' Social Trust," *Journal of Adolescence* 35, no. 3 (2012): 549–60, doi:10.1016/j.adolescence.2011.09.006.

20. Hardy et al., "Moral Identity and Psychological Distance"; Miklikowska and Hurme, "Democracy Begins at Home"; Wray-Lake and Flanagan, "Parenting Practices."

21. Miklikowska and Hurme, "Democracy Begins at Home"; Pratt et al., "Earth Mothers (and Fathers)."

22. UN Committee, *General Comment 12*, 21.

23. Campbell and Rose-Krasnor, "The Participation Rights of the Child," 218–19; L. Johnny, "UN Convention on the Rights of the Child: A Rationale for Implementing Participatory Rights in Schools," *Canadian Journal of Educational Administration and Policy* 40 (March 2005): 1–20.

24. R. B. Howe and K. Covell, "Towards the Best Interests of the Child in Education," *Education and Law Journal* 20, no. 1 (2010), 22–23.

25. K. Bickmore, "Teaching Conflict and Conflict Resolution in School," in *How Children Understand War and Peace*, ed. A. Raviv, L. Oppenheiner, and D. Bar-Tal (San Francisco: Jossey-Bass, 1999), 242; C. Parker, *Peacebuilding, Citizenship, and Identity: Empowering Conflict and Dialogue in Multicultural Classrooms* (Boston: Sense, 2016).

26. Justice for Children and Youth, *Children's Right to Be Heard in Canadian Administrative and Judicial Proceedings*, 2013, 3, http://jfcy.org/wp-content/uploads/2013/10/UNDiscussionPaper.pdf.

27. A. Brown and M. Zuker, *Education Law* (Toronto: Carswell, 2007), 267–76.

28. L. Barnett, *Freedom of Religion and Religious Symbols in the Public Sphere* (Ottawa: Library of Parliament, 2004), 10–13; Brown and Zuker, *Education Law*, 267–74.

29. D. Gereluk, *Symbolic Clothing in Schools* (London: Continuum, 2008).

30. J. Wilson, *Wilson on Children and the Law* (LexisNexis, 2016), 8.73–8.82.

31. Ibid., 8.120–8.123.

32. T. Collins and M. Paré, "A Child Rights-Based Approach to Anti-Violence Efforts in Schools," *International Journal of Children's Rights* 24, no. 4 (2016): 764–802, doi:10.1163/15718182-02404005; Campbell and Rose-Krasnor, "The Participation Rights of the Child," 220–21; Johnny, "UN Convention on the Rights of the Child."

33. R. B. Howe and K. Covell, *Empowering Children: Children's Rights Education as a Pathway to Citizenship* (Toronto: University of Toronto Press, 2007), 29–35.

34. Collins and Paré, "A Child Rights-Based Approach"; K. Covell, "Children's Rights Education: Canada's Best-Kept Secret," in Howe and Covell, *A Question of Commitment*, 244–51; Johnny, "UN Convention on the Rights of the Child."

35. Covell, "Children's Rights Education," 241–63.

36. P. Pitula, "Hollywood and Human Rights in the Curriculum," *Education & Law Journal* 17, no. 3 (2008): 275–90.

37. UN Committee on the Rights of the Child, *UN Committee on the Rights of the Child: Concluding Observations: Canada*, June 20, 1995, CRC/C/15/Add.37, http://www.refworld.org/docid/3ae6af5a14.html; UN Committee on the Rights of the Child, *UN Committee on the Rights of the Child: Concluding Observations: Canada*, October 5, 2012, CRC/C/CAN/CO/3-4, http://www2.ohchr.org/english/bodies/crc/docs/co/CRC-C-CAN-CO-3-4_en.pdf.

38. R. G. Simmons and D. A. Blyth, *Moving into Adolescence: The Impact of Pubertal Change and School Context* (New York: Aldine de Gruyter, 1987).

39. S. Berman, *Children's Social Consciousness and the Development of Social Responsibility* (New York: SUNY Press, 1997); D. Oswell, *The Agency of Children: From Family to Global Human Rights* (New York: Cambridge University Press, 2013).

40. Bickmore, "Teaching Conflict and Conflict Resolution in School."

41. R. B. Howe and K. Covell, *Education in the Best Interests of the Child* (Toronto: University of Toronto Press, 2013).

42. C. Katsenou, E. Flogaitis, and G. Liarakou, "Exploring Pupil Participation within a Sustainable School," *Cambridge Journal of Education* 43, no. 2 (2013): 243–58, doi:10.1080/0305764X.2013.774320; E. Quintelier and M. Hooghe, "The Relationship between Political Participation Intentions of Adolescents and a Participatory Democratic Climate at School in 35 Countries," *Oxford Review of Education* 39, no. 5 (2013): 567–89.

43. K. D. Konings, S. Brand-Gruwel, and J. J. G. van Merrienboer, "An Approach to Participatory Instructional Design in Secondary Education: An Exploratory Study," *Educational Research* 52, no. 1 (2010): 45–59.

44. D. McIntyre, D. Pedder, and J. Rudduck, "Pupil Voice: Comfortable and Uncomfortable Learnings for Teachers," *Research Papers in Education* 20, no. 2 (2005): 149–68.

45. C. Flanagan, "Teaching a Larger Sense of Community," *Analyses of Social Issues and Public Policy* 14, no. 1 (2014): 423–25; Katsenou, Flogaitis, and Liarakou, "Exploring Pupil Participation."

46. Covell, "Children's Rights Education."

47. L. Lundy, "Voice Is Not Enough: Conceptualizing Article 12 of the United Nations Convention on the Rights of the Child," *British Education Research Journal* 33, no. 6 (2007): 927–42.

48. Lundy, "Voice Is Not Enough."

49. Howe and Covell, *Empowering Children.*

50. Howe and Covell, *Education in the Best Interests of the Child.*

51. Ibid.

52. Ibid., 176.

53. Ibid., 177–84.

54. UN Committee, *General Comment 12,* 9.

55. Ibid., 3, 12, 15.

56. M. Denov, "Youth Justice and Children's Rights," in Howe and Covell, *A Question of Commitment,* 163–64.

57. N. Bala, A. Evans, and E. Bala, "Hearing the Voices of Children in Canada's Criminal Justice System," *Child and Family Law Quarterly* 22, no. 1 (2010): 21–45.

58. *Civil Code of Québec,* 1991, Book 1, title 2, chapter 2, article 34 (updated 2016).

59. D. Goldberg, "Judicial Interviews of Children in Custody and Access Cases," in *Children and the Law*, ed. S. Anand (Toronto: Irwin Law, 2011), 197–223.

60. N. Bala and C. Houston, *Article 12 of the Convention on the Rights of the Child and Children's Participatory Rights in Canada*. Report to the Family, Children and Youth Section, Department of Justice Canada, 2015, 33–46, http://www.justice.gc.ca/eng/rp-pr/other-autre/article12/Article12-eng.pdf.

61. Ibid., 16–17.

62. Canadian Coalition for the Rights of Children, *Katelynn's Principle: The Child Must Be at the Centre*, 2016, http://rightsofchildren.ca/uncategorized/katelynns-principle-the-child-must-be-at-the-centre/.

63. Ibid.

64. Ontario Ministry of Children and Youth Services, "Ontario Strengthening Child Welfare, Improving Outcomes for Youth," 2016, http://www.children.gov.on.ca/htdocs/English/index.aspx.

65. B. MacLaurin and N. Bala, "Children in Care," in *Canadian Child Welfare Law*, ed. N. Bala et al. (Toronto: Thompson, 2004), 111–38.

66. T. Waldock, "The Rights of Children in Care: Consistency with the Convention?" in Howe and Covell, *A Question of Commitment*, 307–9.

67. Bala and Houston, *Article 12*, 47–52.

68. Wilson, *Wilson on Children*, 12.12–12.14.

69. Bala and Houston, *Article 12*, 50–52.

70. Ibid., 8–12.

71. Wilson, *Wilson on Children*, 2.2–2.3. However, if Bill C-78 (pending in 2018) becomes federal law, the *Divorce Act* will be amended to require that the views of children be one of the criteria for determining the best interests of the child.

72. Bala and Houston, *Article 12*, 9.

73. Ibid., 12–25.

74. N. Semple, "The Silent Child: A Quantitative Analysis of Children's Evidence in Canadian Custody and Access Cases," *Canadian Family Law Quarterly* 29, no. 1 (2010): 7–43.

75. R. Alaggia, E. Lambert, and C. Regehr, "Where Is the Justice? Parental Experiences of the Canadian Justice System in Cases of Child Sexual Abuse," *Family Court Review* 47, no. 4 (2009): 634–49.

76. K. Chong and D. A. Connolly, "Testifying through the Ages: An Examination of Current Psychological Issues on the Use of Testimonial Supports by Child, Adolescent, and Adult Witnesses in Canada," *Canadian Psychology* 56, no. 1 (2015): 108–17.

77. Alaggia, Lambert, and Regehr, "Where Is the Justice?"

78. Chong and Connolly, "Testifying through the Ages."

79. N. Bala et al., "Children's Voices in Family Court: Guidelines for Judges Meeting Children," *Family Law Quarterly* 47, no. 3 (2013): 379–408.

80. Bala et al., "Children's Voices in Family Court."

81. Ibid.

82. K. P. Roberts and S. C. Cameron, "Observations from Canadian Practitioners about the Investigation and Prosecution of Crimes Involving Child and Adult Witnesses," *Journal of Forensic Psychology Practice* 15, no. 1 (2015): 33–57.

83. Ibid.

84. Ibid.

85. C. Peterson, "Children's Autobiographical Memories across the Years: Forensic Implications of Childhood Amnesia and Eyewitness Memory for Stressful Events," *Developmental Review* 32, no. 3 (2012): 287–306, doi:10.1016/j.dr.2012.06.002.

86. K. Winter, "The Perspectives of Young Children in Care about Their Circumstances and Implications for Social Work Practice," *Child and Family Social Work* 15, no. 2 (2010): 186–95.

87 P. Polkki et al., "Children's Participation in Child-Protection Processes as Experienced by Foster Children and Social Workers," *Child Care in Practice* 18, no. 2 (2012): 116, doi:10.1080/13575279.2011.646954.

88. Polkki et al., "Children's Participation in Child-Protection Processes," 117.

89. J. A. Quas et al., "Maltreated Children's Understanding of and Emotional Reactions to Dependency Court Involvement," *Behavioural Sciences & the Law* 27, no. 1 (2009): 97–117, doi:10.1002/bsl.836.

90. C. Bettenay et al., "Changed Responses under Cross-Examination: The Role of Anxiety and Individual Differences in Child Witnesses," *Applied Cognitive Psychology* 29, no. 3 (2015): 485–91, doi:10.1002/acp.3125.

91. A. D. Evans et al., "The Effects of Repetition on Children's True and False Reports," *Psychiatry, Psychology and Law* 19, no. 4 (2012): 517–29, doi:10.1080/13218719.2011.615808.

92. J. E. Newman and K. P. Roberts, "Subjective and Non-subjective Information in Children's Allegations of Abuse," *Journal of Police and Criminal Psychology* 29, no. 2 (2014): 75–80, doi:10.1007/s11896-013-9133-y.

93. Newman and Roberts, "Subjective and Non-subjective Information."

94. See for example K. Saywitz, L. B. Camparo, and A. Romanoff, "Interviewing Children in Custody Cases: Implications of Research and Policy for Practice," *Behavioural Sciences & the Law* 28, no. 4 (2010): 542–62, doi:10.1002/bsl.945.

95. Bala et al., "Children's Voices in Family Court."

96. M. K. Brunet et al., "How Children Report True and Fabricated Stressful and Non-Stressful Events," *Psychiatry, Psychology and Law* 20, no. 6 (2013): 867–81, doi:10.1080/13218719.2012.750896; A. D. Evans and T. D. Lyon, "Assessing Children's Competency to Take the Oath in Court: The Influence of Question Type on Children's Accuracy," *Law and Human Behaviour* 36, no. 3 (2012): 195–205.

97. S. M. Williams et al., "Is the Truth in Your Words? Distinguishing Children's

Deceptive and Truthful Statements," *Journal of Criminology* 2014 (2014), Article ID 547519, 9 pages, doi:10.1155/2014/547519.

98. Williams et al., "Is the Truth in Your Words?"

99. R. Bosisio, "Children's Right to Be Heard: What Children Think," *International Journal of Children's Rights* 20, no. 1 (2012): 141–54, doi:10.1163/157181811X573462; S. D. Block et al., "Abused and Neglected Children in Court: Knowledge and Attitudes," *Child Abuse & Neglect* 34, no. 9 (2010): 659–70, doi:10.1016/j.chiabu.2010.02.003; J. Cashmore, "Children's Participation in Family Law Decision-Making: Theoretical Approaches to Understanding Children's Views," *Children and Youth Services Review* 33, no. 4 (2011): 515–20; V. Weisz et al., "Children's Participation in Foster Care Hearings," *Child Abuse & Neglect* 35, no. 4 (2011): 267–72, doi:10.1016/j.chiabu.2010.12.007.

100. Block et al., "Abused and Neglected Children in Court."

101. Weisz et al., "Children's Participation in Foster Care Hearings."

102. Bosisio, "Children's Right to Be Heard."

## CHAPTER 8

1. L. A. White, "Understanding Canada's Lack of Progress in Implementing the UN Convention on the Rights of the Child," *International Journal of Children's Rights* 22, no. 1 (2014): 164–88, doi:10.1163/15718182-02201002; see also Canadian Coalition for the Rights of Children, *Right in Principle, Right in Practice* (Ottawa: Canadian Coalition for the Rights of Children, 2011).

2. UN Committee on the Rights of the Child, *UN Committee on the Rights of the Child: Concluding Observations: Canada,* October 5, 2012, CRC/C/CAN/CO/3-4, http://www2.ohchr.org/english/bodies/crc/docs/co/CRC-C-CAN-CO-3-4_en.pdf.

3. M. Bernstein, "Transforming Child Welfare in Canada into a Stronger Child Rights-Based System," in *Transforming Child Welfare: Interdisciplinary Practices, Field Education, and Research,* ed. H. Montgomery et al. (Regina: University of Regina Press, 2016), 24–25.

4. L. Monsebraaten, "Ontario Introduces 'Historic' Changes to Child-Protection Laws," *Toronto Star,* December 8, 2016, https://www.thestar.com/news/gta/2016/12/08/ontario-introduces-historic-changes-to-child-protection-laws.html.

5. Bernstein, "Transforming Child Welfare," 8–9; R. B. Howe and K. Covell, "Conclusion: Canada's Ambivalence toward Children," in *A Question of Commitment: Children's Rights in Canada,* ed. R. B. Howe and K. Covell (Waterloo, ON: Wilfrid Laurier University Press, 2007), 400–407.

6. Senate of Canada, Standing Committee on Human Rights, *Children: Silenced Citizens* (Ottawa: Senate Standing Committee on Human Rights, 2007), 195–98.

7. Amnesty International et al., *Promise and Reality: Canada's International Human Rights Implementation Gap* (Joint NGO Submission to the United Nations Human Rights Council in relation to the February 2009 Universal Periodic Review of Canada, September 8, 2008), http://www.socialrightscura.ca/documents/UPR/JS1_CAN_UPR_S4_2009_SocialRightsAdvocacyCentre_Etal_JOINT.pdf.

8. United Nations, "Vienna Convention on the Law of Treaties," May 23, 1969, http://legal.un.org/ilc/texts/instruments/english/conventions/1_1_1969.pdf.

9. Also noted by Senate Standing Committee on Human Rights, *Children: Silenced Citizens*, 17–22.

10. S. Grover, "Advocating for Children's Rights as an Aspect of Professionalism," *Child and Youth Care Forum* 33, no. 6 (2004): 405–23; R. B. Howe, "Factors Affecting the Impact of Child Advocacy Offices in Canada," *Canadian Review of Social Policy* 62 (2009): 17–33.

11. "Mandate," Canadian Council of Child and Youth Advocates, 2017, http://www.cccya.ca/content/index.asp.

12. Howe and Covell, "Conclusion," 403–7.

13. Howe and Covell, "Conclusion," 402–3; Senate Standing Committee on Human Rights, *Children: Silenced Citizens*, 195–98.

14. P. Burnstein, "The Impact of Public Opinion on Public Policy: A Review and an Agenda," *Political Research Quarterly* 56, no. 1 (2003): 29–41.

15. R. B. Howe and K. Covell, *Empowering Children: Children's Rights Education as a Pathway to Citizenship* (Toronto: University of Toronto Press, 2007), 3–5.

16. Ibid., 3.

17. A. Pellatt, *The United Nations Convention on the Rights of the Child: How Does Alberta's Legislation Measure Up?* (Calgary: Alberta Civil Liberties Research Centre, 1999), 1.

18. K. Campbell and L. Rose-Krasnor, "The Participation Rights of the Child: Canada's Track Record," in Howe and Covell, *A Question of Commitment*, 209–39.

19. G. Esping-Andersen, *The Three Worlds of Welfare Capitalism* (Princeton, NJ: Princeton University Press, 1990); G. Esping-Andersen, *Social Foundations of Postindustrial Economies* (Oxford: Oxford University Press, 1999).

20. K. Covell and R. B. Howe, *Children, Families and Violence: Challenges for Children's Rights* (London: Jessica Kingsley, 2009), 211–19.

21. N. Mandela, "Lighting Your Way to a Better Future" (speech, University of the Witwatersrand, Johannesburg, South Africa, July 16, 2003), http://db.nelsonmandela.org/speeches/pub_view.asp?pg=item&ItemID=NMS909. Some of this statement was used much earlier, in a speech delivered June 23, 1990; P. Schworm, "Nelson Mandela's 1990 Visit Left Lasting Impression," *Boston Globe,* December 7, 2013, http://www.bostonglobe.com/metro/2013/12/07/mandela-visit-boston-high-school-left-lasting-impression/2xZ1QqkVMTbHKXiFEJynTO/story.html.

22. UN Committee on the Rights of the Child, *Committee on the Rights of the Child. General Comment no. 1: The Aims of Education,* UN/CRC/GC/2001/1 (Geneva: United Nations, 2001); see also J. C. Blokhuis, "Student Rights and the Special Characteristics of the School Environment in American Jurisprudence," *Journal of Philosophy of Education* 49, no. 1 (2015): 65–85.

23. K. Covell, "Awareness, Learning and Education in Human Rights," in *The SAGE Handbook of Human Rights*, ed. A. Mihr, and M. Gibney (London: Sage, 2014), 821–39.

24. K. Covell, R. B. Howe, and J. K. McNeil, "If There's a Dead Rat, Don't Leave It: Young Children's Understanding of Their Citizenship Rights and Responsibilities," *Cambridge Journal of Education* 38, no. 30 (2008): 321–39, doi:10.1080/03057640802286889.

25. Howe and Covell, *Empowering Children*, 146–49; K. Covell, R. B. Howe, and J. K. McNeil, "Implementing Children's Human Rights Education in Schools," *Improving Schools* 13, no. 2 (2010): 1–16.

26. K. McMullen, "Postsecondary Education Participation among Under-represented and Minority Groups," Statistics Canada, 2011, http://www.statcan.gc.ca/pub/81-004-x/2011004/article/11595-eng.htm.

27. K. M. Campbell and K. Covell, "Children's Rights Education at the University Level: An Effective Means of Promoting Rights Knowledge and Rights-Based Attitudes," *International Journal of Children's Rights* 9, no. 2 (2001): 123–35, doi:10.1163/15718180120494883.

28. Ibid.

29. S. A. Myers-Clack and S. E. Christopher, "Effectiveness of a Health Course at Influencing Preservice Teachers' Attitudes toward Teaching Health," *Journal of School Health* 71, no. 9 (2001): 462–66.

30. C. Hertzman, "The Significance of Early Childhood Adversity," *Pediatric Child Health* 18, no. 3 (2013): 127–28.

31. J. Coyne and L. Kwakenbos, "Triple P-Positive Parenting Programs: The Folly of Basing Social Policy on Underpowered Flawed Studies," *BMC Medicine* 11 (2013): 11, doi:10.1186/1741-7015-11-11.

32. L. Sylwander, *Child Impact Assessments* (Sweden: Ministry of Health and Social Affairs, Sweden, Ministry for Foreign Affairs, 2001).

33. C. M. Lee et al., "The International Parenting Survey—Canada: Exploring Access to Parenting Services," *Canadian Psychology* 55, no. 2 (2104): 110–16.

34. Ibid.

35. E. Romano, T. Bell, and R. Norian, "Corporal Punishment: Examining Attitudes toward the Law and Factors Influencing Attitude Change," *Journal of Family Violence* 28, no. 3 (2013): 265–75.

36. M. J. Letarte, S. Normandeau, and J. Allard, "Effectiveness of a Parent Training Program, 'Incredible Years' in a Child Protection Service," *Child Abuse & Neglect* 34, no. 4 (2010): 253–61, doi:10.1016/j.chiabu.2009.06.003.

37. "EDI Mapping Wave 2. British Columbia School Districts," 2013, Human Early Learning Partnership, http://www.earlylearning.ubc.ca/edi.

38. S. Popova et al., "Comorbidity of Fetal Alcohol Spectrum Disorder: A Systematic Review and Meta-Analysis," *The Lancet* 387, no. 10022 (2016): 978–87; S. Semenic et al., "Decision-Making and Evidence Use during the Process of Prenatal Record Review in Canada: A Multiphase Qualitative Study," *BMC Pregnancy and Childbirth* 15 (2015): 78.

39. P. R. Britto et al., "Nurturing Care: Promoting Early Childhood Development," *The Lancet* 389, no. 10064 (2017): 91–102, doi:10.1016/S0140-6736(16)31390-3.

40. Senate Standing Committee on Human Rights, *Children: The Silenced Citizens*, 202–14.

41. Ibid., 206–14.

42. Ibid., 209–10.

43. M. Flekkoy, "The Ombudsman for Children: Conception and Developments," in *The New Handbook of Children's Rights: Comparative Policy and Practice*, ed. B. Franklin (London: Routledge, 2002), 404–19.

44. Bernstein, "Transforming Child Welfare," 9–10; "UNICEF Canada Statement on Third Optional Protocol to the Convention on the Rights of the Child—Complaints or Communications Procedure for Violation of Children's Rights," UNICEF Canada, 2011, http://www.unicef.ca/en/press-release/unicef-canada-statement-on-third-optional-protocol-to-the-convention-on-the-rights-of-.

45. L. Lundy et al., *The UN Convention on the Rights of the Child: A Study of Legal Implementation in 12 Countries* (London: UNICEF-UK, 2012).

46. R. Howard-Hassmann, *Compassionate Canadians: Civic Leaders Discuss Human Rights* (Toronto: University of Toronto Press, 2003).

47. R. J. Norlander, "A Digital Approach to Human Rights Education?" *Peace Review* 24, no. 1 (2012): 70–77, doi:10.1080/10402659.2012.651025.

48. M. Klein, "Online Partnerships for Human Rights Education Praxis," *Peace Review* 24, no. 1 (2012): 61–69, doi:10.1080/10402659.2012.651022.

49. H. Shue, *Basic Rights* (Princeton, NJ: Princeton University Press, 1980), 75.

50. R. E. Petty, D. T. Wegner, and L. R. Fabrigar, "Attitudes and Attitude Change," *Annual Review of Psychology* 48 (1997): 609–47.

# Selected Bibliography

## BOOKS, JOURNAL ARTICLES, AND REPORTS

Referenced legal cases and useful websites are listed separately. Website, magazine, newspaper, and other resources are included in the notes for each chapter.

Afifi, T. O. "Child Maltreatment in Canada: An Understudied Public Health Problem." *Canadian Journal of Public Health/Revue Canadienne de santé publique* 102, no. 6 (2011): 459–61.

Afifi, T. O., H. L. MacMillan, M. Boyle, K. Cheung, T. Taillieu, S. Turner, and J. Sareen. "Child Abuse and Physical Health in Adulthood." Statistics Canada. March 16, 2016. http://www.statcan.gc.ca/pub/82-003-x/2016003/article/14339-eng.htm.

Afifi, T. O., H. L. MacMillan, M. Boyle, T. Taillieu, K. Cheung, and J. Sareen. "Child Abuse and Mental Disorders in Canada." *CMAJ: Canadian Medical Association Journal/Journal de l'Association médicale canadienne* 186, no. 9 (2014): E324–32. doi:10.1503/cmaj.131792.

Aitken, S. C. "Children's Geographies: Tracing the Evolution and Involution of a Concept." *Geographical Review* 108, no. 1 (2018): 3–23. doi 10.1111/gere.1228.

Akdeniz, Y. *Internet Child Pornography Laws*. Aldershot, UK: Ashgate, 2008.

Alaggia, R., E. Lambert, and C. Regehr. "Where Is the Justice? Parental Experiences of the Canadian Justice System in Cases of Child Sexual Abuse." *Family Court Review* 47, no. 4 (2009): 634–49.

Albanese, P. *Children in Canada Today.* Toronto: Oxford University Press, 2016.

Alderson, P. "Common Criticisms of Children's Rights and 25 Years of the IJCR." *International Journal of Children's Rights* 25, no. 2 (2017): 307–319. doi:10.1163/15718182-02502001.

Al-hamandi, M. "The Case for Stringent Alcohol Warning Labels: Lessons from the Tobacco Control Experience." *Journal of Public Health Policy* 35, no. 1 (2014): 65–74.

Archard, D. *Children: Rights and Childhood*. 3rd ed. New York: Routledge, 2015.

Archard, D., and C. M. Macleod, eds. *The Moral and Political Status of Children*. Oxford: Oxford University Press, 2002.

Ard, K., and M. Fairbrother. "Pollution Prophylaxis? Social Capital and Environmental Inequality." *Social Science Quarterly* 98, no. 2 (2017): 584–607. doi:10.1111/ssqu.12324.

Bacon, B., and B. McKenzie. "Parent Education after Separation/Divorce: Impact of the Level of Parental Conflict on Outcomes." *Family Court Review* 42, no. 1 (2004): 85–98.

Baker, J. A., R. W. Kamphaus, A. M. Horne, and A. P. Winsor. "Evidence for Population-Based Perspectives on Children's Behavioural Adjustment and Needs for Service Delivery in Schools." *School Psychology Review* 35, no. 1 (2006): 31–46.

Baker, M., J. Gruber, and K. Milligan. "Universal Child Care, Maternal Labor Supply, and Family Well-Being." *Journal of Political Economy* 116, no. 4 (2008): 709–45. doi:10.1086/591908.

Bala, N. "Child Welfare Law in Canada: An Introduction." In Bala et al., *Canadian Child Welfare Law*, 1–25.

———. "Pornography and Prostitution: Does Canada Comply with the Convention?" In Canadian Council on Children and Youth, *On the Right Side*, 22–26.

———. "Setting the Context: Child Welfare Law in Canada." In *Child Welfare: Connecting Research, Policy, and Practice,* 2nd ed., edited by K. Kufeldt and B. McKenzie, 1–18. Waterloo: Wilfrid Laurier University Press, 2011.

Bala, N., R. Birnbaum, F. Cyr, and D. McColley. "Children's Voices in Family Court: Guidelines for Judges Meeting Children." *Family Law Quarterly* 47, no. 3 (2013): 379–408.

Bala, N., A. Evans, and E. Bala. "Hearing the Voices of Children in Canada's Criminal Justice System." *Child and Family Law Quarterly* 22, no. 1 (2010): 21–45.

Bala, N., and C. Houston. *Article 12 of the Convention on the Rights of the Child and Children's Participatory Rights in Canada.* Department of Justice Canada, 2016. http://www.justice.gc.ca/eng/rp-pr/other-autre/article12/Article12-eng.pdf.

Bala, N., M. K. Zapf, R. Vogl, and J. P. Hornick, eds. *Canadian Child Welfare Law: Children, Families, and the State.* 2nd ed. Toronto: Thompson, 2004.

Ballentine, J. A. *Ballentine's Law Dictionary: With Pronunciations*, 3rd ed., edited by W. S. Anderson. San Francisco: Bancroft-Whitney, 1969.

Barnett, L. *Freedom of Religion and Religious Symbols in the Public Sphere.* Ottawa: Library of Parliament, 2004.

Barnett, W. S., and E. Frede. "The Promise of Preschool: Why We Need Early Education for All." *American Educator* 34, no. 1 (2010): 21.

Barrett, N., and M. Shaw. *Laws to Combat Sex Trafficking: An Overview of International, National, Provincial and Municipal Laws and Their Enforcement.* Canadian Women's Foundation, 2013. http://www.canadianwomen.org/sites/canadianwomen.org/files//NB%27s%20Nov%20%2014%20FINAL%20REPORT%20Laws%20to%20Combat%20Sex%20Trafficking.pdf.

Battle, K. *Child Benefits and the 2015 Federal Budget.* Ottawa: Caledon Institute of Social Policy, 2015. http://www.caledoninst.org/Publications/PDF/1064ENG.pdf.

————. *Child Benefits in Canada: Politics Versus Policy.* Ottawa: Caledon Institute of Social Policy, 2015. http://www.caledoninst.org/Publications/PDF/1074ENG%2Epdf.

————. "Child Poverty: The Evolution and Impact of Child Benefits." In Howe and Covell, *A Question of Commitment,* 21–44.

Baumrind, D. "Child Care Practices Anteceding Three Patterns of Preschool Behaviour." *Genetic Psychology Monographs* 75, no. 1 (1967): 43–88.

————. "Current Patterns of Parental Authority." *Developmental Psychology Monographs* 4, no. 1 (1971): 1–103.

Becker, J. *Campaigning for Children: Strategies for Advancing Children's Rights.* Stanford, CA: Stanford University Press, 2017.

Bell, E. R., D. B. Greenfield, R. J. Bulotsky-Shearer, and T. M. Carter. "Peer Play as a Context for Identifying Profiles of Children and Examining Rates of Growth in Academic Readiness for Children Enrolled in Head Start." *Journal of Educational Psychology* 108, no. 5 (2016): 740–59. doi:10.1037/edu0000084.

Bell, S. *Young Offenders and Youth Justice: A Century after the Fact.* Toronto: Nelson, 2012.

Belsky, J. "Infant Day-Care: A Cause for Concern?" *Zero to Three* 6, no. 4 (1986): 1–7.

Bennett, M. "Aboriginal Children's Rights." In Howe and Covell, *A Question of Commitment,* 275–78.

Benzies, K., R. Mychasiuk, J. Kurilova, S. Tough, N. Edwards, and C. Donnelly. "Two-Generation Preschool Program: Immediate and 7-Year-Old Outcomes for Low-Income Children and Their Parents." *Child & Family Social Work* 19, no. 2 (2014): 203–14. doi:10.1111/j.1365-2206.2012.00894.x.

Berlin, L. J., J. Brooks-Gunn, C. McCarton, and M. C. McCormick. "The Effectiveness of Early Intervention: Examining Risk Factors and Pathways to Enhanced Development." *Preventive Medicine* 27, no. 2 (1998): 238–45. doi:10.1006/pmed.1998.0282.

Berman, S. *Children's Social Consciousness and the Development of Social Responsibility.* New York: State University of New York Press, 1997.

Bernard, C., and J. Shea, eds. *Giving Children a Voice: The Transforming Role of the Family.* Newcastle upon Tyne, UK: Cambridge Scholars Publishing, 2009.

Bernstein, M. "Transforming Child Welfare in Canada into a Stronger Child Rights-Based System." In *Transforming Child Welfare: Interdisciplinary Practices, Field Education, and Research,* edited by H. Montgomery, D. Badry, D. Fuchs, and D. Kikulwe, 3–26. Regina: University of Regina Press, 2016.

Bernstein, M., and K. Reitmeier. "The Child Protection Hearing." In Bala et al., *Canadian Child Welfare Law,* 71–73.

Bettenay, C., A. M. Ridley, L. A. Henry, and L. Crane. "Changed Responses under Cross-Examination: The Role of Anxiety and Individual Differences in Child Witnesses." *Applied Cognitive Psychology* 29, no. 3 (2015): 485–91. doi:10.1002/acp.3125.

Bezeau, R. N., and J. R. Hoskins. *The Fallen Feather* [video recording]. Surrey, BC: Fallen Feather Productions, 2007.

Bickmore, K. "Teaching Conflict and Conflict Resolution in School." In *How Children Understand War and Peace*, edited by A. Raviv, L. Oppenheiner, and D. Bar-Tal, 233–59. San Francisco: Jossey-Bass, 1999. http://fcis.oise.utoronto .ca/~csjcse/article.html.

Biggieri, M., J. Ballet, and F. Comim, eds. *Children and the Capability Approach.* Basingstoke, UK: Palgrave Macmillan, 2011.

Bittle, S. "Still Punishing to 'Protect.'" In *Selling Sex: Experience, Advocacy, and Research on Sex Work in Canada,* edited by E. van der Meulen, E. Durisin, and M. Love, 279–96. Vancouver: UBC Press, 2013.

Black, M. *Children First.* New York: Oxford University Press, 1996.

Blackstock, C. "The Canadian Human Rights Tribunal on First Nations Child Welfare: Why if Canada Wins, Equality and Justice Lose." *Children and Youth Services Review* 33, no. 1 (2011): 187–94.

Blair, C., D. Berry, R. Mills-Koonce, and D. Granger. "Cumulative Effects of Early Poverty on Cortisol in Young Children: Moderation by Autonomic Nervous System Activity." *Psychoneuroendocrinology* 38, no. 11 (2013): 2666–75. doi:10.1016/j.psyneuen.2013.06.025.

Block, S. D., H. Oran, D. Oran, N. Baumrind, and G. S. Goodman. "Abused and Neglected Children in Court: Knowledge and Attitudes." *Child Abuse & Neglect* 34, no. 9 (2010): 659–70. doi:10.1016/j.chiabu.2010.02.003.

Blokhuis, J. C. "Student Rights and the Special Characteristics of the School Environment in American Jurisprudence." *Journal of Philosophy of Education* 49, no. 1 (2015): 65–85. doi:10.1111/1467-9752.12096.

———. "Whose Custody Is It, Anyway? 'Homeschooling' from a *Parens Patriae* Perspective." *Theory and Research in Education* 8, no. 2 (2010): 199–222. doi:10.1177/1477878510368628.

Blokhuis, J. C., and A. Smoke. "The Extraordinary Cases of J. J. and Makayla Sault." In *A Question of Commitment: The Status of Children in Canada,* edited by T. Waldock. Waterloo, ON: Wilfrid Laurier University Press, 2018.

Boivin, M., and C. Hertzman, eds. *Early Childhood Development: Adverse Experiences and Developmental Health.* Ottawa: Royal Society of Canada, 2012.

Bonthius Jr., D. J., Z. Winters, B. Karacay, S. L. Bousquet, and D. J. Bonthius. "Importance of Genetics in Fetal Alcohol Effects: Null Mutation of the nNOS Gene Worsens Alcohol-Induced Cerebellar Neuronal Losses and Behavioural Deficits." *Neurotoxicology* 46 (January 2015): 60–72. doi:10.1016/j.neuro .2014.11.009.

Boots, D. P., and K. M. Heide. "Parricides in the Media: A Content Analysis of Available Reports across Cultures." *International Journal of Offender Therapy and Comparative Criminology* 50, no. 4 (2006): 418–45. doi:10.1177/0306624X05285103.

Bosisio, R. "Children's Right to Be Heard: What Children Think." *International Journal of Children's Rights* 20, no. 1 (2012): 141–54. doi:10.1163/157181811X573462.

Braza, P., R. Carreras, J. M. Muñoz, F. Braza, A. Azurmendi, E. Pascual-Sagastizábal, J. Cardas, and J. R. Sánchez-Martín. "Negative Maternal and Paternal Parenting Styles as Predictors of Children's Behavioural Problems: Moderating Effects of the Child's Sex." *Journal of Child and Family Studies* 24, no. 4 (2015): 847–56. doi:10.1007/s10826-013-9893-0.

Brennan, S. (2002), "Children's Choices or Children's Interests: Which Do Their Rights Protect?" In Archard and Macleod, *The Moral and Political Status of Children*, 53–69.

Brisebois, K. "Caseworker Attitudes of Kinship Care in Ontario." *Qualitative Social Work* 12, no. 3 (2013): 289–306.

Brisebois, K., P. D. Kernsmith, and A. I. Carcone. "The Relationship between Caseworker Attitudes about Kinship Care and Removal Decisions." *Journal of Family Social Work* 16, no. 5 (2013): 403–17. doi:10.1080/10522158.2013.832459.

Britto, P. R., S. J. Lye, K. Proulx, A. K. Yousafzai, S. G. Matthews, T. Vaivada, R. Perez-Escamilla, et al. "Nurturing Care: Promoting Early Childhood Development." *The Lancet* 389, no. 10064 (2017): 91–102. doi:10.1016/S0140-6736(16)31390-3.

Bronfenbrenner, U. *Making Human Beings Human: Bioecological Perspectives on Human Development*. London: Sage, 2005.

Brown, A., and M. Zuker. *Education Law.* Toronto: Carswell, 2007.

Brown, A. S., G. W. Holden, and R. Ashraf. "Spank, Slap, or Hit? How Labels Alter Perceptions of Child Discipline." *Psychology of Violence* 8, no. 1 (2018): 1–9. doi:10.1037/vio0000080.

Brown, N. N., L. Burd, T. Grant, W. Edwards, R. Adler, and A. Streissguth. "Prenatal Alcohol Exposure: An Assessment Strategy for the Legal Context." *International Journal of Law and Psychiatry* 42–43 (2015): 144–48. doi:10.1016/j.ijlp.2015.08.019.

Browne, D. T., and J. M. Jenkins. "Health across Early Childhood and Socioeconomic Status: Examining the Moderating Effects of Differential Parenting." *Social Science and Medicine* 74, no. 10 (2012): 1622–29. doi:10.1016/j.socscimed.2012.01.017.

Brunet, M. K., A. D. Evans, V. Talwar, N. Bala, R. C. L. Lindsay, and K. Lee. "How Children Report True and Fabricated Stressful and Non-Stressful Events." *Psychiatry, Psychology, and Law* 20, no. 6 (2013): 867–81. doi:10.1080/13218719.2012.750896.

Brunnee, J., and S. Toope. "A Hesitant Embrace: Baker and the Application of International Law by Canadian Courts." In *Canadian Yearbook of International Law 40*, edited by D. M. McRae, 3–60. Vancouver: UBC Press, 2002.

Bulanda, J., and T. B. Johnson. "A Trauma-Informed Model for Empowerment Programs Targeting Vulnerable Youth." *Child and Adolescent Social Work Journal* 33 (2016): 303–12. doi:10.1007/s10560-015-0427-z.

Bunzeluk, K. *Child Sexual Abuse Images: Analysis of Websites by Cybertip.ca.* Canadian Centre for Child Protection, 2009. https://cybertip.ca/pdfs/CTIP_ChildSexualAbuse_Report_en.pdf.

Burnstein, P. "The Impact of Public Opinion on Public Policy: A Review and an Agenda." *Political Research Quarterly* 56, no. 1 (2003): 29–41. doi:10.1177/106591290305600103.

Butler, C., ed. *Child Rights: The Movement, International Law, and Opposition.* West Lafayette, IN: Purdue University Press, 2012.

Campaign 2000. *2017 Report Card on Child and Family Poverty in Canada.* Toronto: Campaign 2000, 2017.

Campbell, K., and L. Rose-Krasnor. "The Participation Rights of the Child: Canada's Track Record." In Howe and Covell, *A Question of Commitment*, 209–39.

Campbell, K. M., and K. Covell. "Children's Rights Education at the University Level: An Effective Means of Promoting Rights Knowledge and Rights-Based Attitudes." *International Journal of Children's Rights* 9, no. 2 (2001): 123–35. doi:10.1163/15718180120494883.

Canada. *Brighter Futures: Canada's Action Plan for Children.* Ottawa: Ministry of Supply and Services, 1992.

Canadian Coalition for the Rights of Children. *The UN Convention on the Rights of the Child: The Canadian NGO Response.* Ottawa: CCRC, 1994. http://www .crin.org/en/docs/resources/treaties/crc.9/Canada_CCRC_NGO_Report.pdf.

———. *The United Nations Convention on the Rights of the Child: The Views of Canadian Youth.* Ottawa: CCRC, 1990.

———. *Right in Principle, Right in Practice.* Ottawa: CCRC, 2011.

Canadian Council on Children and Youth. *Admittance Restricted: The Child as Citizen in Canada.* Ottawa: Canadian Council on Children and Youth, 1978.

———. *On the Right Side: Canada and the Convention on the Rights of the Child.* Ottawa: Canadian Council on Children and Youth, 1990.

Cantwell, N. "The Origins, Development and Significance of the United Nations Convention on the Rights of the Child." In *The United Nations Convention on the Rights of the Child,* edited by S. Detrick, 26. Dordrecht: Martinus Nijhoff, 1992.

Carr, C. P., C. M. S. Martins, A. M. Stingel, V. B. Lemgruber, and M. F. Juruena. "The Role of Early Life Stress in Adult Psychiatric Disorders: A Systematic Review According to Childhood Trauma Subtypes." *Journal of Nervous and Mental Disease* 201, no. 12 (2013): 1007–20. doi:10.1097/ NMD.0000000000000049.

Casavant, L., and J. Robertson. *The Evolution of Pornography Law in Canada.* Ottawa: Parliament of Canada, 2007. http://www.lop.parl.gc.ca/content/lop/ researchpublications/843-e.htm#billc20.

Cashmore, J. "Children's Participation in Family Law Decision-Making: Theoretical Approaches to Understanding Children's Views." *Children and Youth Services Review* 33, no. 4 (2011): 515–20.

Chamberland, C., B. Fallon, T. Black, and N. Trocmé. "Emotional Maltreatment in Canada: Prevalence, Reporting and Child Welfare Responses (CIS2)." *Child Abuse & Neglect* 35, no. 10 (2011): 841–54. doi:10.1016/j.chiabu.2011.03.010.

Chang, H., D. S. Shaw, T. J. Dishion, F. Gardner, and M. N. Wilson. "Proactive Parenting and Children's Effortful Control: Mediating Role of Language and Indirect Intervention Effects." *Social Development* 24, no. 1 (2015): 206–23. doi:10.1111/sode.12069.

Child Care Advocacy Association of Canada. *From Patchwork to Framework: A Child Care Strategy for Canada.* Ottawa: Child Care Advocacy Association of Canada, 2004.

Cho, E. Y. "Child Benefit Portfolios across OECD Countries." *Social Indicators Research* 132, no. 3 (2017): 1099–115. doi:10.1007/s11205-016-1334-1.

Chong, K., and D. A. Connolly. "Testifying through the Ages: An Examination of Current Psychological Issues on the Use of Testimonial Supports by Child, Adolescent, and Adult Witnesses in Canada." *Canadian Psychology* 56, no. 1 (2015): 108–17.

Church II, W. T., J. W. Jaggers, and J. K. Taylor. "Neighborhood Poverty and Negative Behaviour: An Examination of Differential Association and Social Control Theory." *Children and Youth Services Review* 34, no. 5 (2012): 1035–41.

Civil Code of Québec, 1991, Book 1, title 2, chapter 2, article 34 (updated 2016).

Clarke, M. "The Rights and Wrongs of Canada's Policies for Children." In *Human Rights in Canada: Into the 1990s and Beyond,* edited by R. Cholewinski, 198–200. Ottawa: Human Rights Research and Education Centre, 1990.

Collins, T. M. "The Significance of Different Approaches to Human Rights Monitoring: A Case Study of Child Rights." *International Journal of Human Rights* 12, no. 2 (2008): 159–87. doi:10.1080/13642980801899626.

Collins, T. M., and M. Paré. "A Child Rights-Based Approach to Anti-Violence Efforts in Schools." *International Journal of Children's Rights* 24, no. 4 (2016): 764–802. doi:10.1163/15718182-02404005.

Collins, T. M., and L. Pearson. "The Role and Impact of Civil Society upon Child Rights in Canada." *The Philanthropist* 23, no. 4 (2011): 451–61.

Courtney, M., R. J. Flynn, and J. Beaupré. "Overview of Out of Home Care in the USA and Canada." *Psychosocial Intervention* 22, no. 3 (2013): 163–73.

Covell, K. "Awareness, Learning and Education in Human Rights." In *The SAGE Handbook of Human Rights,* edited by A. Mihr and M. Gibney, 821–39. London: Sage, 2014.

———. "Children's Rights Education: Canada's Best-Kept Secret." In Howe and Covell, *A Question of Commitment,* 241–63.

———. *Seen, Heard and Believed: What Youth Say about Violence.* Toronto: UNICEF, 2006.

Covell, K., and R. B. Howe, eds. *A Question of Commitment: Children's Rights in Canada*. Waterloo, ON: Wilfrid Laurier University Press, 2007.

———. *Children, Families and Violence: Challenges for Children's Rights*. London: Jessica Kingsley, 2009.

Covell, K., R. B. Howe, and A. McGillivray. "Children's Education Rights in Schools." In *Handbook of Children's Rights: Global and Multidisciplinary Perspectives*, edited by M. D. Ruck, M. Peterson-Badali, and M. Freeman, 296–311. New York: Routledge, 2017.

Covell, K., R. B. Howe, and J. K. McNeil. "'If There's a Dead Rat, Don't Leave It': Young Children's Understanding of Their Citizenship Rights and Responsibilities." *Cambridge Journal of Education* 38, no. 3 (2008): 321–39. doi:10.1080/03057640802286889.

———. "Implementing Children's Human Rights Education in Schools." *Improving Schools* 13, no. 2 (2010): 1–16.

Cowden, M. *Children's Rights: From Philosophy to Public Policy*. Basingstoke, UK: Palgrave Macmillan, 2016.

Coyne, J., and L. Kwakenbos. "Triple P-Positive Parenting Programs: The Folly of Basing Social Policy on Underpowered Flawed Studies." *BMC Medicine* 11 (2013): 11. doi:10.1186/1741-7015-11-11.

Cross, W. E. Jr. "Ecological Factors in Human Development." *Child Development* 88, no. 3 (2017): 767–69. doi:10.1111/cdev.12784.

Cryan, J. F., and Timothy G. Dinan. "Unraveling the Longstanding Scars of Early Neurodevelopmental Stress." *Biological Psychiatry* 74, no. 11 (2013): 788–89. doi:10.1016/j.biopsych.2013.10.004.

Curren, R. "Developmental Liberalism." *Educational Theory* 56, no. 4 (2006): 451–68.

———, ed. *Philosophy of Education: An Anthology*. Oxford: Blackwell, 2006.

Curren, R., and J. C. Blokhuis. "The Prima Facie Case against Homeschooling." *Public Affairs Quarterly* 25, no. 1 (2011): 1–19.

Daly, M. "Parenting Support as a Policy Field: An Analytic Framework." *Social Policy & Society* 14, no. 4 (2015): 597–608. doi:10.1017/S1474746415000226.

Dearing, E., K. McCartney, and B. A. Taylor. "Does Higher Quality Early Child Care Promote Low-Income Children's Math and Reading Achievement in Middle Childhood?" *Child Development* 80, no. 5 (2009): 1329–49.

Denov, M. "Youth Justice and Children's Rights." In Howe and Covell, *A Question of Commitment*, 163–64.

Detrick, S. *A Commentary on the United Nations Convention on the Rights of the Child*. The Hague: Martinus Nijhoff, 1999.

Dickerson, A., and G. K. Popli. "Persistent Poverty and Children's Cognitive Development: Evidence from the U.K. Millennium Cohort Study." *Journal of the Royal Statistical Society* 179, no. 2 (2016): 535–58.

Duby, J. C., and D. L. Langkamp. "Another Reason to Avoid Second-Hand Smoke." *Journal of Pediatrics* 167, no. 2 (2015): 224–25. doi:10.1016/j.jpeds.2015.04.049.

Duncan, G. J., M. Kathleen, and A. Kalil. "Early Childhood Poverty and Adult Attainment, Behaviour and Health." *Child Development* 81, no. 1 (2010): 306–25. doi:10.1111/j.1467-8624.2009.01396.x.

Durrant, J. "Legal Reform and Attitudes toward Physical Punishment in Sweden." *International Journal of Children's Rights* 11, no. 2 (2003): 147–73.

Durrant, J. E. "Corporal Punishment: A Violation of the Rights of the Child." In Howe and Covell, *A Question of Commitment*, 99–125.

Durrant, J. E., and R. Ensom. "Physical Punishment of Children: Lessons from 20 Years of Research." *Canadian Medical Association Journal* 184, no. 12 (2012): 1373–77. doi:10.1503/cmaj.101314.

Durrant, J. E., and A. Stewart-Tufescu. "What Is Discipline in the Age of Children's Rights?" *International Journal of Children's Rights* 25, no. 2 (2017): 359–79. doi:10.1163/15718182-02502007.

Eekelaar, J. "The Role of the Best Interests Principle in Decisions Affecting Children and Decisions about Children." *International Journal of Children's Rights* 23 (2015): 3–26. doi:10.1163/15718182-02301003.

———. "The Interests of the Child and the Child's Wishes: The Role of Dynamic Self-Determination." *International Journal of Law and the Family* 8 (1994): 42–61. doi:10.1093/lawfam/8.1.42.

Eichler, M. *Family Shifts: Families, Policies and Gender Equality.* Toronto: Oxford University Press, 1997.

Ensign, F. C. *Compulsory School Attendance and Child Labor.* Iowa City, IA: Athens Press, 1921.

Erickson, A. C., and L. T. Arbour. "Heavy Smoking during Pregnancy as a Marker for Other Risk Factors of Adverse Birth Outcomes: A Population-Based Study in British Columbia, Canada." *BMC Public Health* 12, no. 102 (2012). doi:10.1186/1471-2458-12-102.

Esping-Andersen, G. *Social Foundations of Postindustrial Economies.* Oxford: Oxford University Press, 1999.

———. *The Three Worlds of Welfare Capitalism.* Princeton, NJ: Princeton University Press, 1990.

Esposito, T., N. Trocmé, M. Chabot, D. Collin-Vézina, A. Shlonsky, and V. Sinha. "Family Reunification for Placed Children in Québec, Canada: A Longitudinal Study." *Children and Youth Services Review* 44 (2014): 278–87. doi:10.1016/j.childyouth.2014.06.024.

———. "The Stability of Child Protection Placements in Québec, Canada." *Children and Youth Services Review* 42 (2014): 10–19. doi:10.1016/j.child youth.2014.03.015.

Esposito, T., N. Trocmé, M. Chabot, A. Shlonsky, D. Collin-Vézina, and V. Sinha. "Placement of Children in Out-of-Home Care in Québec, Canada: When and for Whom Initial Out-of-Home Placement Is Most Likely to Occur." *Children and Youth Services Review* 35, no. 12 (2013): 2031–39. doi:10.1016/j.childyouth.2013.10.010.

Evans, A. D., M. K. Brunet, V. Talwar, N. Bala, R. C. L. Lindsay, and K. Lee. "The Effects of Repetition on Children's True and False Reports." *Psychiatry, Psychology and Law* 19 no. 4 (2012): 517–29. doi:10.1080/13218719.2011.615808.

Evans, A. D., and T. D. Lyon. "Assessing Children's Competency to Take the Oath in Court: The Influence of Question Type on Children's Accuracy." *Law and Human Behaviour* 36, no. 3 (2012): 195–205.

Evans, G. W., and P. Kim. "Childhood Poverty, Chronic Stress, Self-Regulation, and Coping." *Child Development Perspectives* 7, no. 1 (2013): 43–48.

Fallon, B., J. Ma, K. Allan, M. Pillhofer, N. Trocmé, and A. Jud. "Opportunities for Prevention and Intervention with Young Children: Lessons from the Canadian Incidence Study of Reported Child Abuse and Neglect." *Child and Adolescent Psychiatry and Mental Health* 7, no. 4 (2013). doi:10.1186/1753-2000-7-4.

Fallon, J. *The Psychopath Inside.* New York: Penguin, 2013.

Farrington, D. P., and D. West. "The Cambridge Study in Delinquent Behaviour (United Kingdom)." In *Prospective Longitudinal Research: An Empirical Basis for the Primary Prevention of Psychosocial Disorder,* edited by S. Mednick, A. Beart, and B. P. Backmann, 137–145. Oxford: Oxford University Press, 1981.

Farson, R. *Birthrights.* Harmondsworth: Penguin, 1978.

Feinberg, J. "The Child's Right to an Open Future." In Curren, *Philosophy of Education,* 112–23.

———. "The Nature and Value of Rights." *Journal of Value Inquiry* 4 (1970): 243–57.

Ferns, C., and Friendly, M. (2014). *The State of Early Childhood Education and Care in Canada 2012.* Moving Childcare Forward Project (a joint initiative of the Childcare Resource and Research Unit, Centre for Work, Families and Well-Being at the University of Guelph, and the Department of Sociology at the University of Manitoba). Toronto: Movingchildcareforward.ca.

Finlay, J., and L. Akbar. "Caught between Two Worlds: The Voices of Youth from Four First Nations in Northern Ontario." *Canadian Journal of Children's Rights* 3, no. 1 (2016): 68–99.

Fitzgerald, P. B., A. R. Laird, J. Maller, and Z. J. Daskalakis. "A Meta-Analytic Study of Changes in Brain Activation in Depression." *Human Brain Mapping* 29, no. 6 (2008): 683–95. doi:10.1002/hbm.20426.

Fitzpatrick, C., T. A. Barnett, and L. S. Pagani. "Parental Bad Habits Breed Bad Behaviours in Youth: Exposure to Gestational Smoke and Child Impulsivity." *International Journal of Psychophysiology* 93, no. 1 (2014): 17–21. doi:10.1016/j.ijpsycho.2012.11.006.

Flanagan, C. "Teaching a Larger Sense of Community." *Analyses of Social Issues and Public Policy* 14, no. 1 (2014): 423–25.

Flekkoy, M. "The Ombudsman for Children: Conception and Developments." In *The New Handbook of Children's Rights: Comparative Policy and Practice,* edited by B. Franklin, 404–19. London: Routledge, 2002.

Flekkoy, M., and N. Kaufman. *The Participation Rights of the Child.* London: Jessica Kingsley, 1997.

Freeman, M. "Article 3: The Best Interests of the Child." In *A Commentary on the United Nations Convention on the Rights of the Child,* edited by A. Alen, J. Lanotte, E. Verhellen, F. Ang, E. Berghmans, and M. Verheyde, 1–79. Leiden: Martinus Nijhoff, 2007.

———. *The Rights and Wrongs of Children.* London: Frances Pinter, 1983.

Freeman, M., and B. J. Saunders. "Can We Conquer Child Abuse if We Don't Outlaw Physical Chastisement of Children?" *International Journal of Children's Rights* 22 (2014): 681–709. doi:10.1163/15718182-02204002.

Friendly, M. "Child Care and the Rights of Young Children." In Canadian Council on Children and Youth, *On the Right Side,* 34–37.

———. "Early Learning and Child Care: Is Canada on Track?" In Howe and Covell, *A Question of Commitment,* 45–72.

Friendly, M., B. Grady, L. Macdonald, and B. Forer. *Early Childhood Education and Care in Canada 2014.* Toronto: Childcare Resource and Research Unit, 2015.

Gaetz, S., B. O'Grady, K. Buccieri, J. Karabanow, and A. Allyson, eds. *Youth Homelessness in Canada: Implications for Policy and Practice.* Toronto: Canadian Homelessness Research Network Press, 2013.

Gaetz, S., T. Gulliver, and T. Richter. *The State of Homelessness in Canada.* Toronto: Homeless Hub Press, 2014.

Garbarino, J. *Raising Children in a Socially Toxic Environment.* San Francisco: Jossey-Bass, 1995.

Gardner, F., D. S. Shaw, T. J. Dishion, J. Burton, and L. Supplee. "Randomized Prevention Trial for Early Conduct Problems: Effects on Proactive Parenting and Links to Toddler Disruptive Behaviour." *Journal of Family Psychology* 21, no. 3 (2007): 398–406. doi:10.1037/0893-3200.21.3.398.

Gartsbein, E., H. P. Lawrence, J. L. Leake, H. Stewart, and G. Kulkarni. "Lack of Oral Care Policies in Toronto Daycares." *Journal of Public Health Dentistry* 69, no. 3 (2009): 190–96. doi:10.1111/j.1752-7325.2009.00123.x.

Gelles, R. J. *The Book of David: How Preserving Families Can Cost Children Their Lives.* New York: Basic Books, 1996.

Genereux, A. "Corporal Punishment: Is it Violence Against Children?" In Canadian Council on Children and Youth, *On the Right Side,* 29–33.

Geoffroy, M., S. M. Côté, S. Parent, and J. R. Séguin. "Daycare Attendance, Stress, and Mental Health." *Canadian Journal of Psychiatry/Revue canadienne de psychiatrie* 51, no. 9 (2006): 607–15.

Gereluk, D. *Symbolic Clothing in Schools.* London: Continuum, 2008.

Gershoff, E. T. "More Harm Than Good: A Summary of Scientific Research on the Intended and Unintended Effects of Corporal Punishment on Children." *Law and Contemporary Problems* 73, no. 31 (2010): 31–56.

————. "Should Parents' Physical Punishment of Children Be Considered a Source of Toxic Stress That Affects Brain Development?" *Family Relations* 65, no. 1 (2016): 151–62. doi:10.1111/fare.12177.

Gershoff, E. T., A. Grogan-Kaylor, J. E. Lansford, L. Chang, A. Zelli, K. Deater-Deckard, and K. A. Dodge. "Parent Discipline Practices in an International Sample: Associations with Child Behaviours and Moderation by Perceived Normativeness." *Child Development* 81, no. 2 (2010): 487–502. doi:10.1111/j.1467-8624.2009.01409.x.

Gilbert, N., N. Parton, and M. Skivenes, eds. *Child Protection Systems: International Trends and Orientations.* New York: Oxford University Press, 2011.

————. "Changing Patterns of Response and Emerging Orientations." In Gilbert, Parton, and Skivenes, *Child Protection Systems,* 243–57.

Gilbert, N. L., C. R. M. Nelson, and L. Greaves. "Smoking Cessation during Pregnancy and Relapse after Childbirth in Canada." *Journal of Obstetrics and Gynaecology Canada: JOGC/Journal d'obstétrique et gynécologie du Canada: JOGC* 37, no. 1 (2015): 32–39.

Gilbert, R., C. S. Widom, K. Browne, D. Fergusson, E. Webb, and S. Janson. "Burden and Consequences of Child Maltreatment in High-Income Countries." *The Lancet* 373, no. 9657 (2009): 68–81. doi:10.1016/S0140-6736(08)61706-7.

Goldberg, D. "Judicial Interviews of Children in Custody and Access Cases." In *Children and the Law,* edited by S. Anand, 197–223. Toronto: Irwin Law, 2011.

Gómez-Ortiz, O., E. M. Romera, and R. Ortega-Ruiz. "Parenting Styles and Bullying: The Mediating Role of Parental Psychological Aggression and Physical Punishment." *Child Abuse & Neglect* 51 (January 2016): 132–43. doi:10.1016/j.chiabu.2015.10.025.

Gonzalez, A., H. MacMillan, M. Tanaka, S. M. Jack, and L. Tonmyr. "Subtypes of Exposure to Intimate Partner Violence within a Canadian Child Welfare Sample: Associated Risks and Child Maladjustment." *Child Abuse & Neglect* 38, no. 12 (2014): 1934–44. doi:10.1016/j.chiabu.2014.10.007.

Goodwin-De Faria, C., and V. Marinos. "Youth Understanding and Assertion of Legal Rights: Examining the Roles of Age and Power." *International Journal of Children's Rights* 20 (2012): 343–64. doi:l0.1163/157181812X652607.

Government of Alberta. *Protection of Sexually Exploited Children and Youth.* Government of Alberta, 2004, revised 2010. http://web.archive.org/web/20160409211120/http://www.humanservices.alberta.ca/documents/PSEC-manual.pdf.

Grandjean, P., and P. J. Landrigan. "Neurobehavioural Effects of Developmental Toxicity." *Lancet Neurology* 13, no. 3 (2014): 330–38. doi:10.1016/S1474-4422(13)70278-3.

Griffin, J. "Do Children Have Rights?" in Archard and Macleod, *The Moral and Political Status of Children,* 19–30.

Grover, S. "Advocating for Children's Rights as an Aspect of Professionalism." *Child and Youth Care Forum* 33, no. 6 (2004): 405–23.

————. *Children Defending Their Human Rights under the CRC Communication Procedure: On Strengthening the Convention on the Rights of the Child Complaint Mechanism* (Berlin: Springer, 2015). doi:10.1007/978-3-662-44443-6_3.

————. *The Child's Right to Legal Standing.* Toronto: LexisNexis, 2008.

————. "Oppression of Children Intellectualized as Free Expression under the Canadian Charter: A Reanalysis of the *Sharpe* Possession of Pornography Case." *The International Journal of Children's Rights* 11, no. 4 (2004): 311–31. doi:10.1163/157181804322985150.

Guggenheim, M. *What's Wrong with Children's Rights.* Cambridge, MA: Harvard University Press, 2005.

Hackman, D. A., L. M. Betancourt, R. Gallop, D. Romer, N. L. Brodsky, H. Hurt, and Martha J. Farah. "Mapping the Trajectory of Socioeconomic Disparity in Working Memory: Parental and Neighborhood Factors." *Child Development* 85, no. 4 (2014): 1433–45. doi:10.1111/cdev.12242.

Hackman, D. A., R. Gallop, G. W. Evans, and M. J. Farah. "Socioeconomic Status and Executive Function: Developmental Trajectories and Mediation." *Developmental Science* 18, no. 5 (2015): 686–702. doi:10.1111/desc.12246.

Haeck, C., P. Lefebvre, and P. Merrigan. "Canadian Evidence on Ten Years of Universal Preschool Policies: The Good and the Bad." *Labour Economics* 36 (October 2015): 137–57. doi:10.1016/j.labeco.2015.05.002.

Hafner-Burton, E. M. "Sticks and Stones: Naming and Shaming the Human Rights Enforcement Problem." *International Organization* 62, no. 4 (2008): 689–716. doi:10.1017/S0020818308080247.

Hallett, S., and N. Bala. "Criminal Prosecutions for Abuse and Neglect." In Bala et al., *Canadian Child Welfare Law*, 311–31.

Hammarberg, T. "The UN Convention on the Rights of the Child—and How to Make It Work." *Human Rights Quarterly* 12, no. 1 (1990): 97–105.

Hanson, K., and O. Nieuwenhuys, eds. *Reconceptualizing Children's Rights in International Development: Living Rights, Social Justice, Translations.* New York: Cambridge University Press, 2013.

Hardy, S. A., A. Bhattacharjee, A. Reed II, and K. Aquino. "Moral Identity and Psychological Distance: The Case of Adolescent Parental Socialization." *Journal of Adolescence* 33, no. 1 (2010): 111–23. doi:10.1016/j.adolescence.2009 .04.008.

Hart, H. L. A. *The Concept of Law.* 3rd ed. New York: Oxford University Press, 2012.

Hart, R. "Stepping Back from the 'Ladder.'" In *Participation and Learning*, edited by A. Reid, B. B. Jensen, J. Nikel, and V. Simovska, 19–31. Dordrecht: Springer Netherlands, 2008.

Hart, S. N. "From Property to Person Status: Historical Perspective on Children's Rights." *American Psychologist* 46, no. 1 (1991): 53–59.

Hart, S. N., Y. Lee, and M. Wernham. "A New Age for Child Protection—General

Comment 13: Why It Is Important, How It Was Constructed, and What It Intends?" *Child Abuse & Neglect* 35, no. 12 (2011): 970–78. doi:10.1016/j.chiabu.2011.09.007.

Haugaard, J. J. "Is Adoption a Risk Factor for the Development of Adjustment Problems?" *Clinical Psychology Review* 18, no. 1 (1998): 47–69.

Hay, M. "Commercial Sexual Exploitation of Children and Youth." *BC Medical Journal* 46, no. 3 (2004): 119–22.

Heckman, J., R. Pinto, and P. A. Savelyev, "Understanding the Mechanisms through Which an Influential Early Childhood Program Boosted Adult Outcomes." Vanderbilt University Department of Economics Working Papers, 2012. http://www.accessecon.com/pubs/VUECON/VUECON-12-00011.pdf.

Helie, S., M. Poirier, and D. Turcotte. "Risk of Maltreatment Recurrence after Exiting Substitute Care: Impact of Placement Characteristics." *Child and Youth Services Review* 46 (November 2014): 257–64. doi:10.1016/j.childyouth.2014.09.002.

Herrenkohl, T. I., S. Hong, J. B. Klika, R. C. Herrenkohl, and M. J. Russo. "Developmental Impacts of Child Abuse and Neglect Related to Adult Mental Health, Substance Use, and Physical Health." *Journal of Family Violence* 28, no. 2 (2013): 191–99. doi:10.1007/s10896-012-9474-9.

Hertzman, C. "The Significance of Early Childhood Adversity." *Pediatric Child Health* 18, no. 3 (2013): 127–28.

Heyman, S., K. Penrose, and A. Earle. "Meeting Children's Needs: How Does the United States Measure Up?" *Merrill-Palmer Quarterly* 52, no. 2 (2006): 189–215.

Hill, M., and K. Tisdale. *Children and Society.* London: Addison-Wesley Longman, 1997.

Himes, J. *Implementing the United Nations Convention on the Rights of the Child.* Florence: UNICEF International Child Development Centre, 1992.

Hodgkin, R., and P. Newell. *Implementation Handbook for the Convention on the Rights of the Child.* New York: UNICEF, 2007.

Hohfeld, W. N. "Some Fundamental Legal Conceptions as Applied in Judicial Reasoning." *Yale Law Journal* 23 (1914): 16–59.

Holtz, C. A., R. A. Fox, and J. R. Meurer. "Incidence of Behaviour Problems in Toddlers and Preschool Children from Families Living in Poverty." *Journal of Psychology* 149, no. 2 (2015): 161–74.

Homma, Y., D. Nicholson, and E. M. Saewyc. "A Profile of High School Students in Rural Canada Who Exchange Sex for Substances." *Canadian Journal of Human Sexuality* 21, no. 1 (2012): 29–40.

Howard-Hassmann, R. *Compassionate Canadians: Civic Leaders Discuss Human Rights.* Toronto: University of Toronto Press, 2003.

Howe, R. B. "Evolving Policy on Children's Rights in Canada." In *Readings in Child Development,* edited by K. Covell, 4–27. Toronto: Nelson Canada, 1991.

―――. "Factors Affecting the Impact of Child Advocacy Offices in Canada." *Canadian Review of Social Policy* 62 (2009): 17–33.

―――. "Implementing Children's Rights in a Federal State: The Case of Canada's Child Protection System." *International Journal of Children's Rights* 9, no. 4 (2001): 361–82. doi:10.1163/15718180120495026.

―――. "Introduction: A Question of Commitment." In Howe and Covell, *A Question of Commitment,* 1–19.

Howe, R. B., and K. Covell, eds. "Conclusion: Canada's Ambivalence toward Children." In Howe and Covell, *A Question of Commitment,* 400–407.

―――. *Education in the Best Interests of the Child: A Children's Rights Perspective on Closing the Achievement Gap.* Toronto: University of Toronto Press, 2013.

―――. *Empowering Children: Children's Rights as a Pathway to Citizenship.* Toronto: University of Toronto Press, 2007.

―――. *A Question of Commitment: Children's Rights in Canada.* Waterloo, ON: Wilfrid Laurier University Press, 2007.

―――. "Towards the Best Interests of the Child in Education." *Education and Law Journal* 20, no. 1 (2010): 17–33.

Huston, A. C., K. C. Bobbitt, and A. Bentley. "Time Spent in Child Care: How and Why Does It Affect Social Development?" *Developmental Psychology* 51, no. 5 (2015): 621–34.

Ignatieff, M., ed. *American Exceptionalism and Human Rights.* Princeton, NJ: Princeton University Press, 2005.

Imber, M., T. van Geel, J. C. Blokhuis, and J. Feldman. *Education Law.* 5th ed. New York: Routledge, 2014.

Jack, S. M., N. Catherine, A. Gonzalez, H. L. MacMillan, D. Sheehan, and D. Waddell. "Adapting, Piloting and Evaluating Complex Public Health Interventions: Lessons Learned from the Nurse-Family Partnership in Canadian Public Health Settings." *Health Promotion and Chronic Disease Prevention in Canada* 35, no. 8/9 (2015): 151–59. doi.org/10.24095/hpcdp.35.8/9.07.

Jackson, C., L. Kenriksen, and V. Foshee. "The Authoritative Parenting Index: Predicting Health and Risk Behaviours among Children and Adolescents." *Health, Education and Behaviour* 25, no. 3 (1998): 319–37.

Jacobsen, G. H., ed. *Rights of Children in the Nordic Welfare States.* Copenhagen: NSU Press, 2015.

Jaffee, S. R., and C. W. Christian. "The Biological Embedding of Child Abuse and Neglect: Implications for Policy and Practice." *Social Policy Report* 28, no. 1 (2014). http://www.srcd.org/sites/default/files/documents/spr_28_1.pdf.

Johnny, L. "UN Convention on the Rights of the Child: A Rationale for Implementing Participatory Rights in Schools." *Canadian Journal of Educational Administration and Policy* 40 (March 2005): 1–20.

Joyal, R. *Les enfants, la société et l'État au Québec, 1608–1989.* Montréal: Hurtubise HMH, 1999.

Jung, H., T. I. Herrenkohl, J. Olivia Lee, S. A. Hemphill, J. A. Heerde, and M. L. Skinner. "Gendered Pathways from Child Abuse to Adult Crime through Internalizing and Externalizing Behaviours in Childhood and Adolescence." *Journal of Interpersonal Violence* (August 11, 2015). doi:10.1177/0886260515596146.

Justice for Children and Youth. *Children's Right to Be Heard in Canadian Administrative and Judicial Proceedings.* Toronto: Justice for Children and Youth, 2013. http://jfcy.org/wp-content/uploads/2013/10/UNDiscussionPaper.pdf.

Kakinami, L., T. A. Barnett, L. Séguin, and G. Paradis. "Parenting Style and Obesity Risk in Children." *Preventive Medicine* (2015): 18–22. doi:10.1016/j.ypmed.2015.03.005.

Kakinami, L., L. Séguin, M. Lambert, L. Gauvin, B. Nikiema, and G. Paradis. "Poverty's Latent Effect on Adiposity during Childhood: Evidence from a Québec Birth Cohort." *Journal of Epidemiology and Community Health* 68, no. 3 (2014): 239–45. doi:10.1136/jech-2012-201881.

Kalil, J. A. "Childhood Poverty and Parental Stress: Important Determinants of Health." *UBC Medical Journal* 6, no. 1 (2015): 41–43.

Kant, I. *Grounding for the Metaphysics of Morals.* 1785. Translated by J. W. Ellington. 3rd ed. Indianapolis: Hackett, 1993.

Kant, I. *The Metaphysics of Morals.* 1797. Translated by M. Gregor. Cambridge: Cambridge University Press, 1996.

Kanyal, M., ed. *Children's Rights 0–8: Promoting Participation in Education and Care.* New York: Routledge, 2014.

Karoly, L. A., P. W. Greenwood, S. S. S. Everingham, J. Hoube, M. R. Kilburn, C. P. Rydell, M. Sanders, and J. Chiesa. *Investing in Our Children: What We Know and Don't Know about the Costs and Benefits of Early Childhood Interventions.* Santa Monica, CA: Rand, 1998.

Katsenou, C., E. Flogaitis, and G. Liarakou. "Exploring Pupil Participation within a Sustainable School." *Cambridge Journal of Education* 43, no. 2 (2013): 243–58. doi:10.1080/0305764X.2013.774320.

Kelly, K., and M. Totten. *When Children Kill: A Social-Psychological Study of Youth Homicide.* Toronto: University of Toronto Press, 2002.

Kelly, P. A., E. Viding, G. L. Wallace, M. Schaer, S. A. De Brito, B. Robustelli, and E. J. McCrory. "Cortical Thickness, Surface Area, and Gyrification Abnormalities in Children Exposed to Maltreatment: Neural Markers of Vulnerability?" *Biological Psychiatry* 74, no. 11 (2013): 845–52. doi:10.1016/j.biopsych.2013.06.020.

Khanna, A. *2017 Report Card on Child and Family Poverty in Canada: A Poverty-Free Canada Requires Federal Leadership.* Toronto: Campaign 2000 / Family Service Toronto, November 2017. https://campaign2000.ca/wp-content/uploads/2017/11/EnglishNationalC2000ReportNov212017.pdf.

Kidd, S., and R. M. C. Liborio. "Sex Trade Involvement in Sao Paulo, Brazil and Toronto, Canada: Narratives of Social Exclusion and Fragmented Identities." *Youth and Society* 43, no. 3 (2011): 982–1009.

King, T. *The Inconvenient Indian: A Curious Account of Native People in North America.* Toronto: Anchor, 2012.

Kitcher, P. "Public Knowledge and Its Discontents." *Theory and Research in Education* 9, no. 2 (2011): 103–24.

Klein, M. "Online Partnerships for Human Rights Education Praxis." *Peace Review* 24, no. 1 (2012): 61–69. doi:10.1080/10402659.2012.651022.

Kokko, K., R. E. Tremblay, E. Lacourse, D. S. Nagin, and F. Vitaro. "Trajectories of Prosocial Behaviour and Physical Aggression in Middle Childhood: Links to Adolescent School Dropout and Physical Violence." *Journal of Research on Adolescence* 16, no. 3 (2006): 403–28. doi:10.1111/j.1532-7795.2006.00500.x.

Konings, K. D., S. Brand-Gruwel, and J. J. G. van Merrienboer. "An Approach to Participatory Instructional Design in Secondary Education: An Exploratory Study." *Educational Research* 52, no. 1 (2010): 45–59.

Koponen, T., K. Aunola, T. Ahonen, and J. Nurmi. "Cognitive Predictors of Single-Digit and Procedural Calculation Skills and Their Covariation with Reading Skill." *Journal of Experimental Child Psychology* 97, no. 3 (2007): 220–41. doi:10.1016/j.jecp.2007.03.001.

Kotin, L., and W. F. Aikman. *Legal Foundations of Compulsory School Attendance.* Port Washington, NY: Kennikat Press, 1980.

Kottelenberg, M. J., and S. F. Lehrer. "New Evidence on the Impacts of Access and Attending Universal Child-Care in Canada." *Canadian Public Policy* 39, no. 2 (2016): 263–85.

Kufeldt, K. "Foster Care: An Essential Part of the Continuum of Care." In Kufeldt and McKenzie, *Child Welfare*, 157–59.

Kufeldt, K., and B. McKenzie, eds. *Child Welfare.* Waterloo: Wilfrid Laurier University Press, 2011.

———.. "Critical Issues in Current Practice." In Kufeldt and McKenzie, *Child Welfare*, 558–63.

———. "The Policy, Practice, and Research Connection." In Kufeldt and McKenzie, *Child Welfare*, 575–76.

Landolt, C. G. *The Child Care Debate.* Ottawa: Real Women of Canada, 2009. http://www.realwomenofcanada.ca/wp-content/uploads/2016/01/Brief-127-The-Child-Care-Debate-COLF-Mar.-25-09.pdf.

Landrigan, P. J., and L. R. Goldman. "Children's Vulnerability to Toxic Chemicals: A Challenge and Opportunity to Strengthen Health and Environmental Policy." *Health Affairs* 30, no. 5 (2011): 842–50. doi:10.1377/hlthaff.2011.0151.

Lang, M. "Health Implications of Children in Child Care Centres Part B: Injuries and Infections." *Paediatrics & Child Health* 14, no. 1 (2009): 40–43.

Reaffirmed February 1, 2016. http://www.cps.ca/en/documents/position/child-care-centres-injuries-infections.

Lange, S., C. Probst, M. Quere, J. Rehm, and S. Popova. "Alcohol Use, Smoking and Their Co-occurrence during Pregnancy among Canadian Women, 2003 to 2011/12." *Addictive Behaviours* 50 (November 2015): 102–9. doi:10.1016/j.addbeh.2015.06.018.

Lansdown, G. "Children's Rights to Participation and Protection: A Critique." In *Participation and Empowerment in Child Protection,* edited by C. Cloke and M. Davies, 19–37. London: Pitman, 1995.

Lavoie, F., C. Thibodeau, M. Gagné, and M. Hébert. "Buying and Selling Sex in Québec Adolescents: A Study of Risk and Protective Factors." *Archives of Sexual Behaviour* 39, no. 5 (2010): 1147–60. doi:10.1007/s10508-010-9605-4.

Lee, C. M., S. B. Stern, S. Feldgaier, C. Ateah, M. Gagné, S. Barnes, K. Chan, et al. "The International Parenting Survey—Canada: Exploring Access to Parenting Services." *Canadian Psychology* 55, no. 2 (2014): 110.

Lemay, L., N. Bigras, and C. Bouchard. "Educational Daycare from Infancy and Externalizing and Internalizing Behaviours in Early Childhood: Differential Effect by Children's Vulnerability." *Procedia—Social and Behavioural Sciences* 55 (October 5, 2012): 115–27. doi:10.1016/j.sbspro.2012.09.485.

Letarte, M., S. Normandeau, and J. Allard. "Effectiveness of a Parent Training Program 'Incredible Years' in a Child Protection Service." *Child Abuse & Neglect* 34, no. 4 (2010): 253–61. doi:10.1016/j.chiabu.2009.06.003.

Liebel, M., ed. *Children's Rights from Below: Cross-Cultural Perspectives.* New York: Palgrave Macmillan, 2012.

Liu, M., and F. Guo. "Parenting Practices and Their Relevance to Child Behaviours in Canada and China." *Scandinavian Journal of Psychology* 51, no. 2 (2010): 109–14. doi:10.1111/j.1467-9450.2009.00795.x.

Loeb, S. "Missing the Target: We Need to Focus on Informal Care Rather Than Preschool." *Evidence Speaks Reports* 1, no. 19. Washington, DC: Brookings Institute, 20165.

Lundy, L. "Voice Is Not Enough: Conceptualizing Article 12 of the United Nations Convention on the Rights of the Child." *British Education Research Journal* 33, no. 6 (2007): 927–42.

Lundy, L., U. Kilkelly, and B. Byrne, "Incorporation of the United Nations Convention on the Rights of the Child in Law: A Comparative Review." *International Journal of Children's Rights* 21 (2013): 442–63. doi:10.1163/15718182-55680028.

Lundy, L., U. Kilkelly, B. Byrne, and J. Kang. *The UN Convention on the Rights of the Child: A Study of Legal Implementation in 12 Countries.* London: UNICEF-UK, 2012. https://www.unicef.org.uk/publications/child-rights-convention-2012-report/.

MacKenzie, M. J., E. Nicklas, J. Waldfogel, and J. Brooks-Gunn. "Corporal Punishment and Child Behavioural and Cognitive Outcomes through 5 Years of Age: Evidence from a Contemporary Urban Birth Cohort Study." *Infant and Child Development* 21, no. 1 (2012): 3–33. doi:10.1002/icd.758.

MacLaurin, B., and N. Bala. "Children in Care." In Bala et al., *Canadian Child Welfare Law,* 111–38.

MacMillan, H. L., M. Tanaka, E. Duku, T. Vaillancourt, and M. H. Boyle. "Child Physical and Sexual Abuse in a Community Sample of Young Adults: Results from the Ontario Child Health Study." *Child Abuse & Neglect* 37, no. 1 (2013): 14–21. doi:10.1016/j.chiabu.2012.06.005.

MacMillan, H. L., B. H. Thomas, E. Jamieson, C. A. Walsh, M. H. Boyle, H. S. Shannon, and A. Gafni. "Effectiveness of Home Visitation by Public-Health Nurses in Prevention of the Recurrence of Child Physical Abuse and Neglect: A Randomised Controlled Trial." *Lancet* 365, no. 9473 (2005): 1786–93. doi:10.1016/S0140-6736(05)66388-X.

Malakoff, M. E., J. M. Underhill, and E. Zigler. "Influence of Inner-City Environment and Head Start Experience on Effectance Motivation." *American Journal of Orthopsychiatry* 68, no. 4 (1998): 630–38. doi:10.1037/h0080371.

Marshall, B. D. L., K. Shannon, T. Kerr, R. Zhang, and E. Wood. "Survival Sex Work and Increased HIV Risk among Sexual Minority Street-Involved Youth." *Journal of Acquired Immune Deficiency Syndromes* 53, no. 5 (2009): 661–64. doi:10.1097/QAI.0b013e3181c300d7.

Marshall, D. *The Social Origins of the Welfare State: Québec Families, Compulsory Education, and Family Allowances, 1940–1955.* Waterloo, ON: Wilfrid Laurier University Press, 2006.

Marshall, K. *Children's Rights in the Balance: The Participation-Protection Debate.* Edinburgh: Stationery Office, 1997.

Marteau, T. M., and P. A. Hall. "Breadlines, Brains, and Behaviour." *British Medical Journal* 347 (November 12, 2013): f6750. doi:10.1136/bmj.f6750.

Martin, J. "Conceptualizing the Harms Done to Children Made the Subjects of Sexual Abuse Images Online." *Child & Youth Services* 36, no. 4 (2015): 267–87. doi:10.1080/0145935X.2015.1092832.

———. "'It's Just an Image, Right?' Practitioners' Understanding of Child Sexual Abuse Images Online and Effects on Victims." *Child & Youth Services* 35, no. 2 (2014): 96–115. doi:10.1080/0145935X.2014.924334.

Mason, M. A. *From Father's Property to Children's Rights.* New York: Columbia University Press, 1994.

Masud, H., M. S. Ahmad, F. A. Jan, and A. Jamil. "Relationship between Parenting Styles and Academic Performance of Adolescents: Mediating Role of Self-Efficacy." *Asia Pacific Education Review* 17, no. 1 (2016): 121–31. doi:10.1007/s12564-015-9413-6.

Mathis, E. T. B., and K. L. Bierman. "Dimensions of Parenting Associated with Child Prekindergarten Emotion Control in Low-Income Families." *Social Development* 24, no. 3 (2015): 601–20. doi:10.111/sode.12112.

Matusicky, C., and C. Russell. "Best Practices for Parents: What Is Happening in Canada?" *Paediatrics and Child Health* 14, no. 10 (2009): 664–65.

Maughan, B., S. Collishaw, and A. Pickles. "School Achievement and Adult Qualifications among Adoptees: A Longitudinal Study." *Journal of Child Psychology and Psychiatry* 39, no. 5 (1998): 669–85.

McEwen, A., and J. M. Stewart. "The Relationship between Income and Children's Outcomes: A Synthesis of Canadian Evidence." *Canadian Public Policy* 40, no. 1 (March 2014): 99–109. doi:10.3138/cppCRDCN.

McGillivray, A. "Child Sexual Abuse and Exploitation: What Progress Has Canada Made?" In Howe and Covell, *A Question of Commitment*, 127–51.

McKay-Panos, L. *Using the Coercive Power of the State to Deal with Child Prostitution and Drug Abuse.* Alberta Law Foundation, 2009. http://ablawg.ca/wp-content/uploads/2009/10/blog_lmp_protection_feb2009.pdf.

McIntyre, D., D. Pedder, and J. Rudduck. "Pupil Voice: Comfortable and Uncomfortable Learnings for Teachers." *Research Papers in Education* 20, no. 2 (2005): 149–68.

Meaney, M. J. "Epigenetics and the Biological Definition of Gene x Environment Interaction." *Child Development* 81, no. 1 (2010): 41–79.

Mejdoubi, J., S. C. C. M. van den Heijkant, F. J. M. van Leerdam, M. W. Heymans, A. Crijnen, and R. A. Hirasing. "The Effect of VoorZorg, the Dutch Nurse-Family Partnership, on Child Maltreatment and Development: A Randomized Controlled Trial." *PLOS ONE* 10, no. 4 (2015): e0120182. doi:10.1371/journal.pone.0120182.

Melton, G. "The Child's Rights to a Family Environment." *American Psychologist* 51, no. 12 (1996): 1234–38.

Miklikowska, M., and H. Hurme. "Democracy Begins at Home: Democratic Parenting and Adolescents' Support for Democratic Values." *European Journal of Developmental Psychology* 8, no. 5 (2011): 541–57.

Mill, J. S. *On Liberty.* 1859. Reprinted as "Education and the Limits of State Authority." In Curren, *Philosophy of Education*, 156–58.

———. "Utilitarianism." In *Great Books of the Western World*, vol. 43, edited by R. M. Hutchins, 470–71. Chicago: Encyclopaedia Britannica, 1952.

Miller, A. "Potential Dangers of Unlicensed Daycares." *Canadian Medical Association Journal CMAJ* 185, no. 18 (2013): 1566. doi:10.1503/cmaj.109-4643.

Minaie, M. G., K. K. Hui, R. K. Leung, J. W. Toumbourou, and R. M. King. "Parenting Style and Behavior as Longitudinal Predictors of Adolescent Alcohol Use." *Journal of Studies on Alcohol and Drugs* 76, no. 5 (2015): 671–79. doi:10.15288/jsad.2015.76.671.

Mitchell, R. C. "Postmodern Reflections on the UNCRC: Towards Utilising Article 42 as an International Compliance Indicator." *International Journal of Children's Rights* 13, no. 3 (2005): 315–31. doi:10.1163/157181805775007567.

Moghaddam, M. F., A. Validad, T. Rakhshani, and M. Assareh, "Child Self-Esteem and Different Parenting Styles of Mothers: A Cross-Sectional Study." *Archives of Psychiatry and Psychotherapy* 19, no. 1 (2017): 37–42. doi:10.12740/APP/68160.

Morin, M. "La compétence *parens patriae* et le droit privé québécois: Un emprunt inutile, un affront à l'histoire." *Revue du Barreau* 50, no. 5 (1990): 827–923.

Morrissey, T. W. "Multiple Child-Care Arrangements and Young Children's Behavioural Outcomes." *Child Development* 80, no. 1 (2009): 59–76.

Muckle, G., D. Laflamme, J. Gagnon, O. Boucher, J. L. Jacobson, and S. W. Jacobson. "Alcohol, Smoking, and Drug Use among Inuit Women of Childbearing Age during Pregnancy and the Risk to Children." *Alcoholism, Clinical and Experimental Research* 35, no. 6 (2011): 1081–91. doi:10.1111/j.1530-0277.2011.01441.x.

Myers-Clack, S. A., and S. E. Christopher. "Effectiveness of a Health Course at Influencing Preservice Teachers' Attitudes toward Teaching Health." *Journal of School Health* 71, no. 9 (2001): 462–66.

National Collaborating Centre for Aboriginal Health. *Child Welfare Services in Canada: Aboriginal and Mainstream.* Prince George, BC: National Collaborating Centre for Aboriginal Health, 2009–2010. https://www.ccnsa-nccah.ca/docs/health/FS-ChildWelfareServices-EN.pdf.

Newman, J. E., and K. P. Roberts. "Subjective and Non-subjective Information in Children's Allegations of Abuse." *Journal of Police and Criminal Psychology* 29, no. 2 (2014): 75–80. doi:10.1007/s11896-013-9133-y.

Noël, J.-F. *The Convention on the Rights of the Child.* Ottawa: Department of Justice, 2015. http://www.justice.gc.ca/eng/rp-pr/fl-lf/divorce/crc-crde/conv2a.html.

Norlander, R. J. "A Digital Approach to Human Rights Education?" *Peace Review* 24, no. 1 (2012): 70–77. doi:10.1080/10402659.2012.651025.

Norman, R. E., M. Byambaa, R. De, A. Butchart, J. Scott, and T. Vos. "The Long-Term Health Consequences of Child Physical Abuse, Emotional Abuse, and Neglect: A Systematic Review and Meta-Analysis." *PLOS Medicine* 9, no. 11 (2012): e1001349. doi:10.1371/journal.pmed.1001349.

Nussbaum, M. *Creating Capabilities.* Cambridge, MA: Belknap Press, 2011.

Olsen, G. *The Politics of the Welfare State.* Toronto: Oxford University Press, 2002.

O'Neill, T., and D. Zinga, eds. *Children's Rights: Multidisciplinary Approaches to Participation and Protection.* Toronto: University of Toronto Press, 2008.

Ontario Agency for Health Protection and Promotion (Public Health Ontario), J. LeMar, E. Berenbaum, and G. Thomas. *Focus On: Standard Alcohol Labels.* Toronto: Queen's Printer for Ontario, 2015. http://www.publichealthontario.ca/en/eRepository/FocusOn-Standard_Alcohol_Labels_2015.pdf.

Oshri, A., F. A. Rogosch, M. L. Burnette, and D. Cicchetti. "Developmental Pathways to Adolescent Cannabis Abuse and Dependence: Child Maltreatment,

Emerging Personality, and Internalizing versus Externalizing Psychopathology." *Psychology of Addictive Behaviours* 25, no. 4 (2011): 634–44.

Oswell, D. *The Agency of Children: From Family to Global Human Rights*. New York: Cambridge University Press, 2013.

Oulman, E., T. H. M. Kim, K. Yunis, and H. Tamim. "Prevalence and Predictors of Unintended Pregnancy among Women: An Analysis of the Canadian Maternity Experiences Survey." *BMC Pregnancy and Childbirth* 15 (October 13, 2015): 260. doi:10.1186/s12884-015-0663-4.

Padilla-Walker, L. M., K. J. Christensen, and R. D. Day. "Proactive Parenting Practices during Early Adolescence: A Cluster Approach." *Journal of Adolescence* 34, no. 2 (2011): 203–14.

Padilla-Walker, L. M., A. M. Fraser, and J. M. Harper. "Walking the Walk: The Moderating Role of Proactive Parenting on Adolescents' Value Congruent Behaviours." *Journal of Adolescence* 35, no. 5 (2012): 1141–52.

Parker, C. *Peacebuilding, Citizenship, and Identity: Empowering Conflict and Dialogue in Multicultural Classrooms*. Boston: Sense, 2016.

Peleg, N. "Reconceptualising the Child's Right to Development: Children and the Capability Approach." *International Journal of Children's Rights* 21 (2013): 523–42. doi:10.1163/15718182-02103003.

Pellatt, A. *The United Nations Convention on the Rights of the Child: How Does Alberta's Legislation Measure Up?* Calgary: Alberta Civil Liberties Research Centre, 1999.

Perry, G., M. Daly, and J. Kotler. "Placement Stability in Kinship and Non-kin Foster Care: A Canadian Study." *Children and Youth Services Review* 34, no. 2 (2012): 460–65.

Peters, E., and C. M. Kamp Dush. *Marriage and Family Perspectives and Complexities*. New York: Columbia University Press, 2009.

Peters, R. S. "Education as Initiation." In Curren, *Philosophy of Education*, 55–67.

Peterson, C. "Children's Autobiographical Memories across the Years: Forensic Implications of Childhood Amnesia and Eyewitness Memory for Stressful Events." *Developmental Review* 32, no. 3 (2012): 287–306. doi:10.1016/j.dr.2012.06.002.

Petty, R. E., D. T. Wegner, and L. R. Fabrigar. "Attitudes and Attitude Change." *Annual Review of Psychology* 48 (1997): 609–47.

Phillips, B. M., and J. Lonigan. "Variations in the Home Literacy Environment of Preschool Children: A Cluster Analytic Approach." *Scientific Studies of Reading* 13, no. 2 (2009): 146–74.

Pitula, P. "Hollywood and Human Rights in the Curriculum." *Education & Law Journal* 17, no. 3 (2008): 275–90.

Polkki, P., R. Vornanen, M. Pursiainen, and M. Riikonen. "Children's Participation in Child-Protection Processes as Experienced by Foster Children and Social Workers." *Child Care in Practice* 18, no. 2 (2012): 107–25. doi:10.1080/13575279.2011.646954.

Popova, S., S. Lange, L. Burd, and J. Rehm. "Cost Attributable to Fetal Alcohol Spectrum Disorder in the Canadian Correctional System." *International Journal of Law and Psychiatry* 41 (July 2015): 76–81. doi:10.1016/j.ijlp.2015.03.010.

Popova, S., S. Lange, K. Shield, A. Mihic, A. E. Chudley, R. A. S. Mukherjee, D. Bekmuradov, and J. Rehm. "Comorbidity of Fetal Alcohol Spectrum Disorder: A Systematic Review and Meta-Analysis." *The Lancet* 387, no. 10022 (2016): 978–87. doi:10.1016/S0140-6736(15)01345-8.

Pratt, M. W., J. E. Norris, S. Alisat, and E. Bisson. "Earth Mothers (and Fathers): Examining Generativity and Environmental Concerns in Adolescents and Their Parents." *Journal of Moral Education* 42, no. 1 (2013): 12–27. doi:10.1080/03057240.2012.714751.

Purdy, L. *In Their Best Interest? The Case against Equal Rights for Children*. Ithaca, NY: Cornell University Press, 1992.

Quan, J., J. F. Bureau, and K. Yurowski. "The Association between Time Spent in Daycare and Preschool Attachment to Fathers and Mothers: An Exploration of Disorganization." *International Journal of Arts and Sciences* 6, no. 2 (2013): 415–22.

Quas, J. A., A. R. Wallin, B. Horwitz, E. Davis, and T. D. Lyon. "Maltreated Children's Understanding of and Emotional Reactions to Dependency Court Involvement." *Behavioural Sciences & the Law* 27, no. 1 (2009): 97–117. doi:10.1002/bsl.836.

Quayle, E., and E. Newman. "An Exploratory Study of Public Reports to Investigate Patterns and Themes of Requests for Sexual Images of Minors Online." *Crime Science* 5, no. 1 (2016): 2. doi:10.1186/s40163-016-0050-0.

Quintelier, E., and M. Hooghe. "The Relationship between Political Participation Intentions of Adolescents and a Participatory Democratic Climate at School in 35 Countries." *Oxford Review of Education* 39, no. 5 (2013): 567–89.

Radford, L., N. Lombard, F. Meinck, E. Katz, and S. T. Mahati. "Researching Violence with Children: Experiences and Lessons from the UK and South Africa." *Families, Relationships and Societies* 6, no. 2 (2017): 239–56. doi:10.1332/204674317X14861128190401.

Raphael, D. "Social Determinants of Children's Health in Canada: Analysis and Implications." *International Journal of Child, Youth and Family Studies* 5, no. 2 (2014): 220–39.

Raver, C. C., C. Blair, and M. Willoughby. "Poverty as a Predictor of Executive Function: New Perspectives on Models of Differential Susceptibility." *Developmental Psychology* 49, no. 2 (2013): 292–304.

Reiss, F. "Socioeconomic Inequalities and Mental Health Problems in Children and Adolescents: A Systematic Review." *Social Science and Medicine* 90 (August 2013): 24–31.

Rice, G., and T. Thomas. "James Bulger—A Matter of Public Interest?" *International Journal of Children's Rights* 21 (2013): 1–11. doi:10.1163/157181812X633842.

Rickert, V., A. L. Gilbert, and M. C. Aalsma. "Proactive Parents Are Assets to the Health and Wellbeing of Teens." *Journal of Pediatrics* 164, no. 6 (2014): 1390–95.

Roberts, J. V., and N. Bala. "Understanding Sentencing under the Youth Criminal Justice Act." *Alberta Law Review* 41 (September 2003): 395–423.

Roberts, K. P., and S. C. Cameron. "Observations from Canadian Practitioners about the Investigation and Prosecution of Crimes Involving Child and Adult Witnesses." *Journal of Forensic Psychology Practice* 15, no. 1 (2015): 33–57.

Romano, E., T. Bell, and R. Norian. "Corporal Punishment: Examining Attitudes toward the Law and Factors Influencing Attitude Change." *Journal of Family Violence* 28, no. 3 (2013): 265–75. doi:10.1007/s10896-013-9494-0.

Rowland, A., F. Gerry, and M. Stanton. "Physical Punishment of Children: Time to End the Defence of Reasonable Chastisement in the UK, USA and Australia." *International Journal of Children's Rights* 25, no. 1 (2017), 165–95. doi:10.1163/15718182-02501007.

Ruck, M. D., M. Peterson-Badali, and M. Freeman, eds. *Handbook of Children's Rights: Global and Multidisciplinary Perspectives.* New York: Routledge, 2017.

Ryan, R. M., R. Curren, and E. L. Deci. "What Humans Need: Flourishing in Aristotelian Philosophy and Self-Determination Theory." In *The Best Within Us: Positive Psychology Perspectives on Eudaimonia,* edited by A. S. Waterman, 57–75. Washington, DC: American Psychological Association, 2013.

Ryan, R. M., and E. L. Deci. *Self-Determination Theory: Basic Psychological Needs in Motivation, Development, and Wellness.* New York: Guilford Press, 2017.

Saewyc, E. M., B. B. Miller, R. Rivers, J. Matthews, C. Hilario, and P. Hirakata. "Competing Discourses about Youth Sexual Exploitation in Canadian News Media." *Canadian Journal of Human Sexuality* 22, no. 2 (2013): 95–105. doi:10.3138/cjhs.2013.2041.

Sandbæk, M. "European Policies to Promote Children's Rights and Combat Child Poverty." *International Journal of Environmental Research and Public Health* 14 (2017): 837–51. doi:10.3390/ijerph14080837.

Saunders, B. J. "Ending the Physical Punishment of Children by Parents in the English-Speaking World: The Impact of Language, Tradition and Law." *International Journal of Children's Rights* 21 (2013): 278–304. doi:10.1163/15718182-02102001.

Saywitz, K., L. B. Camparo, and A. Romanoff. "Interviewing Children in Custody Cases: Implications of Research and Policy for Practice." *Behavioural Sciences & the Law* 28, no. 4 (2010): 542–62. doi:10.1002/bsl.945.

Schoon, I., E. Jones, H. Cheng, and B. Maughan. "Family Hardship, Family Instability, and Cognitive Development." *Journal of Epidemiology and Community Health* 66, no. 8 (2012): 716–22. doi:10.1136/jech.2010.121228.

Semenic, S., N. Edwards, S. Premji, J. Olson, B. Williams, and P. Montgomery. "Decision-Making and Evidence Use during the Process of Prenatal Record

Review in Canada: A Multiphase Qualitative Study." *BMC Pregnancy and Childbirth* 15 (2015): 78. doi:10.1186/s12884-015-0503-6.

Semple, N. "The Silent Child: A Quantitative Analysis of Children's Evidence in Canadian Custody and Access Cases." *Canadian Family Law Quarterly* 29, no. 1 (2010): 7–43.

Sen, A. *Development as Freedom.* New York: Oxford University Press, 1999.

Senate of Canada, Standing Committee on Human Rights. *Children: Silenced Citizens.* Ottawa: Senate Standing Committee on Human Rights, 2007.

Shue, H. *Basic Rights.* Princeton, NJ: Princeton University Press, 1980.

Sidebotham, P., J. Fraser, T. Covington, J. Freemantle, S. Petrou, R. Pulikottil-Jacob, T. Cutler, and C. Ellis. "Understanding Why Children Die in High-Income Countries." *Lancet* 384, no. 9946 (2014): 915–27. doi:10.1016/S0140-6736(14)60581-X.

Simmons, R. G., and D. A. Blyth. *Moving into Adolescence: The Impact of Pubertal Change and School Context.* New York: Aldine de Gruyter, 1987.

Simons, E., T. To, R. Moineddin, D. Stieb, and S. D. Dell. "Maternal Second-Hand Smoke Exposure in Pregnancy Is Associated with Childhood Asthma Development." *Journal of Allergy and Clinical Immunology. In Practice* 2, no. 2 (2014): 201–27. doi:10.1016/j.jaip.2013.11.014.

Skrypnek, B., and J. Charchun. *An Evaluation of the Nobody's Perfect Parenting Program.* Ottawa: Canadian Association of Family Resource Programs, 2009.

Slopen, N., G. Fitzmaurice, D. R. Williams, and S. E. Gilman. "Poverty, Food Insecurity, and the Behaviour for Childhood Internalizing and Externalizing Disorders." *Journal of the American Academy of Child and Adolescent Psychiatry* 49, no. 5 (2010): 444–52.

Smith, A. B., ed. *Enhancing Children's Rights: Connecting Research, Policy and Practice.* New York: Palgrave Macmillan, 2015.

Sorhagen, N. S. "Early Teacher Expectations Disproportionately Affect Poor Children's High School Performance." *Journal of Educational Psychology* 105, no. 2 (2013): 465–77.

Sorkhabi, N. "Applicability of Baumrind's Typology to Collective Cultures: Analysis of Cultural Explanations of Parent Socialization Effects." *International Journal of Behavioural Development* 29, no. 6 (2005): 552.

Stasiulis, D. "The Active Child Citizen: Lessons from Canadian Policy and the Children's Movement." *Citizenship Studies* 6, no. 4 (2002): 507–38.

Steiner, H. *An Essay on Rights.* Oxford: Blackwell, 1994.

Stoecklin, D. "General Comment on Children in Street Situations: Insights into the Institutionalisation of Children's Rights." *International Journal of Children's Rights* 25, nos. 3–4 (2017): 817–69. doi:10.1163/15718182-02503014.

Stoltz, J. M., K. Shannon, T. Kerr, R. Zhang, J. S. Montaner, and E. Wood. "Associations between Childhood Maltreatment and Sex Work in a Cohort of

Drug-Using Youth." *Social Science and Medicine* 65, no. 6 (2007): 1214–21. doi:10.1016/j.socscimed.2007.05.005.

Strike, K. *Liberty and Learning.* New York: St. Martin's Press, 1982.

Sugaya, L., D. S. Hasin, M. Olfson, K. Lin, B. F. Grant, and C. Blanco. "Child Physical Abuse and Adult Mental Health: A National Study." *Journal of Traumatic Stress* 25, no. 4 (2012): 384–92. doi:10.1002/jts.21719.

Sullivan, R. *Driedger on the Construction of Statutes.* 3rd ed. Toronto: Butterworths, 1994.

Sullivan, R. *Statutory Interpretation.* Toronto: Irwin Law, 2007.

Sund, L.-G. "The Rights of the Child as Legally Protected Interests." *International Journal of Children's Rights* 14 (2006): 327–37. doi:10.1163/1571811806779050159.

Sund, L.-G., and Vackermo, M. "The Interest Theory, Children's Rights and Social Authorities." *International Journal of Children's Rights* 23 (2015): 752–68. doi:10.1163/15718182-02304002.

Sutherland, N. *Children in English-Canadian Society: Framing the Twentieth-Century Consensus.* Waterloo, ON: Wilfrid Laurier University Press, 2000.

Swift, K. "Canadian Child Welfare: Child Protection and the Status Quo." In Gilbert, Parton, and Skivenes, *Child Protection Systems,* 36–59.

Swift, K., and M. Callahan. "Problems and Potential of Canadian Child Welfare." In *Toward Positive Systems of Child and Family Welfare,* edited by N. Freymond and G. Cameron, 118–47. Toronto: University of Toronto Press, 2006.

Sylwander, L. *Child Impact Assessments.* Sweden: Ministry of Health and Social Affairs, Sweden, Ministry for Foreign Affairs, 2001.

Taillieu, T. L., and D. A. Brownridge. "Aggressive Parental Discipline Experienced in Childhood and Internalizing Problems in Early Adulthood." *Journal of Family Violence* 28, no. 5 (2013): 445–58. doi:10.1007/s10896-013-9513-1.

Taylor, C. A., J. A. Manganello, S. J. Lee, and J. C. Rice, "Mother's Spanking of 3-Year-Old Children and Subsequent Risk of Children's Aggressive Behavior." *Pediatrics* 125 (2010). doi:10.1542/peds 2009-2678.

Terre des hommes. *Children in Street Situations.* 2010. http://www.ohchr.org/Documents/Issues/Children/Study/TerreDesHommes.pdf.

Thakrar, A. P., A. D. Forrest, M. G. Maltenfort, and C. B. Forrest. "Child Mortality in the US and 19 OECD Comparator Nations: A 50-Year Time-Trend Analysis." *Health Affairs* 37, no. 1 (2018): 140–49. doi:10.1377/hlthaff.2017.0767.

Thomas, G., G. Gonneau, N. Poole, and J. Cook. "The Effectiveness of Alcohol Warning Labels in the Prevention of Fetal Alcohol Spectrum Disorder: A Brief Review." *International Journal of Alcohol and Drug Research* 3, no. 1 (2014): 91–103. doi:10.7895/ijadr.v3i1.126.

Thomlison, R. J., and C. E. Foote. "Children and the Law in Canada: The Shifting Balance of Children's, Parents' and State's Rights." *Journal of Comparative Family Studies* 18, no. 2 (1987): 231–45.

Tisdall, E. K. M., A. M. Gadda, and U. M. Butler, eds. *Children and Young People's Participation and Its Transformative Potential.* New York: Palgrave Macmillan, 2014.

Tomoda, A., H. Suzuki, K. Rabi, Y. S. Sheu, A. Polcari, and M. H. Teicher. "Reduced Prefrontal Cortical Gray Matter Volume in Young Adults Exposed to Harsh Physical Punishment." *NeuroImage* 47, no. 2 (2009): T66–T71. doi:10.1016/j.neuroimage.2009.03.005.

Toope, S. "The Convention on the Rights of the Child: Implications for Canada." In *Children's Rights: A Comparative Perspective*, edited by M. Freeman, 51–52. Aldershot, UK: Dartmouth, 1996.

Truth and Reconciliation Commission of Canada. *Final Report of the Truth and Reconciliation Commission of Canada, Vol. One: Summary—Honouring the Truth, Reconciling for the Future.* Toronto: Lorimer, 2015.

Tucker, P., M. M. van Zandvoort, S. M. Burke, and J. D. Irwin. "Physical Activity at Daycare: Child Care Providers' Perspectives for Improvements." *Journal of Early Childhood Research* 9, no. 3 (2011): 207–19. doi:10.1177/1476718X10389144.

Tudge, J. R. H., A. Payir, E. Merçon-Vargas, H. Cao, Y. Liang, J. Li, and L. O'Brien. "Still Misused after All These Years? A Reevaluation of the Uses of Bronfenbrenner's Bioecological Theory of Human Development." *Journal of Family Theory & Review* 8, no. 4 (2016): 427–45. doi:10.1111/jftr.12165.

Turner, S. *Something to Cry About: An Argument against Corporal Punishment of Children in Canada.* Waterloo, ON: Wilfrid Laurier University Press, 2002.

UN Committee on the Rights of the Child. *Concluding Observations: Canada.* June 20, 1995. CRC/C/15/Add.37. http://www.refworld.org/docid/3ae6af5a14.html.

———. *Concluding Observations: Canada.* October 5, 2012. CRC/C/CAN/CO/ 3-4. http://www2.ohchr.org/english/bodies/crc/docs/co/CRC-C-CAN-CO-3-4 _en.pdf.

United Nations Committee on the Rights of the Child. *General Comment no. 21 on Children in Street Situations.* June 21, 2017. https://bettercarenetwork.org/sites/ default/files/GC%20%23%2021%20%282017%29_Street%20Children.pdf.

UNICEF Office of Research. "Fairness for Children: A League Table of Inequality in Child Well-Being in Rich Countries." *Innocenti Report Card 13.* Florence: UNICEF Office of Research, 2016. https://www.unicef-irc.org/publications/ pdf/RC13_eng.pdf.

———. "Child Well-Being in Rich Countries: A Comparative Overview." *Innocenti Report Card 11.* Florence: Office of Research, 2013.

UNICEF Innocenti Research Centre. "Measuring Child Poverty: New League Tables of Child Poverty in the World's Rich Countries." *Innocenti Report Card 10.* Florence: UNICEF Innocenti Research Centre, 2012.

———. "Promoting the Rights of Children with Disabilities." *Innocente Digest no. 13.* Florence: UNICEF Innocente Research Centre, 2007.

Van Daalen-Smith, C. "A Right to Health: Children's Health and Health Care through a Child-Rights Lens." In Howe and Covell, *A Question of Commitment,* 73–97.

Vandenhole, W., ed. *Routledge International Handbook of Children's Rights Studies.* New York: Routledge, 2015.

van Geel, T. R. *Understanding Supreme Court Opinions.* New York: Longman, 2009.

Vandell, D. L., J. Belsky, M. Burchinal, L. Steinberg, N. Vandergrift, and NICHD Early Child Care Research Network. "Do Effects of Early Child Care Extend to Age 15 Years? Results from the NICHD Study of Early Child Care and Youth Development." *Child Development* 81, no. 3 (2010): 737–56. doi:10.1111/j.1467-8624.2010.01431.x.

Veerman, P. "The Ageing of the UN Convention on the Rights of the Child." In *The Future of Children's Rights,* edited by M. Freeman, 16–49. Leiden: Brill Nijhoff, 2014.

Vogl, R., and N. Bala. "Initial Involvement." In Bala et al., *Canadian Child Welfare Law,* 41–43.

Waddell, C., H. Macmillan, and A. M. Pietrantonio. "How Important Is Permanency Planning for Children? Considerations for Pediatricians Involved in Child Protection." *Journal of Developmental and Behavioural Pediatrics: JDBP* 25, no. 4 (2004): 285–92.

Waddell, C., C. Shepherd, C. Schwartz, and J. Barican. *Child and Youth Mental Disorders: Prevalence and Evidence-Based Interventions.* Vancouver, BC: Children's Health Policy Centre, Simon Fraser University, 2014. http://childhealthpolicy .ca/wp-content/uploads/2014/06/14-06-17-Waddell-Report-2014.06.16.pdf.

Waldock, T. "Enhancing the Quality of Care in Child Welfare: Our Obligations under the UN Convention on the Rights of the Child." *Relational Child and Youth Care Practice* 24, no. 3 (2011): 50–61.

———. "The Rights of Children in Care: Consistency with the Convention?" In Howe and Covell, *A Question of Commitment,* 287–319.

———. "Theorising Children's Rights and Child Welfare Paradigms." *International Journal of Children's Rights* 24, no. 2 (2016): 1–26.

Wall, J. *Children's Rights: Today's Global Challenge.* Lanham, MD: Rowman & Littlefield, 2017.

Weisz, V., T. Wingrove, S. J. Beal, and A. Faith-Slaker. "Children's Participation in Foster Care Hearings." *Child Abuse & Neglect* 35, no. 4 (2011): 267–72. doi:10.1016/j.chiabu.2010.12.007.

White, L. A. "Understanding Canada's Lack of Progress in Implementing the UN Convention on the Rights of the Child." *International Journal of Children's Rights* 22, no. 1 (2014): 164–88. doi:10.1163/15718182-02201002.

Whittle, H., C. Hamilton-Giachritsis, A. Beech, and G. Collings. "A Review of Online Grooming: Characteristics and Concerns." *Aggression and Violent Behaviour* 18, no. 1 (2013): 62–70. doi:10.1016/j.avb.2012.09.003.

———. "A Review of Young People's Vulnerabilities to Online Grooming." *Aggression and Violent Behaviour* 18, no. 1 (2013): 135–46. doi:10.1016/ j.avb.2012.11.008.

Williams, J. H. G., and L. Ross. "Consequences of Prenatal Toxin Exposure for Mental Health in Children and Adolescents: A Systematic Review." *European Child & Adolescent Psychiatry* 16, no. 4 (2007): 243–53. doi:10.1007/s00787-006-0596-6.

Williams, M. L., and K. Hudson. "Public Perceptions of Internet, Familial and Localized Sexual Grooming: Predicting Perceived Prevalence and Safety." *Journal of Sexual Aggression* 19, no. 2 (2013): 218–35.

Williams, R., I. A. Elliott, and A. R. Beech. "Identifying Sexual Grooming Themes Used by Internet Sex Offenders." *Deviant Behaviour* 34, no. 2 (2013): 135–52. doi:10.1080/01639625.2012.707550.

Williams, S. M., V. Talwar, R. C. L. Lindsay, N. Bala, and K. Lee. "Is the Truth in Your Words? Distinguishing Children's Deceptive and Truthful Statements." *Journal of Criminology* 2014 (2014). Article ID 547519, 9 pages. doi:10.1155/2014/547519.

Wilson, J. *Wilson on Children and the Law.* LexisNexis Canada, 2016.

Winter, K. "The Perspectives of Young Children in Care about Their Circumstances and Implications for Social Work Practice." *Child and Family Social Work* 15, no. 2 (2010): 186–95.

Wray-Lake, L., and C. A. Flanagan. "Parenting Practices and the Development of Adolescents' Social Trust." *Journal of Adolescence* 35, no. 3 (2012): 549–60. doi:10.1016/j.adolescence.2011.09.006.

Yonge Street Mission. *Changing Patterns for Street-Involved Youth.* Toronto: Public Interest, 2009. http://www.publicinterest.ca/images/YSM_Report_-_Changing_Patterns_for_Street_Involved_Youth.PDF.

Yoshikawa, H., J. L. Aber, and W. R. Beardsley. "The Effects of Poverty on the Mental, Emotional, and Behavioural Health of Children and Youth." *American Psychological Association* 67, no. 4 (2012): 272–84. doi:10.1037/a0028015.

## CASES CITED

*A.B. v. Bragg Communications Inc.*, [2012] S.C.J. no. 46.

*A.C. v. Manitoba (Director of Child and Family Services)*, [2009] S.C.J. no. 30.

*Baker v. Canada (Minister of Citizenship and Immigration)*, [1999] S.C.J. no. 39.

*Canadian Foundation for Children, Youth and the Law v. Canada (Attorney General)*, [2004] S.C.J. no. 6.

*E.T. v. Hamilton-Wentworth District School Board*, [2016] O.J. no. 5997.

*First Nations Child and Family Caring Society of Canada et al. v. Attorney General of Canada (for the Minister of Indian and Northern Affairs Canada)*, [2013] F.C.J. no. 249.

*Gordon v. Goertz*, [1996] S.C.J. no. 52.

*Kanthasamy v. Canada (Citizenship and Immigration)*, [2015] S.C.J. no. 61.

*Kazemi Estate v. Islamic Republic of Iran*, [2014] S.C.J. no. 62.

*M.C. v. L.P.*, [2009] R.J.Q. 945.

*M.M. v. United States of America*, [2015] S.C.J. no. 62.

*Multani v. Commission scolaire Marguerite-Bourgeoys*, [2006] 1 S.C.R. 256.

*P.(D.) v. S.(C.) Droit de la famille—1150 (SOQUIJ)*, [1993] S.C.J. no. 111.

*R. v. B.W.P.; R. v. B.V.N.*, [2006] S.C.J. no. 27.

*R. v. C.D.* and *R. v. C.D.K.*, [2005] S.C.J. no. 79.

*R. v. D.B.*, [2008] S.C.J. no. 25.

*R. v. Drummond*, [1997] O.J. no. 6390.

*R. v. L. (D.O.)*, [1993] S.C.J. no. 72.

*R. v. Morgentaler*, [1988] 1 S.C.R. 30.

*R. v. R.C.*, [2005] S.C.J. no. 62.

*R. v. Sharpe*, [2001] S.C.J. no. 3.

*R. v. T.F. and T.A.F.*, [2016] B.C.J. no. 129.

*Reno v. Flores*, [1993] 507 U.S. 292.

*Trinity Western University v. British Columbia College of Teachers*, [2001] S.C.J. no. 32.

*Troxel v. Granville*, [2000] 530 U.S. 57.

*United States of America v. Burns*, [2001] S.C.J. no. 8.

*V.W. v. D.S.*, [1996] S.C.J. no. 53.

*Winnipeg Child and Family Services v. G.(D.F.)*, [1997] 3 S.C.R. 925.

*Winnipeg Child and Family Services v. K.L.W.*, [2000] S.C.J. no. 48.

*Wisconsin v. Yoder*, [1972] 406 U.S. 205.

*Young v. Young*, [1993] S.C.J. no. 112.

## ONLINE RESOURCES

Beyond Borders ECPAT Canada   www.beyondborders.org

Campaign 2000   www.campaign2000.ca

Canada—Justice Laws   laws-lois.justice.gc.ca

Canada—Public Health Agency of Canada   www.phac-aspc.gc.ca

Canada—Statistics Canada   www.statcan.gc.ca

Canadian Centre for Child Protection   www.protectchildren.ca

Canadian Coalition for the Rights of Children   www.rightsofchildren.ca

Canadian Institute for Health Information   www.cihi.ca

Food Banks Canada   www.foodbankscanada.ca

Global Initiative to End All Corporal Punishment of Children
   www.endcorporalpunishment.org

Ontario Coalition for Better Child Care   www.childcareontario.org

Organisation for Economic Co-operation and Development   www.oecd.org

Repeal 43 Committee   www.repeal43.org

UNICEF Office of Research—Innocenti   www.unicef-irc.org

United Nations   www.un.org

Youth in Care Canada   www.youthincare.ca

# About the Authors

**Katherine Covell** holds a PhD in Psychology from the University of Toronto. She is a professor emerita and former executive director of the Children's Rights Centre at Cape Breton University. She has acted as a national and international advocate for children, and has published widely on children's rights and child development.

**R. Brian Howe** holds a PhD in Political Science from the University of Toronto. He is a professor emeritus and former director of the Children's Rights Centre at Cape Breton University. He has published six books and numerous articles on human rights, children's rights, and children's rights education.

**J.C. Blokhuis** holds a JD from the University of Ottawa and a PhD in Educational Thought and Policy from the University of Rochester. He is an associate professor in Social Development Studies at Renison University College, University of Waterloo, and a former Kluge Fellow at the Library of Congress in Washington, DC.

# Index

# Books in the Studies in Childhood and Family in Canada Series Published by Wilfrid Laurier University Press

*Making Do: Women, Family, and Home in Montreal during the Great Depression* by Denyse Baillargeon, translated by Yvonne Klein • 1999 / xii + 232 pp. / ISBN 0-88920-326-1 / ISBN-13: 978-0-88920-326-6

*Children in English-Canadian Society: Framing the Twentieth-Century Consensus* by Neil Sutherland with a new foreword by Cynthia Comacchio • 2000 / xxiv + 336 pp. / illus. / ISBN 0-88920-351-2 / ISBN-13: 978-0-88920-351-8

*Love Strong as Death: Lucy Peel's Canadian Journal, 1833–1836* edited by J.I. Little • 2001 / x + 229 pp. / illus. / ISBN 0-88920-389-x / ISBN-13: 978-0-88920-389-230-x

*The Challenge of Children's Rights for Canada* by Katherine Covell and R. Brian Howe • 2001 / viii + 244 pp. / ISBN 0-88920-380-6 / ISBN-13: 978-0-88920-380-8

*NFB Kids: Portrayals of Children by the National Film Board of Canada, 1939–1989* by Brian J. Low • 2002 / vi + 288 pp. / illus. / ISBN 0-88920-386-5 / ISBN-13: 978-0-88920-386-0

*Something to Cry About: An Argument against Corporal Punishment of Children in Canada* by Susan M. Turner • 2002 / xx + 317 pp. / ISBN 0-88920-382-2 / ISBN-13: 978-0-88920-382-2

*Freedom to Play: We Made Our Own Fun* edited by Norah L. Lewis • 2002 / xiv + 210 pp. / ISBN 0-88920-406-3 / ISBN-13: 978-0-88920-406-5

*The Dominion of Youth: Adolescence and the Making of Modern Canada, 1920–1950* by Cynthia Comacchio • 2006 / x + 302 pp. / illus. / ISBN 0-88920-488-8 / ISBN-13: 978-0-88920-488-1

*Evangelical Balance Sheet: Character, Family, and Business in Mid-Victorian Nova Scotia* by B. Anne Wood • 2006 / xxx + 198 pp. / illus. / ISBN 0-88920-500-0 / ISBN-13: 978-0-88920-500-0

*A Question of Commitment: Children's Rights in Canada* edited by R. Brian Howe and Katherine Covell • 2007 / xiv + 442 pp. / ISBN 978-1-55458-003-3

*Taking Responsibility for Children* edited by Samantha Brennan and Robert Noggle • 2007 / xxii + 188 pp. / ISBN 978-1-55458-015-6

*Home Words: Discourses of Children's Literature in Canada* edited by Mavis Reimer • 2008 / xx + 280 pp. / illus. / ISBN 978-1-55458-016-3

*Depicting Canada's Children* edited by Loren Lerner • 2009 / xxvi + 442 pp. / illus. / ISBN 978-1-55458-050-7

*Babies for the Nation: The Medicalization of Motherhood in Quebec, 1910–1970* by Denyse Baillargeon, translated by W. Donald Wilson • 2009 / xiv + 328 pp. / illus. / ISBN 978-1-5548-058-3

*The One Best Way? Breastfeeding History, Politics, and Policy in Canada* by Tasnim Nathoo and Aleck Ostry • 2009 / xvi + 262 pp. / illus. / ISBN 978-1-55458-147-4

*Fostering Nation? Canada Confronts Its History of Childhood Disadvantage* by Veronica Strong-Boag • 2011 / x + 302 pp. / ISBN 978-1-55458-337-9

*Cold War Comforts: Maternalism, Child Safety, and Global Insecurity, 1945–1975* by Tarah Brookfield • 2012 / xiv + 292 pp. / illus. / ISBN 978-1-55458-623-3

*Ontario Boys: Masculinity and the Idea of Boyhood in Postwar Ontario, 1945–1960* by Christopher Greig • 2014 / xxviii + 184 pp. / ISBN 978-1-55458-900-5

*A Brief History of Women in Quebec* by Denyse Baillargeon, translated by W. Donald Wilson • 2014 / xii + 272 pp. / ISBN 978-1-55458-950-0

*With Children and Youth: Emerging Theories and Practices in Child and Youth Care Work* edited by Kiaras Gharabaghi, Hans A. Skott-Myhre, and Mark Krueger • 2014 / xiv + 222 pp. / ISBN 978-1-55458-966-1

*Abuse or Punishment? Violence Towards Children in Quebec Families, 1850–1969*, translated by W. Donald Wilson • 2014 / xii + 396 pp. / ISBN 978-1-77712-063-0

*Engendering Transnational Voices: Studies in Families, Work and Identities* edited by Guida Man and Rina Cohen • 2015 / xii + 342 pp. / ISBN 978-1-77112-112-5 (hc)

*The Challenge of Children's Rights for Canada*, Second Edition by Katherine Covell, R. Brian Howe, and J.C. Blokhuis • 2018 / x + 248 pp. / ISBN 978-1-77112-355-6